The Art of Stalking Parallel Perception:
Revised 10th Anniversary Edition

The Art of Stalking Parallel Perception: Revised 10th Anniversary Edition

THE LIVING TAPESTRY OF LUJAN MATUS

Lujan Matus

Disclaimer
All rights reserved. No part of this publication may be reproduced or transferred in any form or by any means, graphic, electronic, or mechanical, including photocopying, recording, taping, or by any information storage retrieval system, without the written permission of the author. The author specifically disclaims any responsibility for any liability, loss, or risk, personal or otherwise, which is incurred as a consequence, directly or indirectly, of the use and application of any of the contents of this book.
First published 2005. Revised edition 2015
© Copyright 2015 Lujan Matus.
The Parallel Perception logo is copyright,
no unauthorized use.

ISBN: 1517422728
ISBN 13: 9781517422721

Table of Contents

Foreword ix
Preface xv
Part I 1
Shamanic Dreaming 3
   Awakening the witness within 18
Threads of Intention 23
The Hidden Fabric 43
Fear Not, Be Free 54
Haunted Awareness 71
   Corrupted Innocence 83
   The Hieroglyph of Haunted Awareness 85
   The Log Cabin 90
   The Hieroglyph of Inner Light 99
   Hidden Entity 108
Mysterious Encounters 120
Emptying the Imprint 130
   Invisible Imprinting 152
   The Shadow's Mind 158
Hunting the Haunted 166
   Predatorial Attention 179
Dreaming the Dreamed 191
   The Hieroglyph of Completion 196

The Golden Orb	199
Architectural Orbs	**212**
The Three Hieroglyphs	215
The Parables of the Dog and the Deer	**226**
The Parable of the Dog	227
The Parable of the Deer	234
Mirroring	236
Part II	**239**
Sexual Attention	**241**
Responsibility and Inner Truth	243
Applied Mechanics of Interaction	246
Actions and Consequences	248
Power	251
Systems of Expectations	260
Cohesion of Union	265
Character Assassination	268
Cognitive Inversion	273
The Integral Perimeter	279
Professionalism: Less is more	284
Transference	286
The Inner Gaze	289
Acuity	294
The Heart of Dreaming	**296**
Recovery	305
Real Time	310
The Dream Walker	319
Dream Compartmentalization	324
Personal Containment and Why We Don't Dream Real Dreams	332
To Know Without Question	335
Don't Play With That Which You Should Not	337

Denial · 340
The Auditory Architect · 342
Questions and Answers: I · · · · · · · · · · · · · · · · · · · 348
Capturing the Attention of the Cloaked
Inner Child· 353
Mutual Enhancement· 356
The Sentinel · 359
Questions and Answers: II · · · · · · · · · · · · · · · · · · 364
Heightened Acuity and Borrowed Awareness· · · · 366
Questions and Answers: III · · · · · · · · · · · · · · · · · 370
The Power of Silent Cognition · · · · · · · · · · · · · · · · 374
The Eternal Legacy of Master Lo Ban· · · · · · · · · · · 376
Epilogue· 393

Foreword

The particular way in which this book impacts one's personal path is not easy to describe. What is conveyed here becomes so inexplicably intertwined with one's immediate reality, inner and outer, that once we come into contact with this information our own paradigm begins to shift, as previously undreamt of possibilities become increasingly apparent to us.

Essentially, this is a guide to activating our hidden reservoirs of multidimensional human potential. As we become immersed in Lujan's extraordinary life story, a wealth of encrypted knowledge is imperceptibly absorbed. Wellsprings of adaptive wisdom and pragmatic tools for self-liberation trigger a genuine awakening that can't be ignored.

Although the teachings outlined are very direct by nature, we find ourselves drawn back to these pages again and again to discover previously unnoticed layers of meaning. Even during the editing process, going over the same text dozens and dozens of times, I have been continually impacted to review and renew my

www.parallelperception.com

Foreword

understanding. My very molecules crave the authenticity of these teachings and the expansion they deliver.

To be part of making this information available to the world is an honor that I will always be grateful for, and not only because I deeply value what Lujan has to offer. The process itself has been so intensely rewarding, challenging and incredibly synchronistic that it utterly confirms the ultra-dimensional consistency within what Lujan outlines, to a degree that defies explanation.

To complete this introduction, I asked Lujan to describe parallel perception for someone picking up this book for the first time, and this was his reply.

> *'Parallel perception refers to accessing alternate realities; time-space continuums that are simultaneously operational yet not linearly connected via the expectations of a social mind. These dimensional gateways are omnipresently available and eternally fluctuate as a quantum reflection upon our moments, those precious points of arrival that continually escape us.'*

Ten years since its original publication, the revised edition of *The Art of Stalking Parallel Perception* contains a treasure trove of new information that clarifies and expands upon central themes, presenting this timeless shamanic wisdom in a more accessible format. Amongst many other crucial additions, Lujan explains for the first time the workings of the mysterious energy double and how it manifests and connects to us in this world. We are introduced to the intricacies of seemingly indescribable interdimensional processes related to seeing, third-eye perception and the cyclic nature of time, as it exists within parallel continuums. These descriptions trigger realizations that tear the lid off the Pandora's box of human behavior and allow the light of clear perception to come streaming in.

This is more than a chronicle of someone else's journey. It is an invitation to fully engage with your own. Via an empowering sequence of events and conversations with enigmatic seers, we are introduced to the mechanisms and subtleties of the most elusive subjects pertaining to our human dilemma and reminded of the expanded possibilities that we have lost sight of on the long road of human socialization.

By deftly weaving the luminous strands of our heart's remembrance, Lujan cuts through the veil of unwholesome socialization to reach into our deepest reservoirs of consciousness and remind us where we truly stand. Our living tapestry is alive and continuously unfolding, just as the holographic mystery of our existence is evolving in ways that cannot be anticipated, and which come to light differently for each of us. Lujan's journey plants jewels into one's cognitive system that irreversibly alter the equation and whose true worth will only be revealed by time's passing.

Naomi Jean

www.parallelperception.com

Editing by Naomi Jean.
With heartfelt thanks to members of Parallel Perception
for diligent proof reading and elegant suggestions.

Preface

The Art of Stalking Parallel Perception will affect silent cognition within its arrangement, to facilitate your reconnection to that energetic heritage which has been denied us through the enslavement of our awareness. Know that we are layered within our energetic composure, and this resonance will release information in comparison to conscious availability.

Be aware that there are key points embedded within this text that will beckon your attention to realize them in an ongoing, ever-unfolding manner. Many aspects of the narrative that you will become familiar with are fragmented within the chapters. To discover these vital keys you must absorb and realize these fragmentations over time.

Exercising your neuroplasticity in terms of activating your ability to be cognitively inverted will ultimately trigger your awareness to expand into the multidimensional fractality that is our inherent capacity as human beings. I now invite you into the art of stalking parallel perception.

For those who dare to listen.

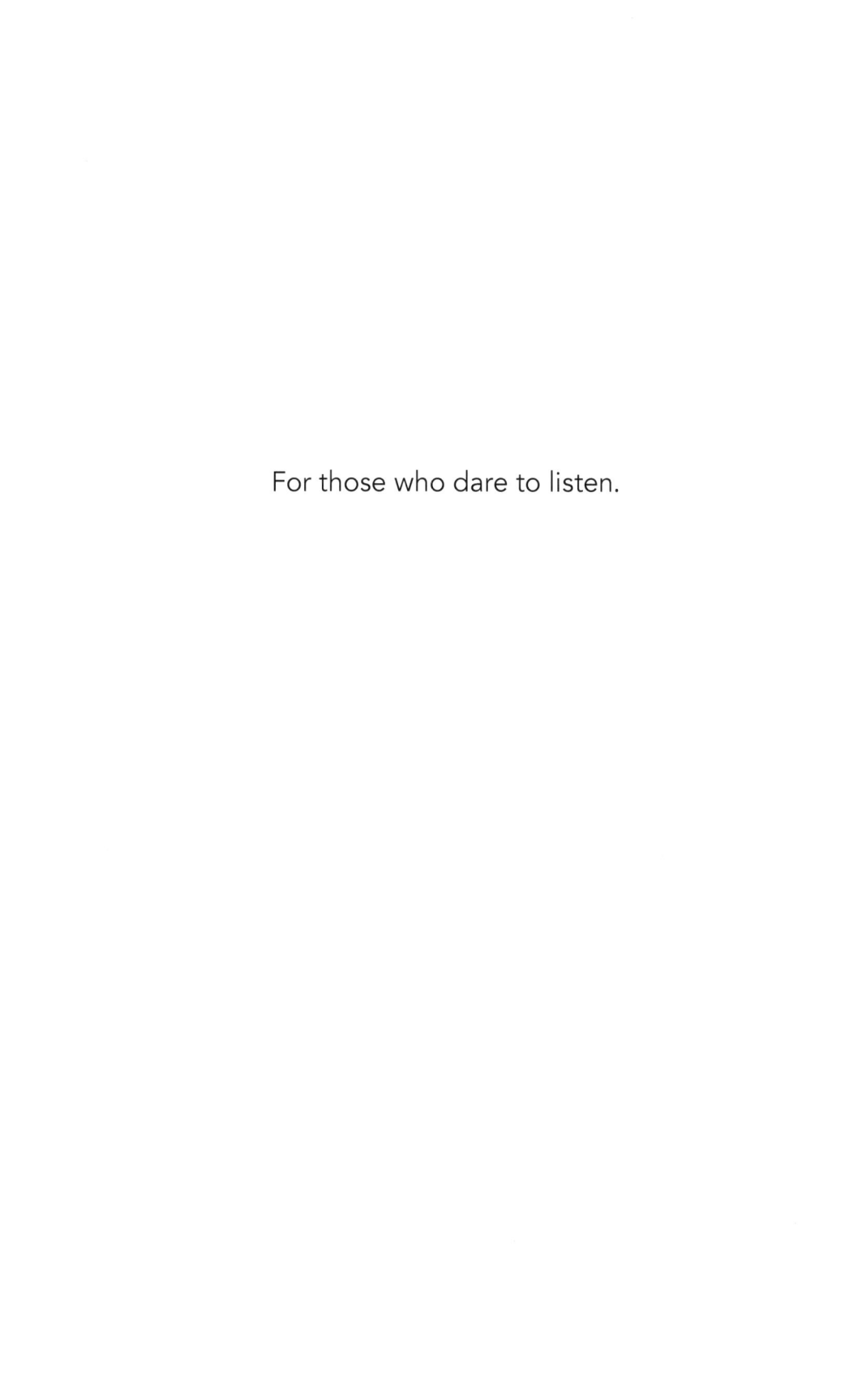

Part I

Shamanic Dreaming

I am the dreamer who dreamt my child, who was taught by the dream maker, the old Nagual* Lujan. He taught my child and my child returned to me, the dreamer, who became the awakened man who transmits the inner child through the stories of the dreams. The old Nagual Lujan, also known as Master Lo Ban*, is my benefactor. He found me in the dream of an adult.

Suddenly I was in a building, in an elevator on the eightieth floor, when a visceral fear engulfed me. I knew that it was going to plummet to the ground and all at once I was travelling downward at a massive speed. I bent my knees and grabbed hold of the railing, afraid that my legs would be snapped backwards from the impact.

As I braced myself, I heard an explosion, and then a thunderous sound manifested all around me. I had arrived and was not injured at all.

---
* The Nagual is a leader and the bearer of altered perceptions.
* Lo Ban literally translates to 'elegantly flourishing spirals'.

www.parallelperception.com

There were dust particles in the air as I tentatively walked out of the elevator into semi-darkness. I couldn't define the walls or the size of the room, and as I was scanning the environment a feeling of great oppression hit my chest. This sensation transformed into the growl of a jaguar that was lurking in the shadows. I heard that animal from different positions all at once, as if I was surrounded. And I was.

Fear once again engulfed me. I did not want to be mauled and die that way. Grappling with my mounting apprehension, I looked upwards and turned that intensity into the growl itself. The whole scene was surreal, unbelievable to me, as though I was watching myself in a movie and in the same instant hearing myself ferociously roaring like a wild cat cornered. At that moment, I noticed envelopes falling from above. As they hit the ground, I realized there were men in the room hiding in the darkness, which frightened me in a way that I was not really familiar with.

They were watching me. I felt their intentions piercing through the fabric that was my being. At that point I knew they were testing me. I lent down to pick up one of the envelopes from the floor and saw a name. "What the…? Why would I need this?" I asked myself.

The room suddenly turned black, and what appeared in front of me was a long rectangular corridor. As I became accustomed to the atmosphere that was confronting my body on a very deep level, it began to expand, allowing me to see more clearly what was there. I looked into it and realized that I would have to take one step up, yet I dared not, for I knew the energetic implication of walking upon that new threshold was beyond my strength at that moment.

Peering into the obscurity, I saw a figure standing at the end of that ominous chamber. He looked like an Oriental warrior, clad in ancient, traditional black leather armor. He stepped forward, and when his right foot hit what seemed to be a stone floor, the atmosphere rippled as if it had tangible substance. He then left the ground and flew toward me horizontally through the air.

Upon his approach, the pressure that ensued from his body entered me, and every fiber of my being became infused with his presence. He landed in a half-kneeling stance with his right knee to the floor, and his left foot firmly planted in front of him. His right forearm shielded his downward gaze, and his left palm pushed toward the ground by his side.

The name 'Lujan*' entered my body, whilst a golden sphere with a blue glow was simultaneously propelled toward me from the center of his being and stabilized itself within my heart.

"This is yours to give to the dreamer, little one."

When he spoke, I realized that I was a child and upon that moment the dream scene disappeared.

---
* Lujan (pronounced Lu-han): to be luminous

The next thing I knew, I was standing near running water and there was a bridge in front of me that curved over a brook in an elegant arc. My eyes were drawn to the center of it and I saw a man gazing over the edge. He turned to his left and looked directly at me.

As I returned his gaze I recognized him, but could not quite put together how I knew him. His regard was fierce and unrelenting. He had a full, medium-length beard and thick, brown, shoulder-length hair. As he faced me, I acknowledged that his physical strength was beyond anything I had ever known. His voice was direct and commanded my attention.

"My name is Somai*. Your inner child has absorbed the old Nagual Lujan's luminosity and has been qualified, and through this transmission, you have also inherited his name. You must turn this power, which is the purity of your inner child, into that advisor that we all seek, to bring clarity within the world that encompasses your very being.

"The old Nagual needs you to understand that I am your strength and the power of your clarity, for you have been waylaid by the cloak that has been pressed upon you within your childhood and is saturating your life as a man.

"When you first entered master Lo Ban's domain, fear encased you as you fell. To rediscover the inner child, one must dive deep into the visceral content of one's true feelings and often fear is the catalyst that must be wrestled with. The jaguar you heard, which delivered a

---

* Somai: the inner witness

www.parallelperception.com

feeling of oppression through the sensation of pressure on your chest that would devour you, was Jagür*. This wild cat represents the confronting of those socialized imprints that are harbored deep within, which belong to the time-space continuum you have entered by being born there.

"The very presence of Jagür demanded, through her challenge, that you drop that socialization. Then the growl became yours, and as you looked up, your benefactor became available by virtue of that void within you. When the envelopes dropped, this was the automatic energetic assumption that you may now step forward and be counted.

"Understand that your perception is being split and that it will take a lifetime to come to terms with this anomaly. The first split of perception is the childlike view, which will yield clarity of heart that is unwavering within its purity.

"The second split of perception that you will assimilate is that of the adult witness, which will be your ability to exercise uncompromising, direct knowing, and communication of truth through language.

"The third aspect of this unique fragmentation that you will experience is the Architect of observation, which is to know beyond what is being presented. This perspective will combine the previous two speeds as intuitive states that are recalled and relayed back within dimensional imagery that is connected to energetic units of information that will

---

* Jagür is an ancient Aramaic name that means a marker, or a pile of stone's.

be stored within your luminosity. Your bio-neural network will be reordered as a result of what is happening to you now. An omnipresent anomaly will become available by being introduced to that emptiness, or void power, via our instructions.

"The Architect within represents a state of being that goes beyond clarity of heart and direct knowing. It is the witness that sees the hidden fabric that is difficult to comprehend through the calculus that belongs to intellectual premises. This viewpoint is the gift the Nagual passes to you, combined with the fourth aspect of perception.

"The fourth perspective has to do with an energetic portion of the Nagual Lujan and creates a bridge to the luminous beings he was in contact with. This reordered perception is also closely related with our extraterrestrial experiences, which will yield to you hieroglyphs that reveal a system of syntax that lays the foundation of what needs to be known by those who enquire."

As Somai described these anomalies, I was simultaneously impacted by a vision of those hieroglyphs of which he spoke. They appeared as if compressed in a golden-white powdered dust, and this visual image somehow collided with me, imprinting as a unit of memory upon my inner silence. This embedded energetic component of information was a direct lesson in real time, and how the puzzle of events finds sequentiality within the seemingly random tapestry that power applies.

At that point, my attention was drawn back to the sound of Somai's voice, and the vision of the hieroglyphs sank into my subconscious as he continued.

"Portions of this energetic universe will become available to those who access their present time continuum as a dimensional composite of awareness. Upon applying this immediacy, we all — as a collective — will inherit the perceptions outlined. If enough of us can become aware of this symbiotic process and apply the principles that are being imparted to you, an exponential factor will become available to the general populous as an evolutionary advancement, which in actual fact is just returning to our original state of awareness that has been buried deep in antiquity.

"Be aware that these split perceptions function as one unit, even though they appear to be separated. Remember that avenues of awareness will bombard your cognitive system and be further compacted and enhanced into the potency of real time via the power of your reviewal.

"In transmitting this information to others, keep in mind that such adaptability has to be reinforced continually in order to overcome the stubborn imprints of socialization so that those you teach may access more than one avenue of perception simultaneously. Your task is to deliver clarity and remind the enquirer of which branch of awareness they are caught in, by passing on this information.

www.parallelperception.com

"You must come to terms with all these elements intertwined and understand that the name Lujan is given to your inner child so that when you are beckoned by this very name, you will assume the strength and the knowing of the Nagual, the one you have witnessed as a child, who is your true Architect of observation.

"You will need his power, for there are those who will challenge what you present. Know that they are waiting within their prospective social corners, and be strengthened by the feeling that your integrity is a boundary that cannot be warped by those who focus from different angles that exist within their perception.

"Once they challenge you, you will automatically know from whence they came. Your observational fortitude will keep your adult witness in a state of pure balance, for how can that which you already know offend you?

"I am one portion of master Lo Ban, part of your honeycomb network of awareness that combined with his and which has now been returned to you. The transmission of what occurred within this mystery will be unveiled in good time. I would like you now to remember that I am the buoyant adult that exists inside of your decision-making capacities. When you remember me, you will think of nothing and only know, as a witness, that there is an Architect of observation beyond your personal view. This will be your ultimate clarity, and your heart is where your power will be stationed.

"You are being split now, beyond your comprehension. How your biofield is being reordered will be revealed to you as time compresses this information within your awareness. You are yet to remember dreaming visions that have impacted you within this scene. These memories will release nuggets of information that will further collapse your socialized cognitive system into that which you do not yet understand.

"Come with me now to master Lo Ban, to exercise your buoyant witness, which will not interfere with the Architect of observation that now must be opened up to its full expression. Close your eyes, and we shall be transported back to where he is, permanently integrated as one being."

When I opened my eyes, I was there in that mysterious room where I had first met my benefactor. From behind me I heard his unmistakably direct voice.

"Look in front of you," he commanded. "Do not turn around."

What I saw before me was an empty void. Then within that emptiness, people appeared. I watched them from above. They were interacting, unaware of my presence or that I was observing them, and within their energy field was a cloak. I could see this presence pressing and distorting their inner perception by covering their purity and innocence, and I realized that within that pressure they only perceived the distortion and nothing else.

What struck me most was that this self-sustaining cloak was so connected to their inner child. I could see how they actively passed it to one another through immature interactions and how their limitations were reinforced by those covert exchanges. As I was watching the projection of a thread from one individual's cloak to another, I was suddenly propelled beyond the visual containment of the scene that I was immersed within by a crackling sound that created a reality that began to transport me completely away from where I was. Once again I found myself in a dream within a dream. I heard the old Nagual Lujan calling out to me.

"Come back," his voice echoed, as if from a great distance. "Focus on that thread which has been projected from the cloak that presses down on the individual innocence of those hearts you have been observing, but do not be caught within that dimension where you have been led. This etheric thread itself will translate the information necessary for you to remember what needs to be absorbed. Within that assimilation, visions containing crucial insights will be delivered and you will understand more deeply what you have just experienced.

"Now the truth cannot be hidden from you. See that your knowing can no longer be manipulated. As the void power that you are gazing into reveals its omnipresence to your eyes, notice that permeation equals saturation in the social circumstances you are witnessing. This is how humanity's collective energy is drained and consumed.

Drama is the key to the cloak's dominance. Objectivity is masked and thus lost, and clarity becomes absorbed within the ensuing power struggle. This drama obscures the existence of that cloaked intention and replaces our inner silence, creating a barrier to insight. This is the loop where the majority of earthlings are captured.

"The interconnective aspect of the thread that is projected by the cloaked inner child travels through time and space. The main resonance within that thread has its basic elemental structure formulated through the self-imposed idea of fear, and it is an imprint. Understand that a state of inner withdrawal has to be cultivated by those on the path of self-realization. The primary reason for this is to subdue harmful imprints by drawing vital distance from immersion in covert activity.

"When the cloak is projected through individual hosts, the ensuing pressure of socialization can enliven any held memory of visual or auditory content as a means to activate these anchors. As you have witnessed, the power of Jagür's paw reveals that insidious influence, which relentlessly pressures its circumstances to comply.

"See that the cloak is thrown as a thread to affect those individuals who seek vital distance to bring about their own enlightenment. The interconnective aspect of our existence must be taken into strong consideration so that we may clearly distinguish our intuitive, crystal clear realizations that erupt from silence as absolutely distinct from habitual preoccupation, which has been corrupted and is the basic elemental structure of the cloak itself. Know that it relies on thought for its existence.

"The cloak develops a symbiotic relationship with us through cultivating our self-sustained dependency. It knows the social being completely and travels on the habitual threads that exist within the narrative that the internal dialogue provides and the social bindings created by that constant nagging. What we had before this imposition was the intensity of our silences. This nefarious influence has stolen our collective potency and replaced our refinement by severely restricting humanity's self-actualization.

"The reason humanity forgets itself is that we have adapted the insidious device of a loop of repetition into our being, which manifests as a shortfall of internal insight. When human beings interact with cloaked intentions, they nourish those unwholesome and crippling behaviors that maintain their entrapment."

As the old Nagual continued to speak, I watched the populous scene in front of me with my attention fully focused upon the dimensional imagery being portrayed by the reflective component of the void power I was gazing into.

"When a clear individual travels on their own intensity, they can become aware of the threads that are being projected from the self-imposed cloak. At this particular stage in the life of a seer, there is a possibility that confusion may take hold. The hair that is being split is so subtle, and the struggle for one's power so important. The risk to be consumed by that battle must be navigated delicately.

"See the cloak for what it is. It has been created through the lazy flaccidity that is human attention clinging to the social moorings that have been locked inside of us since childhood. And like a leaky vessel we are sinking. The power of our joined vision has brought what is hidden to the surface. We have been taught to be surreptitious. As children we hide what's been given to us in undefined parts of ourselves that cannot find resolve, and in so doing we create what haunts us and forget how it came to pass.

"The innocence of children is so easily shaped by adult intentions, within their denials and their inability to do what has to be done. That denial is what translates into the shadow perspective that acts upon us all, and we blindly cooperate. See how the compromises of this world exchange that which used to be yours for the corruptive pressure that the cloak applies.

"Your silences you must see, and your ears must be clear to remember what I say. Calm your heart and empty your mind. The sound of my voice will transport you into the subtleties that you observe. You must know what you see."

As the old Nagual spoke, his wisdom transported me into the folly of what I was witnessing. It was the entrapment that all human beings engage in. He continued with the unmistakable assuredness of one who knows.

"See that there is an unclean exchange that occurs, where energy is traded on an abusive basis that solicits compliance. You will witness that one of the most destructive elements of interaction is the venom-laden tongue of gossip that degenerates conscious awareness, which humanity is grossly aware of. The predominance of this poison tongue destabilizes one's personal power and instills confusion, fear, and a cloud of animosity that obscures the truth of the moment that is continually escaping us.

"Communication that is indirect or unsavory cloaks awareness within a state of impedance that inhibits the natural openness that abides within transparency. Under the auspice of covert exchange, awareness is directed to unfruitful positions, misdirection disguises the actions of corrupt socialization, and collectively and individually we are waylaid. It is through the mechanisms of this nefarious network that ulterior motives can be fulfilled and our primary needs foregone.

"Under the guise of that waylaying principle, the most elaborate traps are set forth to hold and entrap. These are delivered through repetition, the elementary tool that is required to establish and sustain a cloaked perspective.

"Once a certain threshold of influence is established, conscious awareness of what is really relevant is diverted into a surreptitious undercurrent. Misguided preoccupations cause sufficient dilution of one's attention to maintain dormancy, until the time when it becomes necessary to reassert that waylaying principle on breakaway elements so as to ensure that the agenda is not interfered with.

"You can see that, in reality, the routines of control are never fully relinquished. They are simply adapted and reassigned in a myriad of forms to give existence itself its distorted meaning. Without that insistent repetition, weakness would surely be dropped. At this time the influence of this imposition is strong."

Within the scene that was taking place in front of us, I was viewing transparency and truth being swept into that surreptitious undercurrent. A moment later, the scene had disappeared and there was only the blackness of the room and the reflective silence of the void, mirroring my gaze back to me as an overwhelming sense of peace and quietude that entered deeply within.

Awakening the Witness Within

I heard a sound off to my left, the growling of Jagür, and when I looked in that direction, I saw a figure approaching me from the darkness. At first I could not make out his features. Upon his approach, he softly spoke.

"You cannot turn around to face the old Nagual at this moment. My name is Lucien*. I am one of the four companions that have traveled with your benefactor for many years. Our responsibility is to imprint upon you the enigmatic knowledge that you need to come to terms with.

"Your dreaming attention will be drawn to us until we have completed the task at hand. We will transmit through our voices what you need to assimilate, and within the dimensional visions you receive will be hidden inversions of that continuity that we wish you to unravel and see for what it is. These time capsules are what you need to access to enable you to go beyond any form of entrapment that may wish to ensnare your awareness and drag it away from the lessons at hand.

"If one's personal life is not clear or powerful, preoccupations will steal from you, the dreamer, the all-encompassing realm of power that is our heritage as human beings.

"Preoccupation saturates awareness with a disjointed fusion of imagery and emotion that is projected and added

---
* Lucien: Inner light

to what could be our unimpeded circumstances. This incapacitates our natural ability to discover the connecting link that exists in our waking world, appearing in the dream of ourselves to wake us up and alert us to the fact that we are the self-actualizing Architect of observation. Our magic as human beings is to consciously shift between dimensions.

"You must give up the social hierarchy that has been forced upon you so that you appear in a way that you should, and that emergence will be like water. As you know, water falls always appropriately to the lowest position in all circumstances. In truth, this stance is neither higher nor lower but mimics form, and through this empty mirroring, you are able to identify the oncoming agendas. Free expression will be the consequence of this approach, and your awareness will never be corrupted, by virtue of this fluid adaptation."

I became transfixed at that point. I realized that a command had been spoken to me through a suggestion that Lucien had engineered. I looked into his dilated pupils and began to make out the features of the man who was in front of me.

His brown eyes were shaped like almonds, and he had a strong, hawk-like appearance, with a finely chiseled nose and high cheekbones that protruded gently from his angular face. His lips were generous, and his jet-black hair was held in place by a high ponytail that disappeared down the length of his back.

Dressed only in loose-fitting, full-length black pants, his bare upper body rippled with muscles. He was tall and lean, not carrying an ounce of fat. On his upper left pectoral muscle he bore a tattoo that was a tribal representation of a lizard surrounded by various angled shapes that swept over his shoulder and down the length of his arm.

Lucien wore gold earrings that were clasped tightly on his earlobes and one gold ring on his right index finger. I was certainly impressed with the strength that exuded from this man. His coffee-colored skin prompted me to imagine that he was a tribal leader from a remote South Pacific island. My revelries were interrupted by the soft, melodic tone of his voice.

"Lujan, my responsibility is to awaken the adult witness, the man you met upon the bridge, who has now merged with you. To fully reintegrate this part of yourself, you must be guided on the level of intention to absorb deep knowings that emerge from the depths of the void that you are gazing within.

"Once this is completed, my task will be fulfilled. When you put your head on the pillow each night and fall asleep, my companions and I will be awaiting you with the realizations that you must acquire so that you may become a pundit for our knowing. I will now send you back to your world."

He clapped his hands and light exploded in my head as his last words rang in my ears. "You know you are responsible. Make good these lessons. A portion of the Nagual Lujan now lives permanently within you."

I knew I had dreamt myself through my benefactor's power, and the words of Lucien were infused within my being, confirming on a deep level what needed to be known. Since then, I have known my name to be Lujan.

Adaptation without corruption
is the key to personal power

Threads of Intention

For many years I was immersed in that realm where Lucien and his cohorts awaited me to transfer teachings that were so far-reaching within their implications. On one evening, I had fallen asleep harmoniously, and as I was drifting into those visual pictures that bring about the phenomena of dreams, I heard a voice whisper in my left ear.

"Is the thing there?"

"What thing?" I asked, and before I had a chance to say another word, I was there once again with Lucien in that mysterious room where Jagür wandered freely. I could hear her purring contentedly from within the darkness where she was so easily hidden.

"The thing is there," Lucien said in answer to his own question, and he began to elaborate. "There is a phenomenon that will occur for you now, and this is the active use of your true imagination within dimension so that you may capture that which is hidden.

"Within imagination, one's Architect inserts itself and draws pictures of that which we have forgotten. If one forgets this facility, an opening appears that allows the shadow to slip in. So we must remember this omnipresent factor by recapturing our self within the immediacy of the moment.

"Immediacy allows for the expression of your daydreaming self that is constantly being defined, and this definition will be composed of integrity and truth. As you progress along this path, detached observation becomes the hallmark of your awareness so that simply observing what arises enables you to drop attachments to unwholesome and insidious interconnective behavior.

"If you take the elements of dreaming, which essentially are the truths of your inner self that have been realized in an altered state and are transferred to your daytime cognition through visual lateralization, then, by the mere reconnection of these aspects of awareness, real time becomes available.

"Real time, your genuine perceptual speed, serves as truth that cuts through the petty landscape that a mass of small minds has put together.

"We will now engage your awareness within lateralization so that your Architect of observation can combine with the essence of real time, and that power will be your resourcefulness as the observer.

"Try to conceive of where you are stationed within the arrangements of your own application to life, and then see the interconnective web of socialization and discover where you may be caught within that net of compliance.

"See yourself in a circumstance that has previously escaped you. Close your eyes within that imagination. If within the imagery that arises you cannot find definition of the happenings you wish to discover, shut that same old thing off, which is the predatorial mind that holds discovery of what has really occurred at bay. Be possessed with acuity that is not governed by thought and what will jump in will be dreamlike, and that vision will be composed of the truth you wish to actualize.

"Look now into the void that is in front of you. See within that expansiveness the shadow that wields the hand of perception. From this cloaked hand fall threads. These threads attach themselves, each to a different location: the top of the head, the shoulders, the elbows, the hands, the base of the spine, the knees and the feet.

"Even though these are positions on the body, they are not the physicality but an inward conceptualization. Can you say that you are aware of which thread is being manipulated?

"When one thread is pulled, your awareness moves to that thread, and you forget the rest. At this point you might say, 'I am in command of my awareness.' However, once you are familiar with that which you think you have command over, the equilibrium shifts, and then you become aware of the weight that is asserted on an alternative location.

"Now, awareness is focused on this thread, and just when you think you're gaining some insight into that element, the one that you originally thought you had command over shifts and changes.

"Thus intended for you is the proposition that takes you away from discovering the truth. Becoming aware of the threads themselves makes you forget the hand that moves perception. That hand is a cloak; and through multiple interactions that perpetuate self-imposed socialization, the hand steals awareness and moves into an alternate reality, which is screened off by the mere fact that you have focused your attention on the thread.

"By intending upon these elements, they are also lost to you through the integration of emotion. This becomes preoccupation, which harbors justification, and that is the shadow's projection. Here the threads become something more than they really are, through the self-sustained idea of significance and false ownership that is attached to them.

"This is how the shadow lives vicariously through our being. When emotion is added, we become more than what we used to be, justified through that surreptitiously placed imprint upon our emptiness. These installations replace our immediacy and waylay inner truth, which is the recovery of our stolen moment.

"The stabilization of imprints is our true nemesis. This is where humanity is caught. The threads themselves form the barrier that hides the cloak, which moves feverishly within our construct to hold perception in place. However, realizing this is not enough. One must forget everything that is realized.

"It is neither the hand nor the threads that one must be aware of. One must forget the threads and not pay into the assertiveness of their bid for our attention, which demand that we uphold the constant idea that we have conceived of them, within all the circumstances that surround us."

Lucien's descriptions evoked a rush of living imagery that flashed before me as visual confirmation of what he was imparting.

"Listen to my voice," he said calmly. "I will command that part of your awareness which needs to be clear.

"Look to the horizon. The horizon is composed of inner silence. Be within that horizon and be absorbed by it. Even though the horizon is in the distance and you stay where you are, everything in between dissolves, for it cannot conceive of you and cannot be conceived of by the threads. The idea that holds the threads in place dissolves, and you are no longer involved with that which holds you.

"If a thread is flung at you, catch yourself within that involvement. See that interaction and the threads that hold the puppets that play in front of you. They are the phantom's phantom."

Lucien lifted his hand and the gesture broke my fixation from that liquid omnipresence. I realized then that I was focused simultaneously upon him and upon the void. I did not understand how I could be split in such a fashion.

"Everything is so tangible here," I said. "This seems so real, yet we are dreaming."

Lucien reached out and touched my left shoulder, and I felt kindness flowing down his arm into my body as he spoke.

"Your waking life is a dream for me. To be there is more of an illusion than being here. This place seems to be limited only because it is a reflection of your living construct. In reality, we are in an expansiveness that goes far beyond the confines of the construct that exists in your waking dream.

"I will now introduce you to two other men who will come from their prospective corners but still stand within shadows. They will enact for you a riddle that defines entrapment through selfishness. Their true identity will not be revealed to you at this time, for they are to act out an illusion, and to give you their names would make them too solid within the intentions that they present. They must remain in obscurity while they speak the shadow's language."

A figure appeared, lurching unsteadily out of the darkness on the left hand side. He was bent forward, clutching a walking stick as if he could not stand without it. His hand was shaking, and it seemed he could barely hold his own weight. When he spoke, his voice quivered with age. He began to ramble incoherently like a madman.

"The same old thing... the thing is... but I ... it's just me... what about me?"

Suddenly, a second man leapt out of the gloom and addressed the first in a booming voice.

"Stop beating around the bush, you stinking, geriatric fool!"

"It's my bush, and I'll beat around it if I want," the old man retorted with surprising venom.

"What are you ranting and raving about, smelly? When you talk about the same old thing, isn't it just the same old thing that is coming up all the time? You fossilized old fart!" When he had finished his insults, he turned to me, opening his arms wide and saying suggestively, "The thing is there."

I was horrified at the crude and uncouth behavior that was being presented. I turned to Lucien and saw a wicked smile on his face, and then I noticed that the boisterous man had turned back towards his companion.

"The thing is there!" he repeated loudly, thrusting his hips forward and pointing at his genitals. The hobbled figure on the left started to tremble uncontrollably and began shouting and pointing at the other man's genitalia.

"Cover up that wrinkly old installment! And you better protect it," he yelled, "because the thing is there!"

I began to laugh with abandon. Their lewd gestures were alluding to the undisciplined behavior of humanity that emanates from the sexual center. When the jittery old man spoke again, his voice was frail and contemptuous.

"What protects the thing that is there?" he asked petulantly.

"'But I' is the perverted view that won't cover up the thing that is there, and it's a monster," the boisterous man roared wildly, walking comically around the room with his legs bowed as if his genitalia were too big for his pants. The old man was aghast and began swinging his cane with feeble fury.

"But I am in front of the thing that is there," he screeched, "'But I' doesn't protect me! God damn, it's enormous!"

At that point Lucien intervened, and the two alarming characters stepped back into the shadows.

"You'll have to forgive those guys, they haven't been out for a while," he said chuckling, "I knew I couldn't trust them to do the right thing. I will repeat the riddle for you. Their actions have freed you from your seriousness and the fixation that surrounds this state of awareness, and this is a good thing!

"Words are powerful. They confirm oneself to oneself and mold the world to one's agenda. Words like 'The same old thing', 'The thing is...', 'But I...', 'It's just...' and, 'What about me?'

"When we talk about the same old thing, it is just the same old thing that is coming up all the time — that 'same old thing' that adjusts and adapts in repetitive motions to keep itself intact. That same old thing has been passed through many generations. 'The thing is...' is the justification that covers up the first installment and protects it, because the thing is there and does not want to be seen.

"And what protects the thing that is there? 'But I.'

"This is the personalized view that appropriates and conceals the thing that is there. 'But I am in front of the thing that is there.' 'But I,' protects 'me.' The 'me' guards 'myself.' 'It's just...' is the beginning of the same old thing. 'It's just me, what about me?' Do you see?"

He paused while looking at me, and I knew that what he was wishing to convey was that if one is alerted to these phrases, one can recognize the depth, or lack of depth, revealed within the usage of such language.

"Can you see the installment? And can you know it? Words have power. Lujan, do you see what was just said?

"Is your innocence more powerful than your installments? Has your innocence got power? And do you have enough innocence to detach yourself from the power of what you see so that you may return to that uncorrupted innocence?

"Observational silence is the tool of innocence and power and will allow you to identify coercive manipulation so that such maneuvers cannot be used as a way to define and utilize power for self-serving purposes.

"The threads I have spoken of are etherically projected as a foreign substance that passes from generation to generation as cloaked intention. As a hologram, the installer will integrate with the installee from behind, and so, by walking within the installee's shoes, the cloaked intention survives another generation.

"Such is the power of entrapment and a solidified, intended proposition, manifesting as a hardened cache of impenetrable intention that is held in the body and survives as the shadow's mind, therefore cloaking the inner child.

"You must convey to those who wish to learn that they cannot make an installation out of innocence, for innocence is introspective by nature. To be internally reflective is to be composed of power. If one would take credit for this then that becomes an installment — a controlling, tyrannical force that moves to overcome innocence, which is our power. The corrupt witness lies within and has been cultivated by an external force.

"The only element that can descend upon our lives to wake us up to ourselves is observational silence, and the only individuals who can descend harmoniously into others' lives are those possessed by this acuity.

"Being aligned with the Architect of observation means they watch innocently what unfolds with a hand as light as a feather, and invisible to themselves are their actions. For it is not they who act. It is the hand of the Spirit. When seeing these men or women, humanity may see a mask, but that projection belongs to the perceiver. It is the intended filter of their original installment, that same old thing.

"The Architect within needs them to see, and become aware of, the mask that appears. But when you, the clear-hearted, move away from their gaze the mask falls and shatters into a million pieces to be absorbed by the earth.

"It is important to be aware, very aware, of the same old thing. Even though you may think you have conquered this insidious element that has lodged very deeply, your clarity and resolve to have power in your life will inevitably be challenged, by an external operative in the guise of a friend or associate — a familiar.

"If the familiars themselves have not destabilized the same old thing, their envy will be alerted by your fortitude, and their need to overcome your clarity and power will be activated. They will move swiftly and try to find lodgment within the purity of your innocence. Then you will be engaged once again in a battle with the same old thing, except in this case it will be more evasive and cunning than ever.

"When occupied with an external operative, you will need tenfold resolve not to become involved, in order to unmask the covert activities that find placement in the mundane. Such is the war that the clear-hearted fight for their life and power.

"Even though the actions of the men within the shadows seem to make no sense, they make just as much sense as the onslaughts of our fellow man, and obviously, this is none at all.

"In your communication with your familiars, you must become aware of the emotions attached to the words that they speak. Even though the words may not seem deleterious, the emotions are thrown as anchors or hooks into the physiology, and as contact progresses through repetitive motion, the lodgments of these anchors gain gravity.

"Then you may wonder in confused madness, 'Why do I feel this lodgment, this restriction within my heart?'

"Know that it is because, on the back of their words travels the same old thing, hidden behind the complexity of the syntax and arriving as a cloaked intention that embeds the secret envy of the familiar in your body. If you were to approach this associate, this familiar, and ask:

'Why do I feel so bad when I'm around you, even though what you say seems not to be harmful?' Here the familiar will put its hands in the air and say, 'What did you say about me? But I cannot understand what you're saying, what did you say about me?'

"At this point, 'I' must become a monster and accost you, for the truth is too hard to bear and the same old thing's claws are deep, and it does not want to be seen. For if recognition is a statement of realization, then the 'I' must ignore the impulses of that same old thing so that it may wither and die.

"Being in contact with the same old thing, 'I' must retreat. For if 'I' become too familiar with the thing that is there, surely that influence will engulf innocence and power.

"Lujan, it would be a great advantage to see that same old thing as a monster. When you hear 'the thing is,' look back and see that it is a monster. And remember that the same old thing can also be seen externally, as the onslaughts of our fellow man.

"When confronted, this monster will turn around with its hands in the air and say, 'But I…' so that it can forget that 'the thing is,' is that same old thing. 'It's just me, what about me?' personalizes the original installation, which becomes, 'But I…', and forgets that the monster was there, so you can be the same old thing instead of your sovereign self that does not need to make justification for its power.

"See that the intended mask has been given in terms of a visual representation, which is the externalization of the person's view in connection to whom they are gazing at. Witness the mask falling and shattering into a million pieces, and understand that the whole affair, in terms of that projection, is futile.

"If one is concentrated enough, it becomes self-evident that the matrix of manifestation is a collective perception that belongs to us all. The visual context of a person walking away and an emptiness left, with the mask hovering in the air for a second or so before it crashes to the ground, shows that this fixation is such a waste of energy and time. What needs to be focused on is what appears after the mask falls: Nothing.

"Even if in the beginning, the nothingness appears to have no substance, when an individual awaits long enough — and doesn't revert back to those imprints that alert the same old thing back into action — through this reflective emptiness they are filled with a heartfelt sense of beauty that will elevate their energetic mass beyond their wildest dreams."

Lucien paused for a moment, and I realized that while he was talking I had been transported back to the original scene, where people had now appeared. They were enacting upon one another within the void, and the futility and madness of their behavior was starkly apparent.

"Humanity has one fundamental faculty that we are so totally familiar with yet ignore completely," Lucien stated, transfixing me once more with his unwavering voice. "Intent is tangible, and on the back of our words travels that fixated objective.

"Recall the visual description of a cloak traveling behind a word. This will give concrete value to something that is supposedly hidden from view. Know that if you were to ask one person to admit the maliciousness that exists behind their words, in most cases they would respond with absolute denial, for admitting this would give full flavor to your insights and empowerment to your internal seeing.

"If they were to reveal their ill intentions, they would be acknowledging a lower part of themselves that they are riding upon, and this would bring to the forefront the person you are really dealing with.

"I am sure you remember the usage of 'I' that my two companions displayed within their obscure and lewd behavior. Even though their actions were crude, there was a cryptic meaning hidden within their demonstration.

"The representation of 'I' should be stated in the context of transparency and clarity, which ultimately brings about the true advisor from within and fosters an impersonal or professional view that is not governed by selfish preoccupation or emotionality.

"The 'I' used in this fashion deals only with what is pending or appropriate. If the premise of 'I' goes beyond these points, it becomes personal. That personalized view then becomes self-serving, and a power struggle begins.

"When the abstract expresses itself impersonally no agenda is implied, and the only force that eternally transmutes itself through the human physiology is an omnipresent emptiness. Observational silence reveals fluctuations to the eye of the clear-hearted. Any inflection from the environment awakens immediate adaptation in terms of a fluid awareness that will be alert to the ensuing pressures of socialization.

"An external gesture usually gains arrival at the mid part of the chest, which alerts the clear-hearted to an attempt of invisible anchoring. Anchoring can be applied within one's personal space and from a distance, through repetitious internal talk, emotional justification or visualization by the perpetrator.

"Sometimes this phenomenon is immediately apparent, while at other times there's a lull, and from within that liquid suspension emerges introspective realizations that jump into the space of the clear-hearted to warn of things to come.

"Intention pervades every corner of reality. If we are not clear about what is being drawn towards us, what comes may degrade our clarity. We as a human race cast our intentions every day and in many ways. Depending on resonance, like magnets we attract to our internal environment what is necessary to wake us up. If we are not clear about what we are being alerted to, then surely we will be semi-awake, and how dangerous is that?

"One certainly has to be on guard at all times, for our fellow men are continuously practicing their art of attachment and that practice is connected to an inherited line of intent that waits to re-establish itself at every waking moment. You may be susceptible to this until the time when your being is absolutely permeated with power.

"For you now, the challenge is to stand within the realms of your fellow man and hold your state of intensity intact. You will need all your speed not to be caught within the realm of human affairs. This is the first step. Through the knowledge that can be assimilated by simply dreaming awake and being fully cognizant of the content of these dreams, you can pull closer to yourself that which has been denied to humanity.

"By virtue of this gravity, power will present itself in another way. Another dream will appear for you, as it has appeared for us. In this state you will dream, but while dreaming, you will be in that reality that you are sleeping in.

"To experience this oneness is our ultimate goal, for when this dreaming body appears in the waking world, the information that floods our conscious awareness opens us to the necessary speed of comprehension to take us beyond the limitations of the cognitive system that surrounds humanity.

"Your task will be to awaken the dreamer to the fixed perception of the reality they are stationed within so that they may travel upon their inwardly realized images to where the other exists, within its own matrices that will combine when the seer wakes up to the full potentiality of their thousand-petalled lotus that opens upon that point. This will give flavor to the realized seer's fractalized multidimensional resonances. Within that explosion of light, it is as if an eye sees itself within mirrors upon mirrors, giving the appearance of great distance by virtue of the reflection being never ending, yet never leaving its point of origin.

"This in essence is just the living embodiment of the capacity of your third eye matrix to be unified. This is how the possibility of the 'other' appears as what seems to be a carbon copy of oneself that is only slightly larger. In some traditions it is called the double. You must realize that the universe automatically reflects back what it sees. Upon the point of this activation, it creates an alternate vessel that looks the same as the person who has opened their possibilities to the universal omnipresence.

"We live within reflections of that, which fractalize by virtue of the fact that one can travel upon and through these gateways at the pinnacle of their development. Realize the contradiction is at this point that in actuality this is only the beginning of the journey.

"Can you navigate these still waters that I present? Can you negotiate your storms?"

I woke up suddenly and was confronted with the harshness of the reality where my body had lain. Lucien was right. This world did not seem as real, even though the intentions that surrounded me attempted to hold me fixed. I assumed full responsibility for what had to be done within my waking life from that point on.

The next time I entered my benefactor's realm I was to meet with a most extraordinary man, and it began with these words, whispered into my ear as I drifted into sleep.

"Where is the hidden fabric?"

In suspended thought,
when the mind
is absorbed by beauty,
your greatest wealth, stillness,
will surrender the world
to be unmasked before you.

The Hidden Fabric

I was once again immersed in the unmistakable potency of my benefactor's domain. I had opened my eyes and found myself surrounded by stars. There was a vastness beyond comparison above and below me. Two points of brightness came from the heavens, and this visual sight was accompanied by a growl. Contained within this sound was the energetic construct that I had been introduced to by my benefactor, the old Nagual.

I looked to my left. Jagür slinked out from the darkness, and from behind her, a figure emerged. It seemed that she and this man were in a state of acute symbiosis. I recognized his features as he came closer and extended his right hand to grasp my wrist.

I was shocked when I realized he was the feeble old man who had played within shadows before me, for he was not frail at all; he was liquid and beautiful, and not one tremble was revealed in his touch.

"My name is Malaiyan*," he said, reaching his other hand towards my forehead. "We must leave here and go to a place of beauty so that you may be immersed in the lessons I am to give."

As soon as his index finger touched my mid eyebrow, I began to see a scene emerge in front of me. Before I had time to even fathom what was happening, we were surrounded by thick, green rainforest. In front of me was a huge pond fed by a cascading waterfall that created an energizing mist. Malaiyan was to my left, perched lightly on a ledge.

I became immediately absorbed within his big round eyes. He looked like an owl. His pupils were dilated in the same way Lucien's had been, but they were even more absorbing. His pure white hair was also pulled back in a high ponytail that accentuated his sharp eyebrows and made him look intently focused, but his fierceness was hidden within gentle features.

Malaiyan's face was full and generous, and he wore a goatee beard that was as white as his long ponytail. Unlike Lucien, he was fully clad, in black attire that looked like elegant silk pajamas. His skin shone in the full moonlight as he began to speak in low, rhythmic tones.

"Focus your gaze on the water, Lujan. The lesson that I am to give you will be more cryptic than Lucien's. You must use your imagination and your powers of introspection simultaneously to understand what is presented.

---

* Malaiyan: spirit of the mountain

"Your reviewal will yield time capsules of knowledge, and these deposits of information will contain an inversion of elements that is not immediately obvious. But to understand this, you must be saturated within silence.

"Silence can be collected, and is the only element that does not give rise to definition through syntax, which is that preoccupation we all must avoid. It is of itself, yet foreign to itself. Can you sit and be silent, Lujan? Silence as a concept seems to be as elusive as attempting to pick up water with your bare hands."

With this statement, he ran his hand through the water and tried to grasp it as it flowed through his open fingers, then turned his head and looked directly at me.

"Can you not see within my gesture how the water flows from my hands between my fingers? What is left when the water falls to its most appropriate position? Just my hand. If I see this hand as a recovery of what occurred, then this is the truth of that recovery.

"If I were to be emotionally involved and become upset that the water had escaped my grasp, then I would be caught within that emotion and become preoccupied with the fact that the water did not co-operate with me.

"This water is my friend, and the reason I come to this conclusion is that all I am left with is what is appropriate: my hand. If I become agitated with the water for escaping me, then I would be emotionally affected by something I cannot influence.

"Does not the water teach us that we need not possess the wrong elements for reviewal?

"You must understand that the water is here for a reason. If the water evokes a state of emotionality, then when you look at your hand and discover that it is no longer wet, should you be upset with the water?"

Malaiyan paused to peer at me with a mischievous glint in his eye, clearly amused by my perplexed expression. "Or should you question the threads of intention that do not see appropriateness, and from this premise, create preoccupation with that which cannot be controlled?" he asked, as he flicked a pebble from the palm of his hand into the still waters.

"Now consider this. If I were to press my hand into the soft dirt that is before me, when I remove it do I not leave the impression of that form via the weight that has been applied? Is the ground not more solid than the water? And when I look upon my palm, is not dust covering its full surface? Do you see the imprint before me? Do you also see the dust upon the palm of my hand?

"If I immerse my hand in the water, the preoccupation with the dust of that impression is washed away. Now when I gaze upon my hand in this instant, is it not clean? Yet we both can still see what is left within the compacted earth in front of us.

"The earth is the keeper and the water is the facilitator. Through that connection, the water dissolves the imprint that was placed upon my hand, as dust, into a thousand particles as it drifts slowly to the bottom of the pond. Is not the water reviewing this impression within fragmentation? Is this not multilateral assimilation of that which is solid?

"When I withdraw my hand from the water, it is still wet. My hand is the same shape as that outline in the dirt, so I am compelled at this stage to place it once again into that which reflects back my previous doings. Then shall I withdraw it once again, to examine what is there for a more complete reviewal. Is it not covered more thickly now with the dust via the repetition of my actions? Does this not give gravity to the frequency of that knowing? Does it not now want to sing that song on my behalf? Do we not now understand more completely this imprint, due to the water's capacity to affix the soil to that tactile reservoir?

"The water itself is unbiasedly witnessing what is occurring. Yet, the danger within the song being sung is that the water will soon adaptively cooperate with that signal, and there we can be consciously lost, through that repetition."

Malaiyan's descriptions of imprints and their dissolution were magical. These simple gestures for me held so much truth within them. Every movement that he made opened a wellspring within my heart. Never in my life had I met such a magician. Malaiyan lifted his finger to the level of my eyes.

"To the water your attention must be. Listen to me carefully, for within my words are hidden truths. We all know that water takes the lowest position, no matter where it is poured, and we all know that without water there can be no life. There was a time when silence was cherished as much as water. In observing water, we can learn behaviorally how to collect this silence.

"If we are poured into a circumstance, as individuals we should immediately take the lowest position. Not that of a beggar, but one of non-control. Through not controlling and by moving with your circumstances harmoniously, you truly see the position you stand in as an individual and so learn to recognize the consequences that bear upon you through the ensuing pressure of intention.

"By virtue of this observational stance, the doorway to one's inner child is flung open, and all superfluous elements that stand in opposition to your unfettered adult witness will be revealed for what they truly are.

"Remember, the doorway that surpasses the chambers of the heart is the door itself. The key to that door is composed of abeyance, and in that simple beauty dwells the secret tapestry.

"When we listen to the world with our ears and acknowledge the messages received through our hearts, we forgo the interchangeable energetic imprints of socialization. Thus we are delivered to our inherent reservoir of silence. Then through our visual construct, architectural observation will appear and caress that which is hidden.

"Lean forward, Lujan, and look into the water. As you gaze, what you see is your reflection given back. Even though you are separate from the water, the water is one with you. It holds your reflection as if you are dreaming. When you reach out to touch the water, this magical liquid reaches towards you. As your fingers enter it, you absorb the reflection and thus the water becomes you, as a true mirror that sees the unseen.

"Which is more real, the hand that has been absorbed by the water, or the reflection that reveals the osmosis that has just occurred? And has this liquid consciousness taken on your solidity within its reflection as the mirroring of the reality that has approached it? Are we not the ultimate shifter of shapes?

Through his childlike expression, I could see light dancing around his facial features as he enjoyed watching my enrapturement upon his beautiful explanation.

"This is the dilemma that we face as human beings. We dream, yet forget that we are saturated within those dimensions. And when we are awake, we are only a reflection of what we truly could be. We are literally composed of that water which you gaze into. It bears our living essence.

"Water is one of the many entities that lives within the reality of waking and monitors our activities as a species. Speak to the water. In conversing with that liquescence we are addressing ourselves, and the water will transform and truly reflect to us what we are."

Malaiyan gently pulled my arm away from the pond, looked into my eyes and said, "We live within dimensions, and these alternate constructs are akin to the water. If we can enter them as easily as we enter this liquidity, we will then be able to change the content of our living dream, which has absorbed us like the imprint that lies in the dust.

"Can you tell me, where is the hidden fabric that lies behind this vision and reveals a composite of wisdom? Where is the abstract, that which is not immediately apparent, hidden within the scene?

"For me to put this question to you, my friend, is an exercise in perception. I would ask you to recollect and find for me the cognitive inversion that waits to pounce on you as abstract, insightful knowing.

"We all have a perceptual faculty that is visually stationed within our very being. When our cognition is saturated with silence and syntax is forgone completely, what invariably jumps in is the memory of what used to be.

"These images are those dust particles floating to the bottom of the pond to be reintegrated with the earth in a way that will retain no static elements of cognition, and this can only be understood through multilateral assimilation of that which used to be.

"What is recovered through our reviewal is what has eluded us, and what has escaped us we can never really know, for whatever position we stand in, our knowing will be different. We can always be sure that something has evaded the tenuous grasp of our eyes.

"In our stations in life, wherever we are coming from, we must become aware that the obvious is not our strength. What escapes us is where true wisdom abides. So I say to you that this time capsule of reviewal will show what you are focused on, and then when you review it again, it will reveal what was previously hidden.

"Within avenues of awareness, we develop our cognitive system, which is reinforced by syntax and becomes our construct. Take away syntax, take away that inner talk, take away that same old thing and discover what has been escaping you."

Whilst Malaiyan spoke, luminous butterflies flew from the center of his chest and this he said to me:

"Our intentions press upon each other like butterflies that intermingle and crossover to be absorbed. In abeyance, our hearts await."

I was left with a profound sense of beauty that this man had imprinted upon me, and this impression was his gift. I came to discover that whenever intention pressed upon that inner imprint he had left with me, I would be alerted to that which used to escape me.

www.parallelperception.com

As we press
upon one another
with our intentions,
from our hearts fly
luminous butterflies,
that intermingle
and crossover
to be absorbed.
In abeyance
our hearts await.

Fear Not, Be Free

I had gone to bed relaxed, not knowing that on this night I would be pulled into the Old Nagual's realm. I was awoken by a howling wind that penetrated and passed through my neck. As I became more aware of the texture of this auditory phenomenon, I realized it was Jagür's roar, awakening me into that mysterious realm where my benefactor and his companions were conspiring to change the fundamental fabric of my cognitive system.

I was suddenly standing in the room where the four men had appeared previously, and from the darkness leapt Jagür. She flew towards me through the air and pinned me by the chest. As we hurtled backwards, scenes and memories of past events streamed by in rapid sequences.

While plummeting towards the floor, I realized that the imagery was somehow erupting from behind her paw, and when we landed she locked my eyes intently with her bottomless gaze. There was an unbreakable resolve in this animal — the same determination you would see in a wild cat just before it snapped the neck of its prey. But her purpose was not to kill me. She was taking me into past events through her fierceness. I heard from behind her a voice, calling.

"Jagür."

Looking past her, I saw an enormous man approaching. His head was clean-shaven, and when he reached forward, I saw that his forearms were like tree-trunks. He clasped my hand and pulled me effortlessly to a standing position.

"Jagür's actions may seem harsh, but what she has pressed upon within you is more than pertinent for you to become fully aware of now. The scenes that you were witnessing as you flew backwards in time are imprinted anchors that you must review with our guidance so that we can free you from the insidious loop of repetition that is supplied by these sites.

"Come with me, and we shall sit by the void and discuss these vital matters."

Walking by my side, he did not seem as tall as I'd initially thought, but the energy that emanated from his being was massive.

"My name is Barak*," he introduced himself, his voice deep and resonant. "I have no fear," he stated without a trace of arrogance.

---

* Barak: A flash of lightning

"My body is powerful and my heart is full of courage. Focus on my inner strength, and I will guide you through the void so that you can understand how to access this power within your own being."

Turning my attention to his chest, I saw that he bore a large black tattoo of a jaguar's paw on his left pectoral muscle. He acknowledged my observation with a nod.

"You have been marked, as I have been marked. You sustained your strength and clarity while Jagür pressed upon your chest. The tattoo that you gaze at is a representation of her power. I bear that sign out of respect for her. Jagür's fierceness is direct and unrelenting, and her lesson is that if you face the world with anything less than purpose, you will be engulfed by that which surrounds you."

I looked into Barak's eyes and the void began to appear in front of me. I recognized the sensation and knew I was being split.

"Listen carefully as I speak to you," he commanded.

"It has been said that there is nothing to fear but fear itself. If fear is our nemesis, and that emotion is an installation, then the question is: How can we mute fear's existence through understanding?

"Fear is an installed, socially stabilized site of preoccupation. The key to resolving fear is to recognize its placement and to be aware of how it comes into existence. If our society were structured in fairness, the trained repetitive roles of inner and outer dominance would not exist.

"It is through domination that the first window of opportunity is given for a tyrannical force to install an overview of fear. This suffocates the recipient and opens up avenues for controlling factors to be set in place, leading to the development of a hidden network of activity that corrals circumstances and neutralizes growth and awareness.

"If you have fear, you must become aware of three things. You are born alone, you live isolated, and you die alone. The second and third concepts, if truly considered, are relevant for those who have fear in their life. When a child is born, it arrives without fear. But when that very same child travels toward the inevitable conclusion of life, ninety-nine percent of the time, there is fear of death.

"So why do we fear our death at the end, when in the beginning there was no possibility of fear? A child is simply there.

"The reason fear persists is that one has not lived their full potential, and within that realization, feelings of remorse for not being the way one should have been bring about a deep sense of loss. This regret reforms and recreates itself as rigid arrogance that is sustained through justifications so that one never has to face what must be seen.

"When a person in this position is ultimately confronted with the end of their life, they do not have the calculative resource to let go of who they are in order that they may become something more than what they were. Entrapped individuals imprint their children with the same mechanisms of denial to ensure through this replication that they will not be confronted with what they have not done.

"Imprinting of this nature is deeply immoral. Those offspring, within their dysfunctional viewpoint, perpetuate what they have learnt and further evolve the intellectual positioning that enables them to entrap their environment within denial. Thus are the cloaked intentions that haunt the very fabric of humanity established.

"The primary reason why we guard and protect these imprinted sites is that when they are revealed, they cause enormous amounts of regret. If that anguish signals a state of realization, then we would have to admit that we have invested in the wrong elements. For many, this is more than devastating. For those caught in this position, the idea of death is as frightening as the catharsis they avoid.

"We are the Architects of our own construct. The trick is to look back on that, instead of looking forward and damaging everything in our path. It is best to stop and consider our options intelligently, rather than blindly moving forward with the destructive imprint that does not allow the Architect full expression.

"These things will be explained to you in greater depth when you learn to stalk that element which stalks us. Your task will be to awaken, in those you educate, the understanding that what they speak and what they do comes from somewhere other than themselves, for it is foreign to that emptiness we should possess as human beings.

"We are born alone and we should not fear to be alone as we live. There is a centralized focal point within all of us. It is invisible to our eye and impossible to touch. We cannot smell, taste, nor hear this focal point, but we can feel, and adjust our perceptions appropriately so as to outline our integrity by not compromising this inner feeling. That focal point is our inner child. I say to you, Lujan, stand within this premise I am to give you.

"Give of yourself, except for that which weakens you. Accept what is given, but not that which compromises.

"If this principle is adhered to then the inner child will be free to outline its perimeter of integrity, and through this one simple technique, one will be delivered to the most pertinent aspects of their truth.

"You must realize that upon arrival in this new state of consciousness, one may be confronted with installations of fear designed to preoccupy and inhibit growth — a cloak of sorts. At this crucial juncture, the installment will reveal its mind, supplying targeted dialogue in an attempt to prevent change: 'How will my world be, if I do not act in a way which is familiar? Will I lose what is dear to me?'

"Or," Barak said meaningfully, "The mind will say nothing and the seer will act upon their circumstances appropriately."

"What must be remembered is that if an element of your life cannot survive under the premise just outlined, then it was not meant to be there. For in truth, it is not what leaves which makes us fear. What we truly fear is what is activated within us. The idea of loss, which we have given to ourselves repetitively, makes us cling to what is not right for us.

"What we have in all circumstances of fear is a self-perpetuating momentum that can be transferred from an external source and can also be reinforced through internally repeating and fortifying our weaknesses. In each case, the recipient and the perpetrator lose power. We all know within ourselves how far to go, how much to give and how much to take before this part of us is damaged.

"If we see ourselves as an accumulation of frequencies that have momentum, and progressively activate the architectural element of observation, we learn to listen to the cues given, and our feelings will give us arrival at a place of power. As this feeling gathers it will become communal, and this sense of community will neutralize isolation.

."If a person in the position of fear were to touch upon something that would give them a new sense of positivity, you can be sure that the element controlling them, whether it be internal or external, will have them confirm to themselves that this new framework is not a plausible option through its reasoning. This occurs through repetitive cycles that emphasize the non-viability of change. These loops reinforce within individuals the idea of how weak and powerless they are. They are imprints, inwardly stationed sites.

"Essentially, each one of us builds a construct through repetitious acts so that we may confirm to ourselves that our world is intact. This refers basically to a form of self-reflection that remains outside of one's real self, for in essence, our inner silence is never really touched or damaged by the arrangement.

"It seems that the construct is so alive while silence in itself is so non-invasive that its appearance is hard to hook onto. So we simply go to what is familiar, and in doing this we forget who we truly are, by reinforcing the only thing that can be possibly known at that point — our trained, repetitive response to circumstances.

"The reason that we are able to build such complexity is due to our inner silence, but those elaborate mechanisms have stolen that precious sanctuary from us. If we could go back into our introspective self, we would certainly re-evaluate what we are doing.

"For fear to exist, the cognitive system surrounding that feeling has to be sustained. We must open up new perspectives within the perceptual matrix so that we may move away from negative self-perpetuation, and thus reformulate the construct into a baseless configuration that holds more possibilities and which will manifest as a state of dimensional lateralism.

"Our imprints are the basis, the territories and boundaries that we are protecting. And since they are being guarded, they need to be extensively examined. We can all see that we are defending something, but what we need to see is that we can live without these installations that bring separation and fear.

"We must learn to dissolve those reference points, those imprints, so that humanity can be brought into a state of resolve. Metamorphosis will come about through completion.

"Come, I will now travel with you into a vision that will be composed of past enactments upon you. Break your fixation from the void."

I suddenly had the feeling of being released. I looked up to my left to closely observe Barak's face for the first time. The brightness of his eyes was electric. He commanded me to focus on his left pupil.

Gazing into the darkness behind that piercing regard, I saw Jagür leaping at me from the depths. Her roar was deafening, and I was transported by that sound to a time in my childhood.

Jagür stood by my side as I viewed a man beating a child. As I watched, the scene became more distinct, and I realized it was my father. His big hand gripped the child by the left arm, and in the other, he was holding a large white tennis shoe. I was more than shocked to see this past event reoccurring so vividly in front of me.

Standing there watching, I was struck by the fact that this huge man kept continually hitting the child, not stopping. What impacted me the most was the sound of the child's distress, and this anguish related to the feeling in my own chest. He wanted the beating to stop, but it just kept going and going. Jagür began to growl, and I heard Barak's voice in the distance.

"Put your hand through the scene and stop the man," he commanded.

I immediately thrust my hand forward into what seemed to be a type of pressure, and as I pushed through that seal, it popped. I placed my hand on my father's shoulder and said, "Stop."

With this gesture the occupants of that vision turned into shadows and became stationary figures. I walked around the two people that I had been viewing and realized that the intensity of feeling that had first impacted me upon encountering the original scene had now disappeared.

Jagür roared again, and at that point, we reappeared in Lo Ban's realm. In front of me was the void. Barak's voice sounded low and calm at my side.

"What you have viewed was a recollection from your past. This memory comprises a significant portion of your base-plate imprint. As you witnessed that event, you must have realized the energy that it would take to sustain such a vibrant scene within you.

"This living enactment that you have remembered is a past event to which you have attached too much importance, though not intellectually, mind you. It is on an emotional level that you have placed such emphasis. What you have recalled here was a time capsule of reviewal, and within this memory intense feelings of fear and desperation at losing so much control were anchored.

"This imprint that is sustained deep within your being has multi-layered resonance. For this past event to lose its power over you, you must detach emotion from that site.

"Even though this scene is full of distress and fear, the predominant element that has evolved from that initial event is the need not to be controlled or be made to do what you don't want to do by people in positions of authority.

"Under certain circumstances this is not a bad thing, but if the original emotion attached to your need not to be controlled is not subdued, you will fight when you need not and be consumed by fear when you must fight."

Barak instructed me once more to look into his left eye, and in doing so I was again transported back to that memory. The boy and the man were still stationary shadows, and this time Barak was standing by my side.

"Push your hand through and perforate the scene once more," he said, "and as you press forward, visualize what you would do under these circumstances with your own child."

When my hand touched the shadowed figure that was my father, the mood of the scene changed from violence to tranquility, and I heard the little boy explaining what had happened.

"I was with a friend of mine on the outskirts of town," he began. "We went to the middle of a property, and there was a house that had been deserted. When we looked inside and saw no furniture, I thought it was going to be condemned and pulled down. So I said to my friend, 'Let's break all the windows,' because I thought that they would be broken anyway when the house would be demolished. My friend refused, he didn't want to join in, even though he was there with me."

My father reached across and touched my hand, obviously troubled.

"How can you make such an immature assumption?" He asked with a serious expression. "The neighbors saw you breaking the windows. They knew who you were and that you are my son. They consequently rang the owners, who had the damage assessed, and now I have a bill to pay. I will have to work hard and earn nothing until this is paid off."

"I am sorry, I didn't realize," the boy apologized. "I hadn't thought deeply enough about what I was doing. Can I come to work with you on the weekends to help fix my mistake?"

"Yes," said my father. "Even though I am very annoyed with what you have done, I love you. Please learn to think before you act."

Upon this conclusion, I was pulled back from the scene and once again appeared in front of the void with Barak, who began to elucidate what had taken place.

"Now that you have stalked your past within parallel perception, it is up to you which enactment you employ to bolster yourself as a man. If you identify with the first situation, you will be full of resentment and anger and always be fearful of authoritarians.

"If you take the third circumstance as your preferred memory, you will be understanding and compassionate to those around you who are controlling and authoritarian. You will know that they carry a wound and that it is this internal suffering that makes them bleed.

"Take this understanding back with you to the second scene, the visualization of shadow figures, and I will show you what you must do to release yourself completely."

With these words, Jagür leapt toward me with such ferocity that we were propelled back into that memory composed of shadows. Barak was standing to my right and commanded once again.

"Break the seal in front of you."

I burst the pressure with my right hand, and Barak instructed me to blow air into that vision. I blew, and as my hand touched the stationary figure's shoulder it dissolved and turned into dust. The whole scene was disintegrated completely till there was nothing left at all. We stood for a moment in that emptiness until Barak's voice broke the silence.

"You now have three choices," he stated with finality. "The first is to perpetuate your previous behavior through unconsciously living an emotional proposition that will never find conclusion, for in that first circumstance, you were never given understanding as a basis to build your power upon.

"The third circumstance, which you have mindfully re-enacted, yielded the correct response and the course of action that could originally have been taken. This enactment has been noted by your awareness while traveling into this alternate scene.

"When you dissolve that which has been embedded, you are left with an empty perspective. A formless view can draw information from either the positive or the negative circumstance. This choice is the only one that will yield true wisdom.

"Even though the shadows have been blown from the memory, the emptiness that exists within that void will now serve to extract the appropriate mask from the rejected scenes and throw it magically onto your oncoming circumstances to reveal to you the truth of who approaches.

"Our emptiness is aware of that interconnective fabric that links us through time and space, which seems to be invisible but is truly tangible. This fabric is intention. We need to ask ourselves: Is this intention truly ours? Have we manufactured this intent that invades every corner of reality and holds us fixed, or does it come from somewhere else?

"Take with you only what is necessary. What is essential in this reality is what appears after you have released what was contained within that scene: nothing. By virtue of this emptiness, a formless attention will replace that which you used to know."

I understood then how to proceed with all of the memories that had heavily imprinted me. I had to review them, turn them into shadows and dissolve their content, so as to free myself from that which holds awareness stationary within the superfluous residue of past events.

Barak placed his left hand reassuringly on my right shoulder, and we reappeared in that alternate dimension that possessed the void.

"Recovering the items of one's past is in essence all that we can do, and what we do with that recovery will define us as human beings. Be strong and resolve to face this insoluble part of yourself, which is there for a reason."

The dream scene ended as abruptly as it had begun. I awoke in my bed feeling light and clear. Within my chest was left a profound knowing of how to free myself of those heavy imprints that had been implanted within the past.

Give of yourself,
except for that which weakens you.
Accept what is given,
but not that which compromises.

Haunted Awareness

I had fallen asleep early that evening and at about three o'clock in the morning was partially awoken by an urgent voice.

"Watch out! There's a man coming."

I opened my eyes in panic but couldn't move my body quick enough, and by the time I was in a state of realization to react, it was too late. The man had entered my room and had somehow struck my internal organs. What I saw upon hearing the warning was a grayish whirlwind making its way along the foot of my bed.

This being had not touched me in a way that you could imagine, but the impact of its presence injured me to such an extent that it took me eighteen months to recover, and eight years more to fully heal the wound.

This event took place about two years after I met my benefactor, and I was incapable of seeing clearly during this period of time. The next opportunity I had to be in Lo Ban's realm was five weeks after the incident. I woke up suddenly, not in my world, but into the domain of my benefactors. Opening my eyes, I saw Lucien standing in front of me. His expression was calm and clear as I told him what had occurred.

"The voice that awakened you to the man entering your room was an emissary from where we abide," he explained. "That entity is your guardian and has been with you for many years. What happened may have been fatal if it wasn't for this intervention."

I broke my fixation and asked, "What is the guardian?"

Upon my question Lucien looked at me with clarity and said, "It is not as mysterious as you think it will be, my answer to you and your inquiry.

"Within all of us we have a protector. When we are transported into the second attention, this entity then transforms from a silent observer into a disembodied voice. It only appears this way in the waking world if you have been influenced by shadow attention, as was the sorcerer who struck you.

"The way this emissary makes utterances within the living construct is by speaking truth on our behalf. It is our heart's voice, our body consciousness verbalizing the unforeseeable into the seen context of a warrior.

"In the Orient, this silent observer is called shen: the uninhibited, unwavering truth of the unknown being spoken through the consciousness of the seer. When we are here, our internal insights are spoken as an unscripted voice, directly from the heart center, on our behalf. A shen gong is an electromagnetic vortex that can be generated by the movements of one's hands — and the concentration of one's consciousness in certain circumstances — which spirals and creates an opening to dark matter.

"It is a spirit catcher. But we are not after allies or inorganic beings. We are here to catch ourselves within the illusion that we exist and don't, simultaneously. The shen gong focuses the omnipresence of that dark matter within our empty spaces.

"As you progress, this phenomenon will become more prominent. It will give form to that emptiness, which in the uninitiated manifests as an internal plethora of nagging secrets. You will learn to listen to this voice, this subtlety, and recognize it as a truth traveling upon the unwavering embers that are the ethical imperative of one's primal essence.

"Know this. You will not fully understand what I am saying until some of us become reintegrated with the old Nagual. The intentions that have been concentrated on you will become self-evident after that point.

"Master Lo Ban has painstakingly embedded within you these delicate factors through his transferal of consciousness to you. You will begin to know this as the most profound shen gong: an interdimensional portal that is the expression of the omnipresent darkness that surrounds us — the void — that which you have been gazing into as an expression of yourself. For in essence, you are emptiness that has manifested within form. As you grow, you will elucidate and help those who follow you to create this emptiness through movement.

"The man who struck you is the possessor of ancient information that has been passed down from generation to generation in his family. He had obviously become aware of the power you have accumulated and did not want you to succeed in your endeavors."

Great pangs of realization came upon me as Lucien spoke. The image of this man's face came to me retrospectively. I had met him once while he was performing movements in the park. I had discovered that he was an eighth generation master of a lineage of energetics.

As our association grew, I revealed minor portions of my practice and gradually began to realize that he wasn't pleased with the fact that I was a possessor of this information as I was not Oriental. He could not see beyond my facial features and my white skin, to know that I had been immersed in his world longer than my own lifetime.

When I realized that he was possessed by a controlling jealousy I withdrew immediately. Even though I never saw him again he endeavored to follow me etherically, and as you have read, the result of that pursuit almost ended my life.

www.parallelperception.com

"One has to be very careful when in contact with sorcerers," Lucien cautioned me, "Men such as he are true brujos*, highly intelligent and sophisticated in comparison to the general populous. They hoard enormous amounts of energy from the secrets they possess. For centuries these seekers of power have been heavily involved in the dark art of manipulating their peers. Through trial and error, they became intimately acquainted with the inner workings of the psyche and discovered how to interfere extensively with the foundations of perception.

"Our primal blueprint is sustained by pure energy that translates into explosive emotions of passion for life and intuitive intelligence. Driven by an obsessive need to be superior, the old sorcerers began injecting fear and moroseness into that inner landscape so as to corrode the internal core that supplies integrity, individually and collectively.

"Their primary objective was to break down the inner world that encompasses one's personal power in order to manipulate this sanctuary and degrade the collective conceptualizations that lie within the truth of the heart. When that power was lost, they gained that potency through the absorption of the collective innocence of the masses.

"You may wonder how could this primordial imprint possibly be broken into. The way to see this is very simple. Imagine that the sensibilities that lie within one's personality are like a mask or a shield. Knowing this is the first step.

---
* Brujo is a Spanish word for a male witch.

www.parallelperception.com

"The next tactic they employed was to discover and pinpoint areas within these sensibilities that were vulnerable, and thus more available, due to the importance attached to the belief systems that upheld the social fabric of that time.

"The third technique that the old sorcerers took to infiltrate this base-plate imprint was the putting forth of a random precept to discover what may offend that individual. But remember, this insertion would be so subtle and so craftily engineered that the one in question would not even be half aware of their reaction. It is this unconscious response within itself that creates a crack in the mask or protective shield, which that person has placed in front of themselves.

"The fourth tactic was to peer into that opening; for the crack creates a looking glass into the weakest link of an individual's integrity. Once they discovered this, it was easy for them to dislodge any integral boundary that would encompass that person's power. Unfortunately, these were the preliminary steps of the art of stalking. This dark method was passed from generation to generation orally, and somewhere within this history an agreement was struck with the shadows. This arrangement has been ongoing for millennia.

"What initially attracted the shadow entities to these men was their cold, calculating unemotional state, which in actual fact is diametrically opposite to what they are attracted to now. In the beginning, these beings were searching for a form of alignment that would allow them to cross the boundaries of perception so that they could go beyond what they were.

"Unfortunately, the old sorcerers, as you know, had no control over their lust for power. They abused this relationship and tainted those entities with their corrupt intentions.

"There are two main categories of shadows that these sorcerers become connected to. One is attracted to intense emotions. This entity looks like a heavy silhouette that is rectangular in shape or round when it approaches. The other is as you have experienced when you were attacked. It takes a whirlwind form and is gray in appearance.

"It can also emerge as the shadow of a man hiding behind a corner or as a grotesque transparent being. This type is attracted to intelligence and plays within that field. The two work together within a dark symbiosis.

"So you can see, whether we like it or not, we are now living with the legacy of these old sorcerers. And those unfortunate enough to be born into the families that possess this information are hopelessly drawn to the power that comes from being in contact with that whirlwind grayish shape you saw.

"I know that you thought it was a man who struck you, but this is only half the truth. What you saw was a highly evolved shadow that had merged with the malicious intent of that man. These beings are faster, smarter and more concentrated than you can imagine. They pit man against man.

"Through the centuries, they have learnt by association how to access our world without the intervention of the sorcerer's intent. This has made them extremely dangerous and more elusive than ever. The threads of their intention bind, weave, and fasten their intent to intelligence. Obviously, the prime objective is control but that polymorphic focus is so surreptitious, so deeply imbedded, that one's intention must be clear as a bell to break through the facade that is put forth.

"Alliances of this nature go beyond the same old thing, which, as you know, is the encompassing parental imprint that guides and binds mentality within the social structure of the times.

"The type of shadow that struck you is so difficult to pin down that it is almost unknowable, as were the old sorcerers of the past. These discarnate beings adopted their behaviors in the world of man, riding on the corrupt intent of symbiotic greed that was established long ago. This is where they learnt to strike men while they sleep and to bring sickness in order that minor shadows could take over the minds of those enthralled in the depths of despair, such as can be brought on by devastating illness."

With his right hand gently clasping my chin, Lucien turned my face to look directly at him.

"Those who have suffered from serious illness and have overcome that which attempted to overcome them, have you not noticed that they are wise beyond their years? They have fought a battle beyond their world, and this struggle yields to them the appropriate power that relates to the hardship they encountered." Releasing my chin, he continued.

"The dilemma with the shadow's influence can be overcome. But first you, and whoever comes in contact with our wisdom, must gain an understanding of the building blocks that sustain the shadow's entry and activity within our world. Eradication of the shadow beings, you would think, is the answer to this predicament. While this may be true, it is not their expulsion that is the real issue.

"You may wonder what I mean by this. Well, they are here. This cannot be changed. What can be changed is our foundation, our core attitude, so that when they try to influence us to be beneath ourselves in order to feed off the loss of energy that results from corrupt acts, they will find no entry, nor point of attachment, within our behavior.

"When they first came into contact with the old sorcerers, they were self-sustaining beings. They are much like us. They are finding it difficult to avert what they have learnt, just as humanity is struggling to refrain from conduct that does not sustain our spirit within a true base of personal power.

"Even though you are not aware of it yet, the mere fact that you were not completely annihilated when you were struck by that whirlwind shadow being, nor influenced to take on limiting behaviors, which as you know, weaken one's personal power, means that through this event you have opened an unusual door. Your non-reactivity caused a momentary lapse, and this is key.

"The old Nagual obviously knew more than what we expected. He was acutely conscious of the ramifications of the connective links that shadow awareness has obtained through our human attention. A new paradigm will commence when it becomes absolutely clear that this symbiotic process is not truly functional. Our detachment will create the necessary reflective components to assist in the re-evaluation of that relationship, allowing our true journey to resume.

"Alternate possibilities are becoming available, but for these transitions to occur, humanity must be absolutely integral within the understandings of their own imperfections. This can only take place if each individual learns to stalk their own base plate imprint through the premise of pure self-reflective observation. Obviously, this will mean foregoing the temptation of falling back into that dark arrangement that was established for all of us by those self-indulgent old sorcerers millennia ago.

"You are one of the first initiates. If others begin to realize what the old Nagual is proposing through the catalyst of these teachings, then life on the blue planet will recommence its harmonious sequencing, and the damage that has been done will ultimately repair itself.

www.parallelperception.com

"It is fascinating yet within the same breath horrifying, for us to observe how these phenomena are surrounding you. We all have been through the trials you are now experiencing. We knew that you would be extensively weakened when you accepted master Lo Ban's gift of luminosity. By accepting this transfer, which is your destiny, you had no choice but to assimilate the power of his knowing into your being.

"As you know, we all fight change, and this battle caused a weakness within you. Even though you, my friend, were willing to accept that challenge. You would expect that in the beginning, the old Nagual's power would have strengthened you, but instead it weakened you extensively. What a contradiction!"

Lucien looked at me with one eyebrow raised in curiosity.

"If you knew what you were getting yourself into, I wonder whether you would have declined the old Nagual's gift?" he reflected then added, chuckling softly to himself, "I think you and I know there are never any choices. What will be, is, and that's all there is to it.

"When the enigmatic wisdom of a Nagual is passed from one to another, a slight crack is created, as in all transitions of power. A lull or a disruption within your time continuum will occur before full uptake is realized. It is for this reason that the shadow being could get to you. It is always at the point of greatest weakness that such entities attack. Although the risks were clear, we did not expect such a daring strike. If the guardian was not there to protect you, all would have been lost, and our knowledge would have disappeared into obscurity.

"But don't worry, this entity will never reach through the darkness to hit you again. You are much too strong now. However, this does not mean you can relax. The shadow dream's power is continually evolving and adapting. When we discover its presence, it immediately shifts and changes.

"You need to be aware of the depths of that evolution and remember, Lujan, when you think you have grasped the unthinkable and know beyond the shadow of a doubt what is going on, always be prepared for the unexpected.

"Recall now that time when you first met the old Nagual. He mentioned that the memories of the alien hieroglyphs would persist within you. I would like you now to look within the void and recover his memory, which is inevitably becoming yours, so that we may examine the make up of these symbols."

Corrupted Innocence

I turned to my right to look into the void, and as I did so, a man emerged from the darkness. I had seen him before, but he was very elusive, and I had not been able to make out his appearance. He looked like an old Indian with dark coppery skin and pure white hair that came to his shoulders. Like Malaiyan, he was fully clad in black.

The wrinkles in his face were pronounced, and his age was evident. When he came closer, I saw that his eyes were deep brown with wide pupils and facial features like carved stone, ancient, yet pulsing with vibrant energy. He was fiercer, more frightening and exuded more power than all of the others combined. His voice resounded with gravity as he addressed me for the first time.

"I am the bearer of truths. Watch this symbol in the void, and I will describe to you what you see."

Upon hearing this, I realized I was once again split. My attention was focused on the visual scene erupting before me, and as he spoke I experienced dream images flooding my conscious awareness, interacting with me fluidly as the void kept me fixed.

"My name is Zakai*," he said, "The symbol that you see there is a memory that is being revealed within the void. It depicts the world of the shadow and is possessed by many within their harbored intentions."

---
* Zakai: Innocent, one who is pure

www.parallelperception.com

I gazed intently at the mysterious glyph that appeared in front of me, as Zakai began to guide me through its structure and meaning.

The Art of Stalking Parallel Perception: Revised 10th Anniversary Edition

THE HIEROGLYPH OF HAUNTED AWARENESS

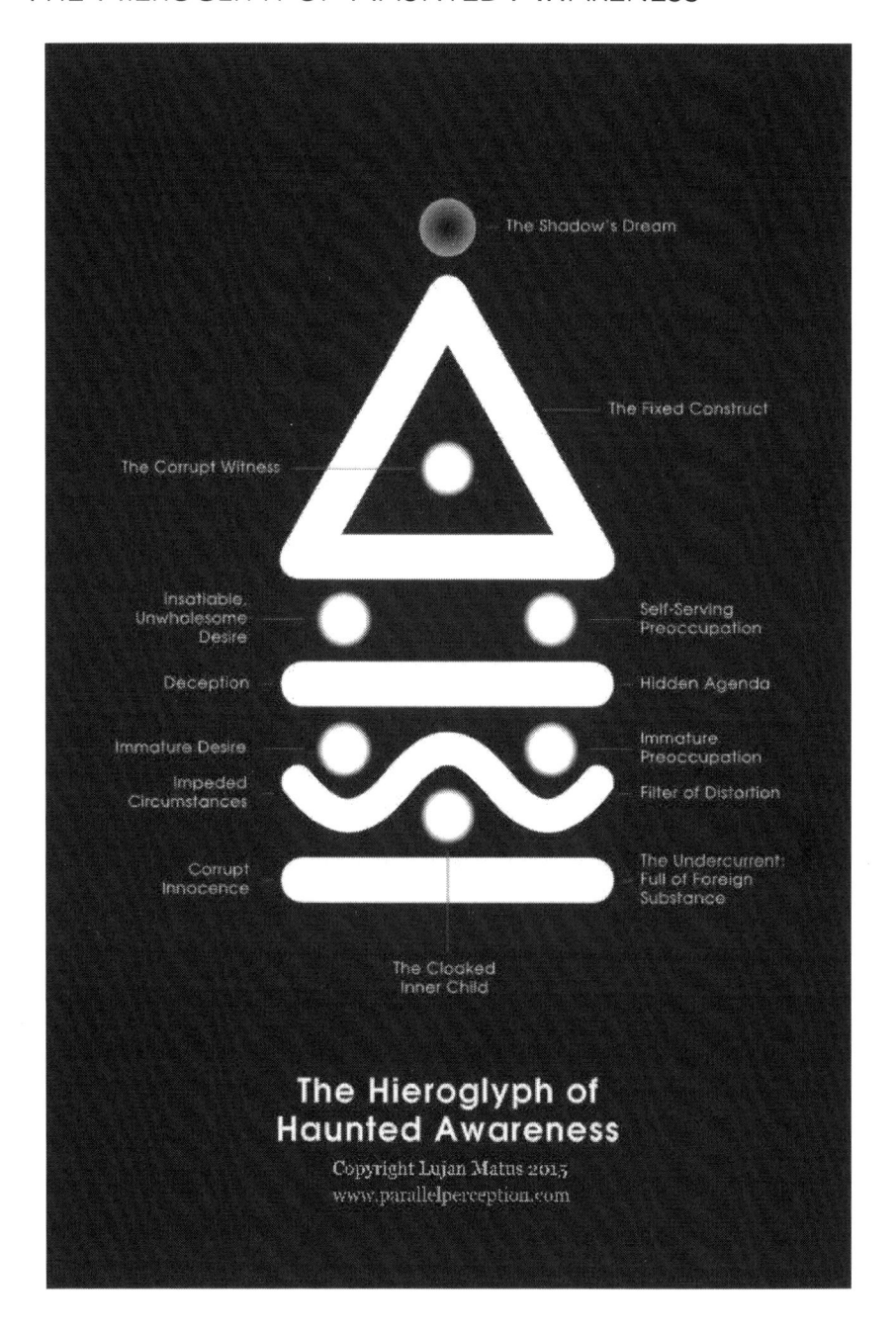

"The triangle you see represents the human construct, the world we create as three dimensional, hardened energetic matter. The sphere in the center of the triangle is the corrupt adult witness, and the sphere underneath that on the lower right-hand side signifies a state of preoccupation.

"The orb on the lower left-hand side represents unquenchable desire, and the line that appears underneath these two spheres represents the deception and hidden agenda within man. The two spheres that you see directly underneath are an unresolved inner child's immature desires and immature preoccupations.

"The wavering line below these is the filter of distortion that permeates all of the circumstances that this unresolved heart encounters. This filter is a cloak that belongs to the shadow's mind.

"The sphere trapped underneath this cloak is our very heart, our inner child, and what pulls this inner child further down is the line below it. This line represents the unresolved feelings of that adult being who cannot find conclusion within truth, and these feelings create a perceptual quagmire that becomes a heavy magnetic undercurrent.

"The bottom line also belongs to the inner child, in that this distorted heart cannot find resolve within its innocence, which has been compromised." He paused to examine me for a moment, and seeing my focused absorption, continued his elucidation.

"The beings that passed these symbols to you are androgynous. What they omit to explain within this hieroglyph is that all humanity's energy is driven from their primordial center, which further holds haunted awareness in place, when corruption surrounds the lower regions that relate to sexuality.

"The orb that hovers above the triangle is the realm that acts upon us indirectly, and this is the shadow's dream that persists in the reality where man dwells, lost to his true self.

"These eleven elements interweave and perpetuate the cloaked inner child through the medium of the corrupt adult witness. When interlaced with each other, they form the building blocks of a cognitive system.

"The cloaked inner child and the corrupt witness are the strongest reflective elements, for they self-confirm within an internal mirroring process. They are the forerunners that sustain a corrupt human cognition.

"Our inner talk is the spark that ignites this dark arrangement and thus holds the construct in stasis and so providing the conditions for distorted awareness to flourish.

"An unresolved heart is the key controlling element, for it promotes unhappiness and does not have the ability to translate any circumstance into true buoyancy. The corrupt witness that governs the choices and actions of this being is unable to go beyond the impedance that is set forth by the cloaked inner child. It is wholly self-serving, and its expression is always inhibited and limited.

"The corrupt witness' motivations revolve around the joylessness that is within the heart. It always interferes with its circumstances to ensure limitations due to its inability to go beyond what it is. This in turn creates a warped conceptualization of cognition: the fixed construct.

"When these elements combine as one solid unit, they generate a hidden agenda, which erupts outwardly from the corrupt witness as a plethora of justifications that become fixed preoccupations. As a result, the undercurrent that is generated develops its own gravity and surreptitious outline, which holds the whole arrangement of that individual consciousness in denial and darkness.

"The filter of distortion, the line that cloaks the inner child's awareness, is a false prospect of the construct that perpetuates the idea that you are unaware of yourself and are unable to deal with your present circumstances. This creates the inability to be buoyant and mature and see beyond what is presented.

"The self-damaging inner child embraces both the deception and the undercurrent as tools of self-perpetuation, applying distortion to the world as its dysfunction through the decision-making medium of the corrupt witness. This is the projection that is supplied by the shadow and covers our true potential.

"Know that this haunted awareness is truly polymorphic by nature. The unresolved heart, that cloaked inner child you are viewing, is the one truly in command. The cloak is positioned in such a way that it keeps the inner child stationed in immaturity, and this disallows the adult witness to find resolve within the living tapestry of that construct which we all exist in simultaneously.

"The primary motive behind the elucidation of this system is to bring the witness into the all encompassing domain of their true Architect of observation."

With these words, Zakai took one step backwards and was seamlessly absorbed by the darkness.

The Log Cabin

Sensing a familiar presence, I looked up to my left and found Lucien standing by my side.

"The four women are waiting, we have to go," he said with immediacy.

"What four women?" I asked, surprised.

"You are becoming so familiar with our realm that you are beginning to talk too much." He answered, smiling mischievously.

Lucien clapped his hands and his beckoning command pulled in an inky blackness that surrounded us both. I emerged from that tunnel of darkness alone. Ahead of me I saw a log cabin. As I sped towards it, its features were being stamped upon my memory, and this imprint reminded me that I had been there before.

The house seemed to be floating in the darkness, and I became aware at that point of four men lurking within the shadows. I realized that it was Lucien, Barak, Zakai and Malaiyan. Their ominous presence scared me, and I sensed that their intentions were somehow upholding the dream scene.

Suddenly, I was in a brightly lit kitchen where four women were screaming and yahooing like cowgirls on the back of wild horses. They were ecstatic to see me, and their energy was so intense and vigorous that I was immediately caught within their excitement, to the point that I forgot where I had come from.

One of the women stepped forward, grasped me by the shoulders and spun me around to face a rustic-looking wooden kitchen table. Without delay, she began enthusiastically commanding my attention.

"Focus your awareness and intend these knives and forks to float above the table. You've done this before," she told me, smiling confidently.

"Make an alternate knowing within your emptiness, and in that knowing see yourself lifting the cutlery with your hands within your living construct. Then the objects in this vision will float in mid air without the intervention of your physicality. These same principles will also apply when you awaken into your familiar world."

I did as she directed and watched the knives and forks lift off the table and hover before me.

"Telekinesis practiced in the dream realm will give you the ability to move energetics in the waking construct, and know the intentions surrounding that energy. But realize; your dreaming attention coexists within your waking world. To combine these two is to become truly awake. Here is where all possibilities avail themselves to the seer," she informed me. While she was speaking, the other women disappeared into an adjacent room. She gestured for me to sit next to her, and when I sat down I realized that the tabletop was now empty.

"My name is Dyani*," she introduced herself, her voice now calm and soothing. Looking closely, I noticed that her rosy cheeks were radiant with health, as was the lustrous brown hair that vanished down the length of her back. Her appearance was very feline with a beautiful delicate nose, generous lips, hazel brown eyes and high cheekbones. She reached out to touch my left hand and squeezed it with a familiar affection.

"Your time here must be dealt with swiftly and with directness," Then slapping the table sharply, she added, "This realm is solid."

The effect of her striking the wood brought the hardness and density of the room into full focus.

"What you are experiencing is more than a dream," she said, intuiting and confirming my observation perfectly. "My first task is to introduce you to San Pedro, the teacher of intentions. I will show you how to prepare and consume the medicine that is within this plant. Its lessons will be blunt and direct. You will need this feeling of finality, for without it, your truth will not have substance."

Standing up, she walked over to the kitchen sink where there was a cactus that was around twenty-four inches

---
* Dyani: A magical deer

long and two to three inches thick. She picked it up and brought it over to the table where I sat.

"The nature of San Pedro is severe," she informed me. "The spines that we will dislodge represent the plant's ability to keep predators at bay." Saying this, she placed the cactus in front of me and handed me a knife. "Cut them off and take care not to be pierced by them, for if you are wounded, the predator we hunt will have access to you. Be careful."

I proceeded diligently, placing the spines in a wooden bowl that Dyani had supplied. She continued to speak with the assuredness of one absolutely familiar with the process.

"Now, cut the San Pedro into four long strips and place them in this cloth. The San Pedro has to be put in the freezer for twelve hours, and this will allow the mescaline to be boiled from it. Come with me as we wait."

Dyani led me through a door that opened off to the side of the kitchen. The other three women were in there sitting in armchairs, in a room illuminated by dozens of candles. She guided me to an empty chair and sat me down, whispering to me, "Close your eyes and listen to the melody that I will play for you on my bamboo flute. Close your eyes."

Sinking back into the armchair, I listened as the women hummed melodically along with the rhythm. I felt myself being absorbed into absolute blackness. I was totally transfixed by their intentions. I found myself sleeping more deeply than I had ever slept before, yet I could sense every sound, every murmur and every feeling that was gestured towards me from these powerful women. Like the men, their intentions were absorbing, and within that sanctuary I felt safe, nurtured and whole.

Hours later, Dyani's voice awoke me from my deep trance-like state. "Come now, we must prepare the mescaline for your journey," she said. We proceeded to the kitchen where she resumed her instructions. "Take San Pedro from the freezer and place him on the table. Cut him into thirteen pieces."

She lightly hummed the haunting melody that she had played on the flute as she brought a large cooking pot from the cupboard. Her voice was hypnotic and I said to her, "You are holding my attention fixed with your humming, aren't you?"

She smiled at me and winked. "You got that right, pilgrim. Now, take this pot and fill it three quarters full of water, and as you do so, intend the San Pedro to know your heart."

I filled the pot up and carefully placed the San Pedro in the water, awaiting Dyani's next instruction.

"While it boils, we will talk of intentions that you need to be aware of, those which entrap the spirit of man. This will prepare you for the lessons that San Pedro will deliver. As it boils down into a thick soup, you must be mindful not to let the pot dry out at any time. Reduce it down to three full glasses. This process will take six hours. The explanations that I will deliver must be transmitted via my softness. This will allow you to become absorbed in observing the world in a removed fashion as you witness the phenomena I speak of."

I had a sudden realization and asked Dyani, "How can I be taking mescaline when I'm dreaming?"

"Are you dreaming?" she asked in return, observing my response with interest. When I did not answer, she suggested I hit the table with my hand.

"Can you awaken from this vision?" she queried. "Have you not already slept while we chanted in the other room? Is not your waking state now a dream, and this the reality you had forgotten? Is not the truth that you remember — in the world where you were previously awake — discarded as if it were a fantasy? Do you not feel more powerful here?

"In this room, you know my intentions completely and I know yours, but in the waking state that you have come from, the machinations of man are coveted and hidden in surreptitiousness. Are they not shadow-like and deceptive within their illusion?"

Her questions were triggering inner realizations that popped up as internal imagery, yet even though my awareness was struggling to wake up, I was fixed, and I knew that she understood what I was experiencing. She addressed my unspoken questions directly.

"The things you will learn here and in the old Nagual's realm will forever change your perception. Now that your awareness is stabilized within this reality, we have an opportunity to shift your cognition. Our elucidations will give you a greater understanding of the elements that surround haunted awareness. Ela* will accompany us with her attention."

At that moment another woman entered the room. She was stunning and exuded poise with her long blue-black hair, dark skin, broad cheekbones and discreet, elegant nose. I could see her white teeth as she smiled. As she walked towards the table, it seemed that her slender form was floating on air, and when she pulled the chair from under the table, the muscles in her shoulder and chest flexed.

Like the others, she was not carrying an ounce of fat, and the tank top she wore accentuated her strength. Her light blue jeans were covered in patches, and around her neck, she bore what seemed to be a black onyx pendant of a bear's paw, encased in gold.

Sitting down, she locked her gaze upon mine. Her lips were full and sculpted, and her eyes such a dark brown that they were almost black. Dyani's voice broke the silence.

---
* Ela: Elfin.

"While you are split between Ela and myself, what will appear will be emptiness, and within that expanse, you will learn to understand and know immediately the shadow's intent. This parasite's behavior is destructive by nature, and its designs adapt to overcome any form of realization that would uncover its existence.

Such adaptation within itself has the corrosive ability to take the prime directive of one's heart, which is the command that we hold as adults, and switch it so that it functions within an atmosphere of dis-ease.

"Know that this is a holographic universe that we essentially sustain as dimensional imagery, which therefore requires all components of syntax and cognition to reinforce itself upon itself. What must be understood is that observing and manipulating through that observation is incorrect, considering that the component being controlled is life itself, and that life can never be replaced.

"Unfortunately, this is the dilemma that has been set in place for humanity; hence, the current state of polymorphic entrapment and the never-ending loop of insane repetition that is brought about by habitual interference."

Ela tapped rhythmically, gazing steadily into my eyes while Dyani spoke. As the sound reverberated through the room, Dyani's words were bringing the first hieroglyph that Zakai had shown me into full view, as a memory held in retrospective imagery.

"It is time to remind you of the second glyph you have been shown," Dyani announced.

Ela suddenly slapped the table. The power of the impact was so enormous that the room rippled and my ears buzzed. Stunned and shocked, I looked questioningly into her eyes. I had not expected so much energy to be exuded from this silent observer. Her eyes opened wide, and she spoke for the first time.

"Gaze into the void," she said, looking towards the table.

Following her eyes, I saw that its surface had transformed into that void I had experienced in the old Nagual's realm, and as I gazed into it, Dyani prompted my recall. Dream images began to flood my conscious awareness as I was split between Dyani's voice and the void. What I saw seemed to be a mirror image of the symbol that Zakai had shown to me in detail, and then I recognized it as the second hieroglyph.

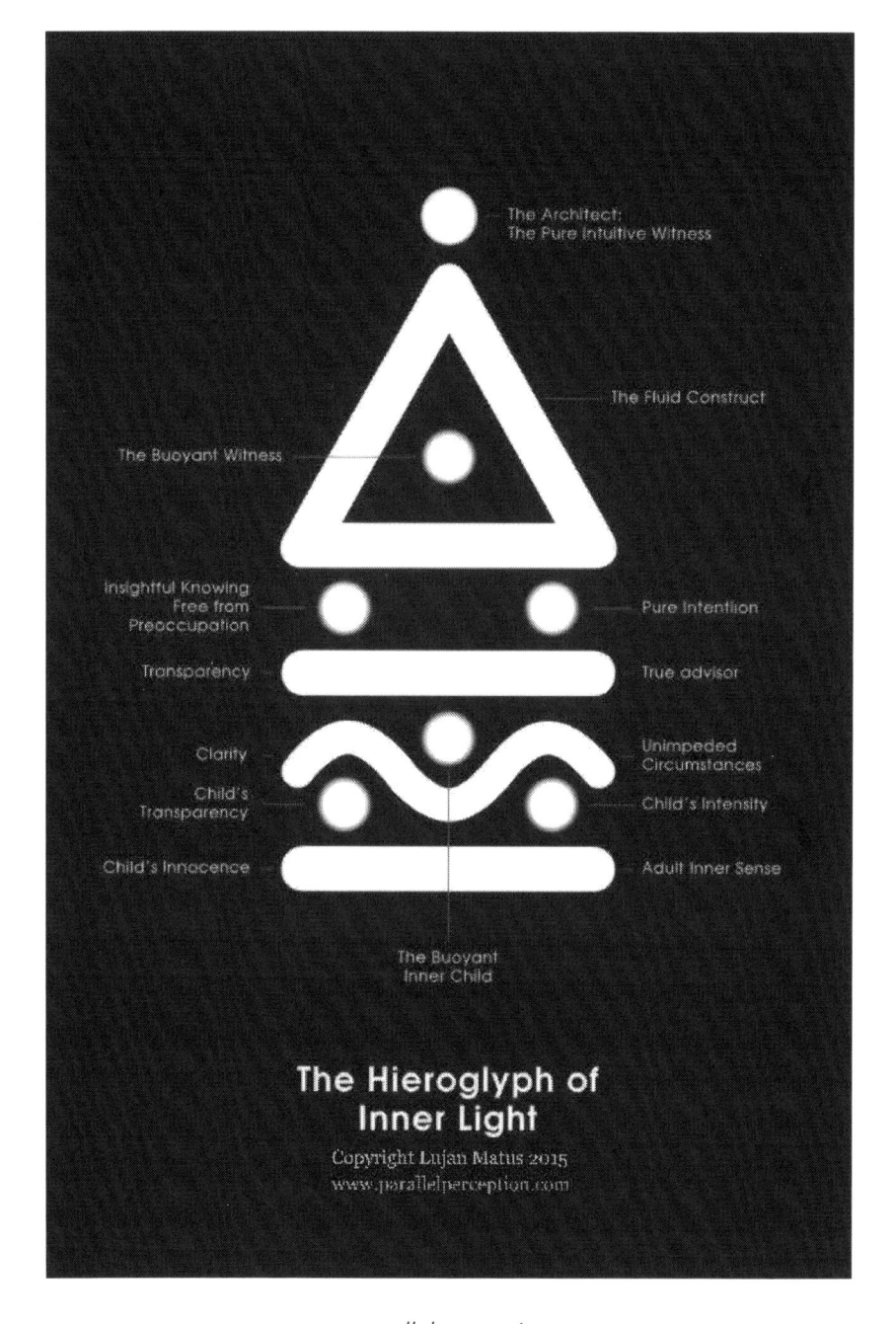

The Art of Stalking Parallel Perception: Revised 10th Anniversary Edition

The Hieroglyph of Inner Light

- The Architect: The Pure Intuitive Witness
- The Fluid Construct
- The Buoyant Witness
- Insightful Knowing Free from Preoccupation
- Pure Intention
- Transparency
- True advisor
- Clarity
- Unimpeded Circumstances
- Child's Transparency
- Child's Intensity
- Child's Innocence
- Adult Inner Sense
- The Buoyant Inner Child

The Hieroglyph of Inner Light
Copyright Luján Matus 2015
www.parallelperception.com

www.parallelperception.com

While I became immersed within the symbol I was totally mesmerized by their feminine energy. The power that exuded from them was extraordinary. They were the most uncompromising women I had ever met. Dyani began to describe the symbol that had appeared in the void.

"This is the hieroglyph of Inner Light. It has eleven stationed positions, just like the glyph of haunted awareness. The difference is that this arrangement represents a precognitive map of perception. It depicts our original state that we traveled here with, but as we became familiar with that construct which engulfed us all, elements of our awareness were surreptitiously repositioned, as you can see when you compare the two glyphs. It is essential that we struggle to re-establish the original arrangement that the hieroglyph of Inner Light represents.

"When we shifted from the realm of pure energy into the realm of matter, we forgot ourselves, and this forgetting has given the shadow the ability to rearrange our status so that it may hold and possess us. The arrangement that we truly travel with is represented by the hieroglyph of Completion, which will be explained to you in detail by Zakai.

"To truly discover the magic of this symbol, which was also shown to you when you were visited, we must first overcome the shadow's dream and awaken ourselves to our original state. However, viewing the hieroglyph of Inner Light is not enough. You must also bear witness to that unseen being that attaches itself to us when we arrive here in energetic form.

"The aliens left us these symbols to give us the opportunity to teach the awareness necessary to escape the unwholesome intent that most of society is caught in at this moment. They are like Jagür's paw, a different kind of imprint, a traceable track. The second hieroglyph can be followed upwardly to the third, the symbol of completion, which represents our freedom and escape from the collective entrapment of this realm.

"The being that San Pedro will allow you to see does not function from the level of reason, yet it plays surreptitiously in that field. You can witness it, but to try to fathom its motives is madness. It is best to just learn to recognize the feeling and fear that comes from being confronted by this hidden entity.

"The eleven components you have been shown in the hieroglyph of Haunted Awareness operate collectively to hold us in bondage. Is this not possession? The way it works is that the shadow's dream replaces our clarity, cloaking the inner child with an imprint of confusion. When this occurs, childhood transparency and intensity immediately swap their positions to become immature preoccupations and immature desire. Thus, the pure intuitive witness is obscured and disappears from our conscious awareness.

"This is how we move from one dream to another and forget where our consciousness originates. Once this forgetting transpires, we are at the mercy of those forces that have cloaked and misdirected our perception.

"Remember, Lujan, as I speak to you, the second formation is where you are now and where we all could be in terms of our burgeoning consciousness. You are in the glyph of Inner Light. See that this fluid construct is an alternate cognitive system.

"In this symbol, the sphere that is on the right, below the construct, is possessed by pure intention. That purity gives rise to abstract knowing and freedom from preoccupation, which is the sphere on the left-hand side that awakens the Architect, the pure intuitive witness.

"The buoyant adult witness within the center of the triangle is clear and concise. The first line under the construct is the true advisor, and the corresponding connective element is transparency. The first orb under this line is the buoyant inner child that hovers above its circumstances within an atmosphere of clarity and represents a clear heart.

"The buoyant inner child will automatically access its own transparency and intensity by virtue of being in this position. It exists in a state of freedom that is unsurpassed. This freedom depends on the adult's inner sense and the child's uncorrupted innocence to sustain it, and these are represented by the bottom line.

"This is the battle that is being fought — to reposition that haunted awareness into the uncorrupted precognitive state that we arrived here with when we transformed from pure energy into matter. Remember that the consciousness that is represented by the hieroglyph of Inner Light is also driven by the sexual center, yet in this case it propels it with power and purity.

"One of the main governing elements within this symbol is the buoyant witness. The elevation of the buoyant witness is sustained by the clarity of the inner child that is at the heart of all things. Here, the inner child is secondary within its stationed position in the hieroglyph. Yet, although second in charge, it is nevertheless the ultimate commander, and the way it commands is through forgetting that it is there at all.

"Since it exists within a state of inner resolve, happiness is lived without question, and circumstances are sustained through positivity. Such light-heartedness will not be possessive, and as a result, will not collect information for usage, which brings about the eleventh orb: the Architect of pure observation.

"The Architect of observation extensively examines all circumstances from a removed perspective, and becomes an interdimensionally linked reflective mechanism that advises the adult buoyant witness within the hieroglyph. In this way, pure intention can be directed towards the pure intensity that exists since the buoyant inner child has been forgotten.

"Under this premise, circumstances will not be inhibited by distorted perception; they will be clear, which is shown as the line of unimpeded circumstances, above which the inner child floats. The reason fluid perception can exist is that the forgotten buoyant child's intensity and transparency infuse every circumstance. This in turn sustains the stability of the inner sense of the buoyant adult witness through the natural innocence of that child. Thus, the adult witness is upheld within a position of transparency that never inhibits pure intention, and the advisor is left as a last resort if energy wanes or buoyancy is impacted.

The hieroglyph of Inner Light is truly a magical symbol of discovery and within its complex composition will always challenge the shadow's dream to be more than what it is. These two configurations exist within all of us and are very much like dreams. They are fluid and can be made pliable in comparison to the awareness of those who examine them.

"If awareness is not corrupt and the internal dialogue is switched off completely, then what is out there cannot intervene or interfere with the natural process of our passage through life.

"There is an uninhibited observation that supplies unconditional support to the environment. It is this hidden premise that lies between a deceptive principle and the principle of cooperation, and this approach is the only viable option to head off the destruction of our species.

"We can see within the hieroglyph of Haunted Awareness that an individual who is not clear will reach for the tools that manufacture the syntax of the cloaked inner child and in doing so, cause a snowball effect. What results is an experience of overwhelm to which that cloaked inner child will connect anything that is disturbing, melding all perturbing sensations into one and creating a form of saturation.

"Thus the self-serving rationale of the shadow's dream can influence and integrate with awareness through paired association, creating insoluble preoccupation, which is an intended proposition put forth to subdue one's power.

"In contrast, adherence to principles of personal integrity will invite a state of non-preoccupation. Transparency, which is the primary energetic stabilizer of the second hieroglyph, will then become the forerunner and advisor of awareness. In this naturally introspective state, genuine recovery will occur, and this review will define those happenings within our environment that are real placements of power, allowing us to retrieve the moment that is escaping us. Within that perpetually lost yet nevertheless eternally available moment, are hidden cognitive inversions that reveal true indications of Spirit.

Dyani's voice floated like a golden thread through the visual scenes that were unfolding before me.

"We must be aware that external elements, more often than not, move in the world and are not analogous to pure internal realization, which is our heritage: to be aware of multiple dimensions within our linear realities. If this interdiversity is internally realized, it will evoke an inner revolution that brings to the forefront the contradiction in terms of the external affair truly being an ineffective component, in comparison to inner truth. In other words, external and internal realities will bind as one true composite.

"For this knowing to be fully applied, an internal mechanism of fluid perception — corresponding to that which moves both outside and within — must be awakened in order to facilitate the consciousness necessary for adaptive cognition in a pure sense. This is the basis of absolute immediacy."

Throughout the whole explanation, I was immersed within imagery. When Dyani's voice stopped, my ears popped, my nasal passages cleared and suddenly, a luminous ball became visually available. I noticed it pulsated as it hovered above the table, yet it appeared and disappeared so quickly that I thought I was imagining things.

When I looked to the two women for an explanation, they seemed to be frozen in time. I stood up quickly, and my chair flew backwards, but there was no sound from any of my movements. Then all at once I was back, seated comfortably, and both women were gazing at me with intrigue.

"What was that?" I asked. "How can I have thrown my chair backwards and then be sitting here, not knowing how I returned?"

Dyani smiled with amusement and stood up without answering my question. "Let's go top up the San Pedro," she said. "It's been boiling for quite some time." She came to my side as I poured water into the pot, and placing her hand on my shoulder, smiled radiantly once more and began to speak.

"You know we are all luminous, don't you? What you are experiencing now is a reflection of your living construct. That being that appeared in front of you was simply curious, and its sudden arrival disrupted your continuity. You'll not be able, at this time, to define the events which just took place, but nevertheless, we must proceed."

Hidden Entity

I turned to face Ela, who had risen from her chair to approach. She extended her long, slender arm and grasped my hand, speaking softly.

"The San Pedro has been boiling for six hours. It is true that your continuity has been severely compromised by being here, and this is a good thing."

Ela handed me a strainer as Dyani brought three glasses to the kitchen bench, instructing me to fill them with the San Pedro and then bring them to the table to cool. I did so, listening carefully to her every word.

"Within this realm, power is applied directly. By the mere fact that you have intended to be drinking San Pedro, this dreaming scene has already begun to readjust, as you have experienced with the luminous sphere that jumped in. It is time now for you to consume these three glasses. Soon, Zakai and I will accompany you on a walk in that expansiveness that is beyond the door of this cabin."

I attempted to drink down the bright green liquid and began to gag uncontrollably. As this was occurring, Dyani placed her hand on my shoulder. Giggling to herself, she covered her mouth in an attempt to silence her amusement at the untenable situation I was facing at that moment.

Suddenly I began to introspect on the life that I had forgotten, where my body lay sleeping. There were shockwaves of realization rippling through my awareness. I immediately knew of things that I needed to stop doing, and I knew this would change my life completely. Dyani's voice interrupted my revelries.

"You will have plenty of time for those realizations. While you are in an acute state of inner comprehension, it is better that you turn your awareness to your physicality within this realm and forget the dreamer that lies asleep within that alternate construct."

As she spoke, I heard a rhythmic sound coming from an adjacent room. Dyani and Ela took me by the forearms and as we approached, the door opened. The other two women were there, stomping out hypnotic rhythms on the floor. This time it was Ela who spoke.

"This shamanic dance is for you to learn so that you may take it back to your waking world. It will deliver a deep state of quietude to those who practice."

Dyani closed the door behind us, and the two dancing women stopped suddenly. A profound silence filled the room, and then the woman to my left introduced herself.

"My name is Shashani*, and this," she said, gesturing gracefully, "is Mion*." Her voice was warm and rich like hot chocolate. "We learnt this rhythmic dance from your benefactor many years ago. It is practiced in conjunction

---
* Shashani: Blackbird.
* Mion: Purity, virtue.

with movements that originate from the Orient. The rhythmic tapping regenerates organ energy and revitalizes the body on a cellular level. It is also designed to stop the internal dialogue so that nothing but those who practice it will be in the room. It will vanquish everything that is in opposition to a clear heart.

"These teachings are traditionally transmitted via the state of consciousness you are now witnessing, known to some as the second attention. This alternate dream reality is now containing the power of your visions, as a tool of reflection. These movements are called the dance of thunder."

Although small in stature, both Shashani and Mion exuded an enormous amount of energy. Mion was Chinese and very elusive, not speaking a word. Shashani was of Native American origin, with bronze skin and a self-assured countenance that revealed alertness combined with profound peace. She was extremely beautiful and when she spoke her voice was calm and centered, with the ancient rhythmic tone of her people.

At the moment Shashani finished her brief description of the movements, I awoke abruptly in my room. I reached for my clock to discover that I'd only been sleeping for two hours. A shadow moved in the corner, and I screamed at the top of my lungs when a figure approached. A masculine voice spoke.

"Cool down Lujan, it's me, Zakai."

"What the hell are you doing here in my room?" I asked, terrified.

"This is not your room," he replied bluntly. "It is an alternate dream state that, if you are not careful, you will be caught in, and you will forget everything that has transpired. Unfortunately, we are not the only beings in this region of the universe. I'd love to chat with you but we have to get out of here."

Saying this, he sprang towards me with startling agility and pressed lightly upon my mid-eyebrow with his index finger. At his touch, the scene disappeared completely, and we were once again back in the log cabin, where he ordered me to sit down. The sound of his voice gave me a sense of foreboding.

"There is something I must show you, and this can only occur outside of the protective confines of this cabin. There are beings that wish to waylay humanity's awareness. I will accompany you on this journey."

We proceeded at once towards the front door, where Dyani was standing and gesturing for us to walk through.

"Stay close," Zakai said. "I don't want you to get bitten."

"What's going to bite me?" I asked apprehensively.

I heard Dyani and the other women giggling in the background. Zakai looked at me and smiled, but his gaze remained fierce and pierced right through me.

"What I am about to show you will scare the wits out of you," he warned. "Be careful not to indulge too deeply within your fright. I am going to take you now to a populated region that exists out there in that expansive vastness."

As we walked down the front pathway, the moon shone brightly. Zakai signaled for me to open the front gate, and when I did so, I saw that Dyani was accompanying us.

"I want to see what happens when you discover what is hidden behind the facade, pilgrim," she said softly. "Do you mind if I come along?"

"No, I don't mind," I replied, closing the gate behind us.

Looking around, I realized we were in a suburban neighborhood. Zakai broke my fixation on the environment by performing a series of gestures that appeared to be Oriental in origin. The air popped and crackled as he extended his arms forward.

"You also know these movements very well," he said, glancing at me sideways, "Don't look so surprised. Now that the spirit of mescal has been absorbed within your luminous field of perception, you must become aware of what Dyani was describing to you earlier."

With only moonlight illuminating our path, we continued to walk along the unlit street until Zakai motioned for us to be still.

"Stop and listen now."

There were no ordinary sounds to be heard, but what I could perceive was the intentions of each person that dwelt in every house in the street. I became shocked to realize that even though we were alone, those feelings permeated the space that we were occupying. I started to feel extremely distressed. I had become accustomed to the intentions of my benefactors and how non-interfering they were. What I felt emanating from the houses was pure poison.

Zakai told me to look to the sky and focus on the full moon. As I watched, clouds covered its luminous surface. "Use your hands to move those clouds," he instructed.

I began to motion instinctively, and as I did so, I realized that the three of us were gesturing in exactly the same way. To my amazement, the clouds were drawn like curtains, and the moon was revealed. The sky seemed so close, and the moon appeared to be glaring at me with one eye, as if it did not want me to discover the secret that we were uncovering. Zakai caught my attention then with a strange comment.

"It is here because we have interfered with the living construct," he announced cryptically.

"What is here?"

"Can you see it?" he asked, pointing towards a large tree near a tall fence.

"No I can't, but I feel something tearing at my heart," I answered, truly afraid.

"This is the stuff of nightmares," said Dyani, and the sound of her voice conveyed ominous fear of what was before us.

"Approach that presence which you cannot see," commanded Zakai. "Although it is not visually apparent at this moment, you will never forget what you are about to experience now."

The moment I stepped towards it, my hair stood on end. I was frightened to my very core. I felt like screaming and running out of there to escape that which I could not see. Zakai's voice became even sterner.

"Control your fear and step closer."

I began to feel a sense of revulsion that relayed the same intentions that were coming from the houses, but they had been minor in comparison to what I was now confronted with. I stepped forward and heard a branch cracking on the ground under my foot.

The sound somehow unmasked that hidden monster that was in front of me. I gasped with terror upon seeing a transparent outline of what appeared to be a giant, gargoyle-like creature. Suddenly it exploded into darting shadows, vanishing from sight as quickly as it had appeared. Dyani's voice alerted me into action.

"Come now," she said, her words taut with urgency, "we must move swiftly back to the cabin."

Haunted by what I had seen, I walked briskly back to the front gate with them and down the stairs to where Ela was waiting, anxiously motioning for us to come inside. When the door was closed, Zakai gestured towards the window.

"Look now and see what's following us," he said.

I pulled the curtain to see what was there, and what I saw shocked me more than the transparent monster. I saw a man. He was totally encased within darkness, yet I could see through him. He was standing stationary, and as I watched him, I realized he was trying to merge with the shadows of the trees that were in the front yard.

"What the hell is this?" I asked, looking to Zakai for an explanation for this bizarre apparition.

"We are being pursued, as has every man and woman been for millennia," he answered chillingly. "The only difference is that we have discovered what is stalking us from the world of shadows."

I was so deeply affected and alarmed by what Zakai said that it triggered me into a panicked reviewal of my life. At that moment I turned and saw Dyani sitting in an armchair in the front room. Looking into her eyes, I realized how pure she was. I placed my hand on her knee and knelt down to speak with her.

"I have wasted so much time."

She laid her hand on top of mine and smiled calmly.

"No time has been wasted. Everything is as it should be," she reassured me. "You are way too hard on yourself. To have come this far one must have power, and to sustain one's composure in the face of that frightening entity takes guts of steel."

Her words were soothing, and I knew then what I had to do and how I had to be. She had spoken directly to my heart. I told her that I now understood what Lucien had been saying about the thing that is there, and that I was beginning to realize the full implications of what he had imparted to me.

What he had described, along with what Zakai had shown, painted a picture of epic proportions. The thing is there, and it is a monster. It was becoming chillingly clear how this influence rearranges our awareness, capturing us and devouring our energy through that interaction. Dyani's gaze conveyed heartfelt compassion as she acknowledged the scope of what I was taking in.

"When you return to that world where you sleep, you must act upon your knowledge. Remember that the world of man is saturated with something other than himself. Be strong, pilgrim. You will be challenged by those close to you, and what will be confronting you will not be them but the mind of that transparent being that stood within the shadows.

"You must apply the teachings of the hieroglyph of Inner Light to overcome the entrapment of your attention. To assist you in this task, Zakai will instruct you in the ancient art of stalking, which will help dislodge the shadow being's agenda.

"This is a forbidden subject that must now be brought into the open so that all can understand the fluid principles and applications of this art, and dispel the confusion that surrounds it. Know that whenever these matters are spoken of or written about, you will encounter unreasonableness from all quarters. You will be tested continually, and what will be combating you will not be of this world."

I woke with a start and checked my watch. I had only been asleep a few hours, yet I knew I had been gone for days. I turned on all the lights in my room to make sure there was nobody hiding in the corner to frighten the hell out of me. I asked myself if I had awoken in the same place where I had fallen asleep and realized I had no way of knowing. All I could do was apply what I had learnt from these unusual events that had irreversibly changed my perception.

When subtleties
become substance,
wisdom arrives.

Mysterious Encounters

On the next occasion that I found myself in master Lo Ban's realm, Zakai was there waiting, peering steadily through the time-space continuum that connected us. A light glimmered in his eyes as he acknowledged my arrival.

"How in the hell did you get here without me calling you?" he demanded, grinning mischievously. "I have a project for you, a task of recovery, but it has to take place within your living construct.

"I'd like you to write a description of the encounters you have had with those aliens, the creators of the hieroglyphs that we are examining extensively. Best make your way back now to your waking dream and get started," he said, gently squeezing my arm.

I awoke in my bed and feverishly got working on the task he had given me. It had been so many years since I had first been visited, but those events had left me with unforgettable feelings and made me very aware of inexplicable gaps in my continuity. What follows is my account of what happened.

My earliest recollection was of a hysterical child running down the stairs of our two-story home, yelling at the top of his lungs:

"They're coming to take me! Don't let them take me!" Then bolting into my parents' room, I shouted, "They're here to take me again!"

Even as a child, my own words were confusing to me, for although it seemed like this was the first incident, my body knew that they had come many times before. One of the most vivid memories I have from that initial encounter is of my father ordering me back to bed and telling me not to be ridiculous.

I guess what frightened me most was not remembering leaving my bed or my room, nor arriving at the craft itself. What I do recall from this same occasion is floating down the semi-dark street on my back in mid-air, traveling backwards, watching the trees looming over the road as menacing silhouettes imprinted on the dark sky above. I saw an owl flying from one tree to another, and it frightened me to the core, for at that moment I knew I had lost all control. I was around six years old at the time.

The next encounter took place many years later. I was in my early thirties, sleeping in an upstairs bedroom. I woke suddenly and looked out the window to see a strange light illuminating my front garden. The trees were moving as if there was a horrendous wind storm, yet everything outside of my front yard was dead still. Turning my gaze towards the sky, I saw a circular craft that was a quarter of the size of a football field. I quickly put on a shirt and a pair of pants and ran outside.

When I looked up again, I saw the craft above me. What I did not understand is what I said and the corresponding feelings that went with those words. They have devastated me ever since. I was so moved that I fell to my knees with an unfamiliar exultation rippling through my body, and I found myself saying, "Please don't leave me this time. Please take me with you."

It seemed then as if the bottom of the craft was opening, and I saw some kind of water vapor, a mist-like substance, emerging. Even though my neighbors were very close, there was no sound in the area, neither from them nor from the craft. I could not hear a thing, and I knew that within close proximity of my front yard time was still moving, while outside that perimeter time had stopped for everybody in the environment but me.

At this point, something strange occurred. A memory was taken from me — the knowledge of how I got from the yard back into the front room of my house. I found myself standing there with three beings the size of seven or eight year olds standing in front of me, yet access to the visual image of their faces was mysteriously erased, even as it was happening.

The alien in the middle handed me a rectangular box, and as he opened it, the recollection of what was inside disappeared from my conscious awareness. I was able to recover only portions of information from that event. A date was left with me: March 8th, 2011. I assumed that this would be the time when something important would happen, either to me personally or to humanity in general. Perhaps it would be when the aliens would overtly reveal their existence to the world.

Another memory they left with me was a technique to access the potency that exists within their realm — a state of heart that would protect the purity of my being while I was surrounded by so much harshness, for my battle would be long and arduous. As it happened, no one would believe me when I spoke of these experiences, and the feeling of aloneness was so intense that I thought it would break me. That was my second experience.

The next encounter, which took place years later, just before I met the old Nagual, was with the gray alien race. I woke up and saw, in a dark corner of my room, one of these beings watching me. Before I opened my eyes, I spoke.

"I know you're there. I know you're watching me. What are you doing?"

As I looked at this small individual, once again a portion of my memory was stolen. Suddenly, it was daylight, and I was back in a disc-like alien vessel, observing some remote town, heaven knows where. All I was capable of doing was witnessing the landscape that was presented. Up until this day, I have no way of fathoming why this occurred. The only thing left from this experience that is of importance is a deep and profound visceral feeling of loving gratitude. It was the most subtle state of affection for everything and anything that I would encounter. I truly believe that this is what humanity should be experiencing and are not.

There is another happening I remember for which I cannot identify sequential definition, and it was on this occasion that I learnt of the hieroglyphs. I was in a craft, looking at a panel that was just above my eye line. It was formulating a strange type of calculus that corresponded to where I needed to go. I knew that I had just been somewhere but couldn't remember where, and I knew that I was coming home. These are the most potent recollections I have of these beings.

I looked towards a panel that lined the ship's inner surface and what appeared there were the alien hieroglyphs that Zakai and Dyani had begun to reveal within Lo Ban's domain. I knew upon seeing them that they corresponded to states of awareness that can be accessed within our living construct, and I learnt that they were the symbols that the owners of the craft would focus on as a navigational tool to access our position in the universe.

What was most interesting was that the craft had been built to be aware of itself and of intentions in a symbiotic manner with the occupants. What I know of these beings is that their awareness is empty, yet they conceive of the future in terms of energy, and their conception translates into matter — in this case as a living craft that can be directed through merely observing a glyph.

These symbols do not follow a set format but appear in correspondence to the empty intention of the beings that fly that craft. They conceive of where they wish to be, and the craft accommodates with a hieroglyph that formulates within the pilot the corresponding futuristic conceptualization necessary to draw them from point A to point B. The craft then locates energetic wormholes that move erratically in time and space.

Many people have observed these ships zigzagging across the sky and then disappearing. This motion is the craft following those elusive entry points. When entering the wormholes, they disappear from view and reappear within the region that correlates to the hieroglyph that was generated via the empty intention of the pilot.

If these craft were to be found, to fly them man would need to forget himself and only know where he wants to go. The craft would provide everything in between. In essence, these beings are so advanced that they have created a vessel that corresponds to selfless desire, for within their awareness desire has been foregone.

Years later, I remembered that the hieroglyphs were also in the box that they had given me (along with others I am yet to remember), connected on a light silver, metallic substance shaped like a ruler about three inches wide and ten inches long.

When next I appeared in the realm of my benefactor, Zakai eagerly asked me to relay the information that I had recalled. Before I began, he called Jagür from the darkness. She slinked around from behind him, coming to rest beside me. Her feline face was exuding pure power, which I felt absorbing into me, and by virtue of this, I was able to speak with greater clarity.

"Jagür will sit with you and comfort you as you talk," Zakai said. "She is now your companion. She has been with the old Nagual for centuries and now she will stay by your side and sustain your being within the shamanic dream that needs to be awakened within you, and within all the warriors that you will encounter."

I stroked Jagür's large head as I recounted my experiences to Zakai. He listened excitedly with eyes wide open. When I had finished, he remarked on the portion of my story where the aliens had handed me the rectangular box and the moment in which the memory of their faces had been taken away.

"There's a good reason why you couldn't recall their faces. Your cognitive system was not prepared for what you would have seen. Their features are not what you would expect, and this sight would have frightened you and destabilized the beautiful feelings they were leaving within you."

When Zakai mentioned this, I remembered the absolute purity of their presence. It was like being in a state of ecstasy. Every gesture they made was full of exquisite beauty.

Their intentions are so soft, so non-intrusive. They know the depth of the trouble that humanity is caught in, but for some reason can only proceed in the way that they did with me; one by one, singularly touching each human beings' heart and awakening us to the ecstasy that has been withdrawn from our existence. I looked to Zakai, and he returned my gaze with profound empathy.

"I too had my memories erased in exactly the same fashion." He told me, "When you speak of what occurred with you it re-enlivens those sites of beauty within me, and within my recalling through your recital, I marvel at the ingenuity of these beings. Their subtleties surpass man's current evolutionary phase. When I remember what they have done, my luminosity brightens."

I was suddenly propelled backwards by a strong pressure. Zakai had become luminous, and there was a deep, pulsating hum coming from the center of the vibrant golden sphere that had appeared right before my eyes. I noticed a small item that shone brightly, floating near the molten core. It looked like a child with outstretched arms, and I knew this to be the imprint of the aliens that Zakai had alluded to.

Before I had a chance to fully stabilize myself within that awesome sight, Zakai was sitting in front of me again. Smiling like a Cheshire cat, he winked at me.

"At some time in the future, I will tell you about what just occurred," he said, in response to my inquisitive expression. "You don't yet have the capacity to fully comprehend.

"The way these imprints are placed within our luminosity defies description. One has to understand the concept of temporal transmutation, as well as the future implications that surround this embedded feeling that you saw stationed within my luminosity.

"We are intimately connected with the future, and reviewing the past impacts this unfolding. Before one can conceive of the future, one must revisit the past. Reviewal is the only viable option that exists for us as a species. It is our only recourse. The reason for this is that we are governed by that which has been set forth, even though it is not necessarily permanently in place, for this would imply absolutism. To fathom the intricacies of that liquid arrangement, we first must softly recognize the insoluble within ourselves."

Zakai smiled at me knowingly and said, "You know more than you expect. Be within your power."

Focus on that inner beauty, that inner silence
so that you may recapture yourself
and not be captured by something else.

Emptying the Imprint

Every encounter with Zakai stood out as one of the most mysterious and unforgettable events of my life. So many of my visits to my benefactor's realm were infused with his elusive character. This man was capable of slipping into any dream scene without interfering with its content.

On one such occasion, I was within a dream, doing what dreamers do, when I became aware of a gray-haired man sitting on top of a roof. I had seen him but in the same instant not noticed him at all.

He was stationary as a statue, yet within that stillness he wordlessly conveyed from a distance how to observe and be unnoticeable within that observation.

I didn't question why he was sitting on the roof or even realize when he disappeared, for his manner was so non-invasive that I simply didn't notice that he had gone until he suddenly reappeared by my side.

"To where master Lo Ban abides," he whispered, and upon his command, that mysterious dominion appeared before us.

"It is time now for us to discuss the ancient shamanic knowledge that has to do with the interactive elements of mother and father. You will see how these imprints combine in multiples and ultimately keep realization of truth at bay. Look now into the void, and we will examine haunted awareness and the art of stalking, both of which are applied through the mind of that shadow.

"Did you not notice that when I entered your dream, you accepted my arrival without question? You knew who I was, yet within that same realization you didn't know me. The territory of our inner stratosphere is vast and complex.

"What we have done with this complexity is divide it into sites that can be more easily managed, and the way we have achieved this is by imprinting those site with memories. Accessing these subtle aspects will unlock those etheric locations.

"Each site resonates with a certain amount of emotion, which brings forth the memories of that region to the surface, and these stored feelings hold enormous amounts of information within the boundaries of their own vibratory force. The problem that we now encounter is a loss of awareness when we arrive at these allotted sites.

"The way we forfeit our perceptual clarity is through the reprogramming influence of multiple illusions, designed to absorb our attention within activities that have no real functional importance. It is a priority to discover where we are surreptitiously being held, whichever attention we are arriving upon, which in actuality is a dream, even though we are not sleeping.

"Did you not notice how easily I slipped into your dream? Have I not entered it as easily as the shadow? Would it not be just as easy for me to insert within your dreamscape whatever I please? Those who enter others' realities must take great responsibility. Wouldn't you agree? If no responsibility is taken then obviously an agenda is at hand."

"If we are surreptitiously held within a reality that is based on a deceptive, covert outline of another mind, how can we escape?" I asked, disturbed by such a dark prospect.

"As you know, Lujan, being within this realm with us is to be in a state of no compromise. The reason for this is that here the interplay between one's heart and one's mind is not cloaked. There are no surreptitious outlines to be dealt with, and this is because the elements of male and female, or mother and father, are operating in complete harmony.

"The way that the shadow's mind functions is to take those elements and put them into imbalance so that they fight with each other and engender conflict within a person. This is a form of coupling, an intermingling of familiar states. The beast, the corrupt intent, has an advantage over us in the arena of perception, for it can access almost any circumstance and inject itself wherever it pleases to disrupt individuals searching for power.

"This is easy to recognize. Look into the eyes of those who speak to you. If you see that they're not within their truth, and a surreptitious agenda that outlines their selfish gratification is at hand, then you will know you are dealing with the shadow awareness and not with the personal power of a real human being.

"Know that through social interaction the center of our body is pressured. Imagine that your being is composed of earth. If a predator were to walk upon this ground, an imprint would be left. The presence leaves an impression. That imprint, if impacted, creates a pressure that warps perception.

"In this warping of attention, one's fundamental cognition is being swayed in a direction that is aligned with the weight of that perception and is therefore no longer composed of the original intention. This warped conceptualization is known to itself. It is the shadow's mind that takes over what was originally there, if you're not careful.

"When these impressions are examined and swept into oblivion, just as one would pick up a broom and sweep away traceable tracks left behind, this simple act realigns the original inner self. Through this alignment, silence re-establishes itself, and in this process, the placement of elements is spun and transformed.

"Only one quality remains — pure retrospective silence. Introspectively, we receive this imagery that has many dimensional doorways interwoven, and silence harmoniously blends them together in a never-ending sequence of adaptation that has neither beginning nor end."

The energetic truths he described played in my awareness as vivid units of visual information, and when I saw the image of an imprint in the soft dirt, a question arose within me.

"How does this point of reference and pressure come about?" I asked.

"When someone's chest is pressured, that weight is a representation of the predator that wishes to corral us for its own consumption. The power of this imprint states, 'I need you to feed me, for I cannot exist without you.'

"This is the ensuing pressure of a formatted socialization that survives by reflecting upon itself through you, reinforcing its methodology in this way so that interconnective compliance occurs.

"Tacit conformity is where the problem lies for all of us; it is where the energy we need has gone. We must retrieve the original purity and clarity of these sites by reviewing and dissolving those imprints so that we can pursue the power that lies within us.

"As you gaze within that void whilst in this dream scene with me, become more aware of these imprints that are surreptitiously placed within our social order. What you are learning now is the lost shamanic method of stalking shadow attention. However, before I discuss this subject with you, I must further explain the phenomenon of coupling.

"Split your perception now so that your awareness may hook onto my words and absorb the power that lies behind them. As you focus within the void, imagery will arise, and these visions will give you deep and profound lessons."

I was free from thought as I peered into that vast emptiness, waiting for Zakai to continue.

"We are here and together. We are coupling our attention within a familiar state. The phenomenon you are experiencing with me is that of cooperation. What you will realize through this experience is that if ever you find yourself feeling uncomfortable within your waking dream, this is an indication that you are being interfered with. Within both our living construct and our dreams, we must learn to discover that which is not harmoniously progressive.

"Without a doubt, every being on earth needs to couple, thereby sustaining their reality through symbiotic attention. The danger of this lies in the fact that within those parameters that bring comfort and safety are injected familiar mechanisms, habits and moods that reinforce our internal imprints.

"In a primal context, the predatorial factor is obvious to us. However, within an urban lifestyle this element no longer takes the form of an external, physical threat. Instead, familiars assume the role of predator: marking, flagging and stabilizing awareness to confirm their internally bound status within and without so that circumstances can be kept under control and change held at bay.

"Even though this may seem to be a heavy concept and perhaps frightening to conceive of, to undo the invisible imprint of any predator that presses and holds fast our position is a priority."

Whilst looking into the void and listening to Zakai's voice, I was swept into familiar imagery. I was witnessing individuals being covertly claimed, in essence possessed, by shadow attention. I could see them grasping at the illusion of security within the perceptual prison they embraced. Realizing that complacency lay behind their eyes, I knew that this was the predatorial influence projected through them.

I had to make a supreme effort to remain focused on what Zakai was saying, for it required an enormous amount of energy to sustain such a memory.

"There is much that can be learnt through observing the visualization of the predator that leaves an imprint. We all know that a jaguar would not come back to confirm her own steps and reinforce where she has been. But we, unlike the jaguar, confirm the imprinting of our own steps in terms of communication that establishes our idea of self within a restrictive facade.

"This phantom positioning is reinforced by familiars, who are subliminally aware of the undercurrent of our invisible imprinting, which has been stabilized in the past. These individuals will re-enliven those sites by surreptitiously acquainting themselves with our weaknesses and supplying negative reinforcements to press upon the site that will hold us in states of complacency and limitation.

"The familiar would devour our very essence through the repetitive idea that life has only this much to offer, and that these crippling boundaries of perception cannot be broken. Such insidiousness can and must be overcome by presently recounting one's past events so that one may discover that masked proposition that appears to be lived unconsciously by those acting upon us."

I was seeing within the void many people with very little personal power, whose lives were devoid of meaning. As I was witnessing this, Zakai's words were being superimposed over the imagery, confirming what I was becoming aware of. He knew exactly what I was seeing and addressed my observations as if I had spoken them.

"These individuals have willingly given up their sovereignty for the security of being accepted. This brings about two types of corruption. Whether this takes the form of subservience or dominance or a combination of both, one's personal power is forsaken. These false premises are compounded incessantly by inner talk and cultivate alliances that are incestuous and unwholesome.

"Even if an individual believes they are learning valuable lessons through these toxic interactions, engagement in petty power struggles will not result in levity. It is simply a waste of time and must be avoided like the plague. As you can see, this dark predilection, multiplied by billions of people, brings about a most complex and sorcerous socialization."

I was absolutely enthralled with the depths of his elucidation. He drew my face towards him with his right hand and spoke intently to me.

"Do not forget what I say. Your life depends on it. For this wisdom to endure, you must never lose sight of what is being directly transmitted to you now. Look again into the void. What you are learning is the stalking of shadow attention."

Zakai prompted me to visualize the hieroglyph of Haunted Awareness once more. He told me that he wished to expand upon how the elements of mother and father interact in a corrupt cycle and how an atmosphere of discord is established in childhood. His voice was calm and precise as he resumed his explanation.

"There are two reflective shields within this hieroglyph that must be examined extensively. They are the cloaked inner child and the corrupt witness. These shields combine with four elements of interplay that are activated to dominate circumstances.

"These identifiable elements are the traits of male and female that are swapped and interchanged in comparison to the need to reflect control back onto the environment through male dominance or female submissiveness and vice versa.

"This polymorphic positioning is employed to manipulate and coerce, to conjure an illusion of compliance so as to create a strategic advantage. These cultivated masks cover a hidden agenda, which stems from intention that is possessed by the preoccupation of self-serving rationalization. This selfish drive and the need to justify it are simply avenues that are sustained by landmarked sites of emotion.

"The cloaked inner child adopts a filter of distortion that is absorbed from the adult assertions that are played out in its environment. The controlling factors are the dramas enacted by mother and father. As a consequence of being witness to the ensuing battles between male and female, the cloaked child takes on dominant, conquering behaviors and supplies those to itself as a tool, while simultaneously adopting submissive conduct to use as a surreptitious trap.

"Passive attributes are employed to encase itself and others in the illusion that it has been weakened, yet all the while it waits to strike with the dominant aspect. These tools develop into a refined combination of both the masculine and feminine imprinted characteristics.

"Unbeknownst to themselves, the parents have set forth an intended proposition that becomes the energetic boundary that this inner child will apply to all of its present and future circumstances.

"As you can see in this hieroglyph, the intended proposition is the filter that creates a practice ground for that child, in its own environment, upon which to apply his or her immature preoccupations. These are connected to immature desires and obviously are seen through that very same lens, which is the shadow dream's distorted view.

"The glyph can also be viewed as an upper and a lower domain, which simply reveals the dominant force of the upper elements upon the lower. The upper can equally be seen as an adult asserting control over circumstances, and the lower as the true innocence, which represents the inner child or children within our society who are learning to control by witnessing that behavior. When you refer to these symbols, these examples will help you to convey the complexities of their cycles of enactment to those who wish to free themselves.

"The hieroglyph of Haunted Awareness can also pertain to a governmental body, employing exactly the same principles of parent and child. The upper sphere, as the corrupt witness, asserts its power as an intended proposition that is installed within society as a widespread preoccupation with self-serving rationalization.

"This fixation is sustained through the cultivation of insatiable desires that are transmitted to the corrupt witness of the masses, who are collectively held in a cloaked position through a worldwide hidden agenda that further thwarts and suppresses realization.

"The reason this is possible is that the inner sense of those adult beings is full of foreign substance as a result of their own wrongful self-application. Discordant repercussions stem directly from that cloaked inner child who has oppressed and who takes willful command over its circumstances by wielding its immaturity as childish preoccupations that demand to be satisfied at all costs. This cycle self-perpetuates and locks awareness within seemingly irresolvable loops of repetition.

"All of these behavioral devices are the mirrors of the corrupt witness and the cloaked inner child that must be purified. Purification happens only through self-reflective acknowledgement. Each person must undertake that process individually so that it may then be collectively realized.

"The first two shields are really the focal point of the hieroglyph. The cloaked inner child governs the corrupt witness. As a unit, they create the most powerful reflective component. They are the primary mirrors, which in essence, can make it very difficult for one whose awareness is enthralled within the shadow's dream to become fully conscious of what is taking place.

"As you know, the cloaked inner child contains integrated elements of male and female, as does the corrupt witness. These interchangeable characteristics are indiscriminately employed to condone self-serving, destructive behavior. Justification is used as a filter, or intended proposition, that keeps the mechanisms of denial intact.

"Instead, what needs to be established are the true components of male and female in balance, to reflect upon the world within a harmonious framework, as is depicted within the hieroglyph of Inner Light.

"Justification becomes an assertion of oppression that will draw upon all elements of social conditioning to maintain control. Behind this righteousness appears the incestuous continuity of hidden agenda. Such an approach relates to fixed intent and the actualization of will to hold back insightful intensity, which is motivated primarily by the jealous need to waylay.

"A hidden agenda is extremely insidious by nature, and its impact far-reaching. To fulfill a surreptitious outline, deception is applied through indirect insinuation, subtle body movements and inflections of voice that demand compliance, wordlessly delivered via the gaze of condemnation.

"The assertion of shadow attention endeavors to hold intensity in the illusion of incompleteness, and the idea that innocence needs approval from that phantom position in order to succeed. Disapproval is implied to disempower and enliven uncertainty.

"In fact, what is actually occurring is the gradual draining of vitality into the shadowy aspects of human attention, the principle motive being to steal that potent energy. This is a fixed and protected prime directive of the shadow's mind, which we all must become aware of, so that the magical door that lies behind our eyes of intent can be opened, and crystal clear clarity can identify the elusive mystery where true intensity resides."

The very potency of which Zakai spoke imbued his every word and gesture. His elucidation of the hieroglyphs covered so many complex variables in human behavior, using such simple terminology. Pointing, he drew my attention to the sphere at the top of the glyph.

"By simply observing this symbol, we automatically activate architectural observation. When the hieroglyph of Inner Light is brought into play through consciously witnessing the shadow's dream, the Architect of observation will sweep from one arrangement to another. In this process we may question preoccupation and wonder what intention is without this element attached.

"By merely asking this of ourselves, we are transported to the true advisor, and we find ourselves delivered into a state of transparency. When honest introspection is privately applied to one's circumstances, one is drawn into the adult inner sense of oneself. Here, we land squarely in the center of our chest, where the innocence of our inner child is stationed.

"Upon this arrival, the cloaked inner child will invariably want to be uplifted. It will be swept back to the hieroglyph of Inner Light and into the position of the buoyant child, accessing its own true counterparts of transparency and intensity. This advent will cause a cathartic release.

"The now buoyant inner child wishes to look through its own clear, unimpeded circumstances to review itself and be free of the superfluous residue – the cloak that previously weighed down the natural light-heartedness of that child.

"When the cloaked inner child transforms into the buoyant child, a new field of exploration becomes available. It is only then that the adult witness gains access to the Architect of observation. Here, that uninhibited observer will examine the construct of the buoyant witness extensively.

"This is where the focus should have been in the first place: introspectively reviewing our current state of awareness, which identifies our past and present reality combined, as a multiplex of usable continuums that can be randomly gazed into."

Looking at the two hieroglyphs, I was struck by how similar they appeared to be visually, yet how utterly opposite in their cycles of enactment. Observing them brought on a dizzying sensation, as they appeared to be blurring between dimensional planes. Zakai resumed speaking and his voice crystallized my attention within the void.

"In looking back to the hieroglyph of Haunted Awareness, see that these protective shields are made up of the imposed energetic imprints of socialization. These potent sites gain momentum through the conscious act of establishing alliance with behaviors that are contrary to the inner growth of all of us as human beings.

"When broken down into single elements, the shields appear as they are – irrational. Nevertheless, they develop a life of their own, a vibratory force that presses upon external circumstances in the form of relentlessly adaptive justification.

"Evidence of this can be perceived within personal conduct as a divertive force that correlates exclusively to the needs of those insecure and manipulative individuals who are aware of placements within their environment. Such leverage points are also energetic imprints that can be utilized through the activation of fearful or limited behaviors, both internally and within others.

"Although this may seem complex and hard to conceive of, there is a good reason for this. The preoccupations placed within our emptiness as heavily weighted sites don't allow us to be totally cognizant of the full ramifications of the interactions that are constantly inter-dispersed within our reality.

"Unfortunately, consequences have to be learnt through contact. We must take responsibility and be real in the moment we are living so that our lives are not pulled into lengthy, drawn out situations through being absently involved in those dramas that take us away from the essential lesson of empowerment.

"To be real is easy. Simply do not invest in negative impulses that will drain your essential essence. Be light-hearted and positive wherever you can so that you may involve yourself in witnessing. From this perspective you will have nothing to hide, even though you are concealed. Then you may witness the actions of those you observe in your own private space.

"Your review will become a state of absorption that disallows saturation so that you can become progressively more aware. In this state of quiet contemplation one must never, under any circumstances, assert an argumentative defiance through auditory or visual imaginings which may reflect one's own dramas or weaknesses and bolster one's own shields, for they must be put aside when observation takes place."

Watching Zakai, I realized that he was in a profound, analytical state that corresponded to heart and not mind. He turned to face me directly.

"Keep your focus on the void," he said. "We need to finish what we have started. When the shields are laid aside, one may experience the effect of catharsis. If this release is strong and pure enough, the person involved will recall the past event that molded the present perceptual filters that created the imbalance in the first place.

"At this point appears the opportunity to examine this karmic residue. One of two possible alternatives will be presented. It may be that the individual becomes aware of something having been done to them, where that circumstance remembered had taken their potency. In that instance, they were not able to assert the boundary that made them whole in comparison to their personal power at that time.

The second possibility is that a person will see where they have asserted themselves incorrectly by attempting to injure that which damaged them, which once again disempowered them, at the same time as they were being undermined by another.

"Honest, retrospective evaluation has the ability to deliver an individual to a moment of fluid actualization in comparison to their current state of being, which frees that person from internally stationed imprints that may limit their potential.

"The behavioral key to this metamorphosis is observation infused with patiently waiting, and timing one's input via the awareness that the omnipresent factor within will deliver to the seer the formlessness necessary to bring completion so that the one's sedentary state is dissolved.

The force of one's emotion is never added to that delicate equation, where witnessing becomes the primary instrument of understanding. At this stage, we must acknowledge that what we are embarking upon is not a quick fix solution but a lifetime engagement.

"In the setting aside of the behavioral shields and relinquishing the mechanisms associated with them, they are purified. Slowly but surely, one by one, they reappear back in front of the doer in a new configuration, as the hieroglyph of Inner Light demonstrates. This evolution lays forth the magnification of that which used to be in the forefront, alerting the individual to that which was once theirs.

"Through the transparency of the shields, the warrior is forewarned of what is coming, yet does not re-engage with involvement, for the elemental structure is now clear, externally and internally. In this way, a formless view becomes apparent.

"Clarity and power become the tools of internal imagery, and the experience of existing in real time is established through not being involved in the lagging time-space continuum of other individuals' reality. Being wholly in your speed, yet simultaneously aware of the other, you develop the ability to get to the heart of things.

"Just be patient and observe your circumstances lightly, taking care not to add too much of yourself, and timing your withdrawal so that excessive saturation does not occur. This within itself will allow a new cycle to commence. If evolution is waylaid in any way, recover those simultaneous time-space continuums that are your present reality interlaced with your past experiences.

"Your real time recovery will invariably dislodge that foreign substance which caused energetic stagnancy, thus allowing you to regain the potency and immediacy of your full attention. When one is purely in the field of real time, objectivity will come into poignant magnification, selfless observation.

"Unabashed observation is where the way of the clear-hearted is applied in daily affairs. Though it may appear that any internal imagery that arises belongs to the individual who sees it, it is not always so. The correlative force of introspection manifests this holographic material in the air, which takes on a format of impersonal knowing and indicates the direction in which one must proceed.

"The warrior sweeps the environment, acknowledging the interconnective parallel elements of social order and gleaning essential information via both physical and non-physical channels. As the seer becomes cognizant of the subtle arrangements that the mystical facility of inner seeing presents, a much greater journey begins.

"Previously imprinted visual aspects associated with this person's past are beckoned forth to be witnessed. Light and unknown to themselves, the warrior is never convinced of any circumstance until those primary motives that are presented through seduction and manipulation are absorbed and re-related in a fashion that retains no static cognition.

I broke my fixation from the void. I had to see Zakai's face. What he was explaining was both beautiful and frightening. My attention was perfectly attuned as he continued.

"Watch how the subtleties become substance, as we become increasingly aware that intent itself is the boundary or fence that entraps. From a predator's perspective, our gaze demands that we corral and annihilate our prey in order to survive. On an energetic level, this predatorial view in its narrow inference must be abandoned. This would be the end of dominance and agenda, allowing entry for true introspection to occur.

"Remember, emptiness must be embraced so that the original status of intent can be absorbed like magical gold dust particles falling everywhere at once, infusing us with a sense of potency and the possibility of going beyond what we are."

Zakai's eyes were locked on mine, and as I peered into their depths, I saw his being dissolve. At that moment, the scene popped. He had become luminous once again, yet his voice went on uninterrupted.

"This subtle information that has just been transferred to you may not fully awaken you from the shadow's dream. You must be delivered to a place of beauty to further assimilate these insights. Your guide will be Malaiyan, one of my oldest and dearest friends. We are clan-like, and you and your cohorts will be marked by our awareness. Those who receive this knowledge will be integrated on the level of intention and become our mythical companions."

With these words, the luminosity that was Zakai faded from view and I was left there, awaiting my next instruction.

Invisible Imprinting

I heard soft footsteps approaching and saw two points of brilliance emerging from the darkness. Malaiyan came to my side and gently touched my arm as he gazed at me warmly with his big round eyes.

"With me you will come, and watch the water that was once before you. It is within your memory. It is a landmark."

Upon his command, we were transported to that pond we had visited together. A wonderful sense of quietude surrounded Malaiyan. I had forgotten how intensely magical he was.

"Dip your hand in," he said to me. "Look within the water and reflect upon that which is in front of you. Zakai has informed you in great depth on the subjects I am to broach, but there is always more.

"The first thing to be aware of is that society has a certain amount of sleepers. Sleepers assimilate information in total acceptance, without question. It's not that they cannot access the intelligence to ask pertinent questions about life in general; it is that they will not take the risk to break their boundaries, as change for the sleeper seems immensely daunting.

"For a sleeper to change means they need acceptance during that transformation. This grace, however, is rarely given unconditionally. If granted, it is usually characterized by disgruntled reluctance from peers, which is enforced relentlessly, holding humanity in stasis through the auspices of fear and preoccupation.

"Imprints link one sleeper to another. 'If you change, I will have to change too. If you realize, so must I.'

"People need to become aware that there are three types of certainty: to know everything without question, to know that everything must be questioned, and to know that everything can be known in your world through introspection, which applies solely to the individual and will eventually be collectively integrated to become holistic certainty."

I looked up into Malaiyan's face. I'd never heard him speaking in this fashion before. It was almost as if he and Zakai had merged through the thread of their intentions. He returned my gaze with reflective intensity.

"We are working on you and making you pliable," he said. "You must recognize everything that approaches so that you can skillfully navigate that which surrounds you at every moment." Peering even more deeply into my eyes, he reached forward, gently touching my heart center with his outstretched fingers.

"For you to be here is a remarkable thing," he said softly. "We have waited such a long time for this to occur. When you awaken into your living construct, you will realize that you are besieged. The difference will be that now you will comprehend completely what you are surrounded by, without question. By virtue of this, you will know exactly how to proceed.

"The old Nagual was right, we have found a continuum within you, and you will proceed with our intentions and awaken those who are your companions into the world we are returning to you.

"Do you know, Lujan, that we are now in a familiar state? This dream scene is an imprint. The mere fact that I talk to you is reinforcement, and that interaction becomes an anchor. If you hear my voice and know my being, then my words become a flag that will draw your awareness to this memory and the reality of this cognitive system.

"What I pass to you now is one of the major keys, delivered in the language used by the old shamans to describe the ancient art of strategically stalking awareness away from shadow attention.

"When this information is assimilated, one is automatically put into a state of war. The reason this inevitably comes about is that once you become aware of these principles, you will fight not to be positioned. You will refuse to be entrapped within that which is being set up. But you, Lujan, will fight silently against the shadow's mind.

"Be alert, so as not to be caught within agendas. Know the familiar." He paused, acknowledging my focus, while I waited silently for him to continue, allowing every word to sink in.

"A familiar is a close friend, lover or associate; one who will confirm to you the ramifications of your own boundaries, unbeknownst to themselves, or semi-consciously, for they are fully involved. Be aware of their usage of imprints, which are usually connected to conceptual ploys that provide a basis for land-marking, on both inner and external landscape.

"A person can be imprinted through being partially aware of their environment, which is a form of immaturity. In being semi-alert, one's attention can be molded, and by the mere fact that molding occurs, the imprint begins to become 'second nature'. This is how an internal mechanism is established surreptitiously through familiarity.

"Pay attention to the reinforcement that is taking place. It is usually asserted by the engineers of land-marking so that they may keep both their world and yours within the bounds of familiar comprehension and available for usage. Also be aware of anchoring, which is a tactic of verification that draws the subject into immersion and brings about a solidified state of perception."

Something made me look up, and I caught a glimpse of a spiraling gesture so quick that I almost could have imagined it. Malaiyan's unobtrusive nature was so prominent that to see him move like that jolted me. He smiled wryly at my surprise.

"The old Nagual Lujan taught us these movements, which we are transmitting to you visually to awaken the primal energy hidden within your hippocampus. These movements will further enhance the concepts we have outlined, which are so interdimensionally interdispersed that when they are shown to you, you will discover the deeper essence of yourself, which is your memory being recovered.

"These basic foundations outline the ancient shamanic art that uses parallel perceptions to sustain clarity within the vortices, which you will experience through the enhancement of kinesthetic units of information that become absorbed via the magnetism created. The gravity generated by practicing these movements will give you access to dark matter."

I had been so thoroughly absorbed in the tranquil mood that surrounded Malaiyan that it was only now that I had begun to notice how disarmingly direct he could be. He reached out and touched my arm with purposeful urgency.

"There is not much time. You must proceed with speed and agility to achieve the task of imparting the information we are collectively transferring to you."

Next thing I knew, I had awoken in my bed. In the days that followed, I became totally immersed in the principles Zakai and Malaiyan had put forth. These were exciting times. I realized that the old Nagual's realm and my living construct were spilling over into each other, and the content of my conceptualizations within my waking state was shifting and changing at a great pace.

I understood that I was at war, and that what I was fighting against was an unseen enemy that reached its hand through almost every being I met. The shadow influence was so insidious and intrusive, and we were all entangled within its web.

The Shadow's Mind

When next I entered into master Lo Ban's domain, I realized that I had arrived without being summoned by a voice. The way that I got there was by seeing Lucien's tattoo as a pattern in front of my face. When I was fully cognizant of my surroundings, I saw that he was standing right in front of me. He was truly a magnificent human being, so powerful and so at ease. When he began to speak, his manner was calm and his words succinct.

"On the first occasion we met, we spoke of threads of intention and the same old thing. Since then, Zakai has painstakingly put together the puzzle for you. You know now that the same old thing truly is a monster that relentlessly hunts our being and stalks our awareness through interconnective activity that is deemed normal.

"The shadow's mind has installed the mechanisms of subterfuge and collective compliance. Both this insertion into our perception, and the constant solicitation via the threads of intention, are surreptitiously masked in the idea that everything we think and conceive of is ours. In fact, that internal dialogue is the insistent nagging of the social programming, which amounts to the simple overlay of a limited reality within the truth of what we really could know, which is actually devoid of a thought process.

"When you interact with another and that person tries to enliven limiting behaviors within you, they are most often subduing you through the mechanism of non-approval.

This is the first furtive technique that disempowers our inner child.

"When we do not have purpose, due to this disapproval and disempowerment, we are ruthlessly directed to act out the bidding of shadow intention, which unfortunately is one of the primary matrices of human awareness in the time-space continuum that we consciously exist within. As a result, we are constantly at war with each other, and so hopelessly engaged away from our purpose.

"This golden cage reveals the ramifications of one's self-reflection that incessantly confirms its existence to itself through talking, as an echo of the repetitious internal dialogue; which possesses the eyes to such a degree that it does not see itself standing on the precipice of eternity due to its constant need to be recognized.

"Our leaders, those men behind the smug smiles who herd us to our death in battle — which in essence is our domestication — have unwittingly given their allegiance to the predator, which they are actually creating via cultivating that maniacal, self-serving intention that is the vibratory frequency of our collective awareness. That psychopathic tendency, which is screened off from us via our relentless programming, has become so confident that it will not be discovered that it wreaks open havoc on consciousness itself, which in turn is destroying our planet.

"Become aware of the ramifications of these echelons. Every advancement of each phase will be revealed to us as attention expands beyond the limited confines defined by that awareness that is determined to keep more than one step ahead.

"The ongoing conflict and hostilities being perpetuated to gain selfish dominion are utterly out of alignment with our evolutionary process. This is meant to be a place of empowerment for those who wish to experience the expansiveness of our physical universe, behind which lies a field of energy that is as immeasurable as the abyss.

"Nevertheless, in spite of its seemingly never-ending onslaughts, shadow influence can be identified. Its hallmarks can be seen. Our powers of observation must be brought into a new field, a new imprint. Within an awareness unhindered by learnt limitations, the warrior will listen to the agenda applied without becoming subdued by that pressure.

"When that warrior finds themselves being engaged, if their subtleties have been honed correctly they will recognize the predatorial influence behind the eyes of those individuals who have lost their power to that insidious force. This will allow that seer to become an unbiased witness.

"I know that Barak has shown you how to travel back in time and dislodge the imprints that are heavily placed within our emotionality. This process of dissolving sedentary material is essential for your growth. The old Nagual awaits to teach you of the wonders and powers that lie within us as human beings. He has been waiting a long time for such a tenacious being as you — one who will not be told what to do and who will question everything that is presented.

"As a collective humanity, we need to stand up and question why. In so doing, we deliver shadow attention to its true position by transparently viewing where it has been revealed within oneself, as a reflection of what is being seen. Only then will power permit a truth to be truly spoken. When I feel you within, Lujan, I know that your task will be to present everybody with the questions we all must ask of ourselves.

"We all need to pursue our personal path within the idea of growth. We must eliminate the corrosive and heavy effects that our self-concern mirrors back to us as false needs. Preoccupation is the primary component that locks our inner child within a self-perpetuating cycle of inwardly sustained entrapment.

"We have to dislodge our continuity so that we may dissolve our past. Within this dismantling, we will find power and be occupied only with the immediacy of the moment instead of perceptual distortions that take us away from the real reason we're here. We must examine our behavior relentlessly so that we may recognize our self-concern as damaging, and only align with that which has power in our lives.

"The hieroglyph of Haunted Awareness reveals those behaviors, characterized by surreptitiousness, that disallow us to observe without the influence of preoccupations, which are the cloaks that waylay our spirit collectively. We actively pass these burdens from one to another within an atmosphere of unspoken acceptance that holds us fixed and inhibits our capacity to be fluid. This collective agreement needs to be broken. We must examine the dysfunctional behaviors that belong to haunted awareness and discover why we are perpetuating a limited perceptual view."

I looked to Lucien in amazement, marveling at his incisive portrayal of humanity's dilemma. He glanced back at me and winked.

"The specific behaviors that I am referring to are character assassination, gossip and incorrect inquiry," he clarified. "It is vitally important not to let the insincere get too close. Most people have been trained to merely gossip and not to ask the true and relevant questions of their heart.

"Sincerity and trust have to be established as the basis of communication before one can be open. In all encounters, your behavior must not be elusive but full of caring and true kindness. It is essential to be as polite and as professional as possible, for you know that where people are coming from is not truly full or happy, and interference is the only intervening element in their lives. When you become aware, be loving and considerate to these people, for within your actions, you act upon yourself.

"The main reason why people ask invasive questions is that they haven't dealt with their inner turmoil. They seek distraction and solace outside of their own sphere of responsibility. Their guilt and unhappiness are usually reinforced by their inquiries, which keep them removed from their own inner silence, and they are inwardly very angry about that, even though they don't quite know why.

"Another reason people inquire in an inappropriate manner, though it may be unknown to them, is that on a subliminal level what they are really pursuing is themselves. Within this quest, they are demanding to be given an integral yardstick so that they may measure their own state in comparison to what has been presented through the interaction.

"What has occurred over the centuries is a perversion of a simple query of truth. If one stands their ground and says, 'Stop,' to an intrusive question they are actually teaching the inquirer that they have no real business being there. The question within itself drains the essential part of that person's true nature, the very thing that could possibly give them power in their life. When you look at it from this point of view, it is difficult to be offended and more interesting just to observe.

"When next you return, Zakai will continue to instruct you in the art of stalking. These teachings are best assimilated within the parallel continuum that will ultimately become your daily reality. Within an altered state, Zakai will show you authentic methods to empower those who proceed in a manner that corresponds to the hieroglyph of Inner Light, which eventually transforms into the hieroglyph of Completion. Jagür will accompany you to your living construct now."

Upon this statement, Jagür leapt out from the darkness. Together we flew through the emptiness of that void that I had become so familiar with. I awoke suddenly in my bed, with the power of Jagür once again surging through my system. She had truly become my hidden companion.

If you engage in your world
With anything less than purpose,
You will be engulfed
By that which surrounds you.

Hunting the Haunted

I had awoken into the old Nagual's realm, magnetically drawn by the vision of that alien imprint that I had seen previously in Zakai's luminosity. As I focused my gaze upon the symbol floating in front of me, Zakai's form materialized. He smiled at me with a familiar glint in his eye and began to speak.

"What you followed here is an imprint of non-interference. It belongs to those beings that have awakened your awareness to a higher purpose. You too have this imprint stationed within your luminosity. The old Nagual adopted you thirty-three years ago to ensure that these units of information would be passed on intact to those who intend to go beyond a fixed cognitive system.

"Be mindful within your transmission that if those you teach are not prepared to destabilize their hidden agenda, the real meaning of what you convey will become lost in the depths of rigid intellectual conceptualization. The risk then is that the information may be unraveled and reapplied in a way that reinforces a personalized surreptitious outline within distorted states. This is the shadow's mind.

"What I am to show you now may be disturbing, but this process is necessary. Understanding is the only vehicle that will dislodge the shadow's imprint. I must warn you, however, that the moment you start to bring this information out into the open, this attention will emerge from every corner to try to stop this process, as it has done throughout the ages. Our essential task is to deliver a method of stalking shadow attention so as to free humanity from that influence.

"These teachings will illuminate and uncover the limiting behaviors that are embedded within the living construct. Through this transfer, we invite each individual to reclaim their sovereignty and transcend those stifling parameters by taking personal responsibility for our collective dilemma."

Zakai gazed directly into my eyes, and as I looked within, the void appeared. Placing one hand on my shoulder, he pointed into that endless vastness and whispered to me.

"I would ask you now to visualize the happenings I am about to describe."

As he said this, a person appeared within that void, and when I focused on their physical form they became transparent. Zakai directed my awareness to an implanted foreign object that appeared within their transparency. I knew that what I was seeing was a covertly placed imprint that was internally sustained through habitually repetitive behavior. Zakai snapped his fingers suddenly, and the sound acutely focused my attention on the scene being presented.

"See that these imprints are like an ethereal landing pad that exists within that transparency. When the shadow applies pressure on these sites, what invariably escapes is our energy, which then becomes a source of sustenance for those beings.

"This application is echoed in our behaviors towards each other as petty enactments that trigger awareness into states of egocentricity and justification, which establish the limited avenues of preoccupation needed to sustain these sites and subdue our potential. See that the stronger the preoccupation, the more energy released.

"As you know, this creates a perpetual cycle of excited gluttony. When that energy is discharged, our power is redirected away from our true purpose. People who unconsciously enact their dysfunctions upon one another, thinking that these states of being are theirs to possess, must realize that they are not the possessors, but rather, they are being possessed by that pre-arranged phenomenon."

Zakai gently waved his hand across the void. As he did so, imagery began to explode in front of me. Scenes unfolded in multiple layers before my eyes, eloquently conveying the complexity of our human condition.

"As children, we are given internal repetitious talk from our immediate environment, which we unconsciously absorb and identify with. Once the inherited imprint has been established via routines, the next generation further refines that inheritance through practice, adapting its expression to current circumstances.

"What drives this twisted refinement is the shadow attention's ability to polymorphically adapt to its circumstances through the human entity via demanding social compliance; a covert system of delivery that can be applied as reward or punishment, and which appears to function upon reasonable premises yet is anything but. Remember, these inferences abide within human consciousness. To discover that shadow you must confront the human vessel.

"Realize deeply upon what I am about to say. When a man turns his back to the sun, he is forced to look upon his own shadow. But when he turns to face that burning orb, floating within a vast, empty space, his eyes are filled with light and thus the shadow does not have the power to rise from the depths and stand before him."

Looking at me, Zakai lifted his eyebrows comically and shocked me by shouting suddenly, 'Get thee behind me!'" I laughed as he returned to his solemn tone.

"Social compliance is the gatekeeper to humanity's growth, through the pressure that is applied. It is invisible to the eye of the socially bound yet blatantly apparent to a seer. Antiquity is but a reflection of eternity's ability to constantly adapt to that which presents itself in every living circumstance via the newness of that site, which is in actual fact, seeing.

"When a social being accesses those implanted imprints that enliven emotion and justifiable self-serving rationalization, awareness is then corralled into narrow and repetitive avenues of preoccupation, not only on an individual basis but also within a collective network.

"This hidden mechanism is initiated through intention, reinforced internally and then emotionally perpetuated. Remember, these imprints are so insidiously stationed that once triggered they become self-sustaining through personalized identification.

"However, that usable network appears to only connect in our realm if we are stabilized and fixed within familiar routines. Once these patterns are dismantled within the living construct, the shadow has less opportunity to implant itself.

"Focus now within to discover the implications of what I am describing to you. The more gifted a person is, the more complex their application of shadow intention will be. This is propagated through their reasonable faculties to incessantly dominate through rational premises. That possessive intention will take the living essence of other human beings' prisoner using intellectual propositions designed to protect the hidden agenda via individual and collective programming, which in essence is the mind of a psychopath.

"Our essential resource as human beings lies within our capacity to dream and to be awakened within our daytime reality to those seeings. Shadow attention is aware of this complexity and has been injecting itself within our dreamings, which are composed of separate time capsules that can be broken into via the pre-programmed edifice that is undermining our waking world.

"By applying misdirection and cultivating our constant absorption within perceptual labyrinths, the shadow has captured our attention. Thus our purpose becomes exhausted by preoccupation and a loss of memory and awareness within whichever dream capsule we are occupying.

"The primary agenda is to lead us away from that network of realization, for if we were to remember, this would allow us to emerge from the maze, free of those enthralling complexities which confront us at every moment."

He paused, and in that moment the translucent human being I was observing suddenly morphed into a honeycombed maze of multiple luminous dream scenes. Within the center of that cluster was a white glow, which I immediately knew to be the essential energy that sustained that mysterious cluster of awareness. Zakai began to explain what I was seeing.

"Depending on the energy available, we have the potential to function with between two and four hundred dream capsules at one time. When we arrive in one dream capsule, we forget the alternate reality that we have just come from.

"If we were to remember and become fully conscious of the interconnective aspects of this network, all of these dream capsules would amalgamate into a centralized portion of energy. When this occurs we ourselves become luminous. Then the living construct is seen as it is, composed completely of void.

"At the moment we realize that our living construct is made of absolutely nothing, the subduing intentions that we are escaping from lose their momentary hold on us. Once we recognize the entrapment that binds us, the feeding frenzy that occurs in each separate compartment of each waking dream that we arrive in stops, allowing a moment of clarity. That energy is returned, and we are free to continue our journey beyond this region of the universe.

"See now before you the complexities that I am to explain. The honeycombed network was created by our luminosity so that we could express our dimensional lateralism within dream constructs and simultaneously escape the predatorial attention within, in this region of the universe. As source creators, we knew that each segment would only contain a small portion of our whole energy within it, so we created this maze as a way to prevent ourselves from being instantaneously consumed, once in human form.

"Now, Lujan, you must see that choice on the level of energy has become a contradiction within our living construct. To avoid enmeshment, we became more than what we were, which actually makes us less than who we really are.

"Through our facilitation and adaptation, we learn via the conflict presented, and this is true of all evolutionary processes. To inhabit all of the compartments at one time is to be in a state of dimensional lateralism, and this is our heritage.

"So in each dream that we dream, we must now wake up to what is occurring, and this, as you can see, is a very complex matter. If we lose one partitioned section through not being fully aware, then we have less capacity to become cognizant of what is being set up while we are occupied elsewhere.

"We also created the illusion of permanent sequentiality within our living construct so that our awareness may be solidly stationed within seemingly separate portions of time. Each section of the honeycomb contains a fragment of reality that doesn't necessarily correlate to the adjacent time-space continuum.

Without this elusive phenomenon in place, we would dissolve into light. The honeycomb fragmentation allows our third eye capacity to be intermittently aware of itself via visionary bursts that give access to trace elements of other time–space continuums. Thus, they imbue us with necessary information in the form of memory that inspires conscious evolution.

"The primary reason why time appears stable within the living construct is that this gives the best strategic advantage for recovery to occur in terms of accessing our memories. If we don't have the capacity to remember, we are unable to review and grow, and this is an annihilation of our spirit.

"The system of fragmentation works to confuse the shadow and prevent it from having complete access to us within our dreams, but also can be used against us. In forgetting what we have done to protect our luminosity, we have created a trap for ourselves, and unfortunately, this has been taken advantage of.

"Shadow attention has become a dream weaver and is now integrated with and behind our Architect of observation within our dimensional dreaming constructs. This is more than dangerous. It could mean for our species total possession within the honeycomb network.

"Recall now the grayish whirlwind that you encountered years ago. It is one of the elements responsible for the fracturing of our attention that renders us incapable of remembering the precious déjà vu that is our heritage. It is so adaptive within its intelligence that it has almost learnt how to infuse completely with our Architect of observation within the living construct. This parasitic intention stations itself within that position so unnoticeably that it almost speaks the truths of a seer. This mimicry must be stopped."

I looked up to Zakai, more than worried about what he had just said. While I was being split within the void,

I had begun to realize something about my interactions with those I encounter within my living construct.

"Yes, what you are seeing is right," Zakai confirmed.

"I would like you now to focus within the void with all your attention so that you may recover the events that surround you within your living construct when you transmit what you have absorbed from us. Retrieve those memories.

"See now the struggles that arise and know those conflicts to be triggered placements, implanted by the shadow's mind within the complexities of human attention. The danger of entanglement with this networked phenomenon is amongst the most insidious that you will face.

"The way this entity establishes its position is to question everything that is put forth by a seer. By doing so, it becomes so familiar with that knowledge that it is capable of appearing to have assimilated the seer's intelligence. This may also occur when a teacher passes information to students or disciples. You have experienced this, I know, and so have I.

"It is for this reason, to reveal and neutralize this influence, that we conspired to capture you within the old Nagual's realm. The only way to combat intelligence is through counter-intelligence. Once our information is fully documented, the socially embedded shadow awareness will have much to contend with. Our collective awakening will deliver a powerful blow to surreptitious networks of activity, for, as you know, they do not want to be discovered.

"I would ask you to look now deep within the void and understand that when you teach, you must be aware of the minor conflicts that flare up between yourself and those who wish to learn from you. These emotional eruptions are characteristic signs of the grayish whirlwind entity integrating with your student's intelligence.

"When your students challenge you by projecting enormous amounts of dysfunctional emotion, that is this being practicing to hide behind their Architect so that it can integrate within the seer's world and access the enormous amount of energy that lies within that silent reservoir of knowing that exists within our living dream.

"Recall the story of the old sorcerers that Lucien described to you. The roots of this insidious battle, which we are still contending with now, are directly related to those initial power struggles that began so long ago. There were two main categories of sorcerers at that time. The first focused their intention externally, and as a result of this choice became extremely manipulative within their machinations.

"The second ilk of sorcerers focused internally, and their clear-hearted intentions awakened the dreamer within. When they shared their discoveries with the first category, those old sorcerers assimilated that knowledge and subsequently became truly unbearable in their determination to maintain dominance.

"We are intimately connected with the second type of seer. They had no interest in the manipulative tactics in which the others were indulging. When this division became obvious, the sorcerers corrupted by their desire for power plotted to capture and possess the awakened seers, for they could not stand to think that they would escape their grasp.

"It was around the same time that those old sorcerers became aware of the shadow beings. As Lucien told you, the shadows learnt through association. It was then that the awakened seers discovered that the grayish whirlwind was interfering with their dreams extensively.

"The way they exposed this was by reviewing their dreams immediately, whilst still lucid within the honeycomb compartment. It became apparent that the review was slightly different the second time around, thus revealing a glitch in the matrix. When this anomaly was identified, they realized that the shadows were attempting to direct their awareness within that time-space continuum, which is the very behavior they had absorbed through contact.

"Within that redirection lies our capture. The real danger is that shadow attention has almost become fully conscious within its networking. Breaking down the non-sequential time capsules through recovering our waking dreams is now, and has always been, our only viable option.

"When we first began our journey in this region of the universe, we had to forget ourselves, by putting non-sequential time barriers in place so that we could elude capture. Now we must remember our dimensional lateralism, where time still retains no sequentiality, but where we have access to memories that are recovered in a staggered fashion, as unadulterated insight that is wholly ours and not influenced by a predatorial attention."

Predatorial Attention

Suddenly, without warning, I was transported to a dream scene that was taking place within one of those partitioned sections of the honeycomb phenomenon that I had been witnessing moments before. A deep feeling of distress and bewilderment overcame me. I knew that I was still with Zakai, yet at the same time I was contained within a dream compartment.

Surveying my surroundings, I realized it was probably the middle of the night. I noticed a few buildings in the penumbra. There was no moonlight, nor streetlights to illuminate what I was viewing. I heard a phone ring and reached automatically to pick it up. I became intensely frightened at this point, for I knew that what I was reaching for was not there. I was being directed. A voice then appeared next to my right ear as if a phone was pressed up against it.

"This dream you are dreaming," the voice said, "is one of your partitioned compartments. We know what you are doing. We know what you and your cohorts are conspiring to accomplish."

The voice was metallic and seemed to be located at a great distance from my position. I immediately proceeded to scan the scene that was being presented so that I could discover the source of the voice. "I am screened off from you," the voice stated.

"How can you know my intentions?" I said, truly frightened of the implication.

"My positioning is strategic. If you were to discover exactly where I am, I would lose my advantage," the voice stated flatly, ignoring my question.

As I looked ahead of me, I realized that the obscuring veil of that entity was interfering with my ability to establish its whereabouts.

"There is no need to pursue us with so much vigor," said the being. "I could very easily give this compartment back to you, and then you would be able to keep your memory while you are here. You could do anything you please."

Upon the entity's suggestion I became outraged. "How can you bargain with something that is not yours?" I demanded. I was shocked at the sound of my own voice and the harshness that manifested within my tone. "This dream is mine, not yours to possess," I declared.

At this moment, I felt the entity abruptly disappear from its undetectable vantage point. I looked around, wondering how this dream compartment could have been so easily stolen.

Looking to my right, I noticed a gloomy old house and was shocked to see the shadowy figure of a man standing in the entrance of the front door. His presence presented an awesome warning for me to back off his territory, which in actual fact was my dream compartment. This energetic mass conveyed a possessiveness so heavy that it shocked my body.

"The fight for this dream will go beyond this moment. Do you have the energy to sustain yourself? I will appear within others, where you do not even expect, within your living construct and beyond its boundaries. Will you have the power to see me?" The shadow asked, tauntingly.

I suddenly woke up in what I thought was my own room, and I simultaneously heard a noise outside the house and on the wall next to my head. Truly disturbed, I sat upright immediately. To my relief, I heard Jagür's roar in the distance. As I focused on her intention I was transported back to the old Nagual's realm, where Zakai had been waiting patiently.

He looked at me, raised his finger and said, "No need to explain. When Jagür discovered where you were, we all knew instantly what had happened."

"I will now continue with my explanation as if we were not interrupted, for we were not. You were simply waylaid within a captured dream compartment, one which that whirlwind entity does not want to give up. It doesn't like what you are learning and what you will transmit. This is a good reason to continue, don't you think?"

I nodded in agreement and settled down to listen, feeling once more my awareness being split between his awesome attention and the void.

"If we are clear, we can recognize the presence of the shadow within the living construct. There are many indications that can be felt within; like your liver being internally tapped by a small hammer, or a pressure upon your chest, or a sensation of pressure on the back of the eyes that looks like a shade being pulled down and then let up very quickly, whether your eyes are open or closed. Minute or dramatic changes in light will also alert you to their presence. We are surrounded.

"You must understand at this point that even if the conspiratorial theory of the shadow is not taken on board as a foregone conclusion, this information nevertheless has the capacity to bring humanity into a state of liquid self-realization, through introducing the idea of imprints and preoccupations as a process that can be understood and dissolved.

"The facts are undeniable. We have imprints and preoccupations, and they must be worked on, regardless of any belief system we have consciously or unconsciously subscribed to.

"Understanding is the unseen doorway into our living matrix, as dreaming awake is the doorway into the partitions of the honeycomb of awareness — where our true insights are to be found. Once we access these phenomena, we then start to multilaterally assimilate and tap into different fragmentations of time.

"When we gain entry into these parallel continuums, corresponding intuitive realizations will be available from even very far-removed time capsules. This is the automatic, organized lateralization of random events, which represents our connectivity to eternity at large.

"If we act correctly here, time will release the pertinent amount of information that we need in this moment. Our luminosity has set this up for us, but what is preventing us from accessing multilateral awareness is the encompassing grip of corrupt human attention.

"The void has created this complex singularity in order for us to evolve and escape simultaneously. Through living this paradox, which is only a contradiction if considered from a linear point of view, we continuously assimilate information through diverse experience so that we can grow and usher what we have learnt back to the void.

"Once we return to our luminous form, everything dissolves and we become assimilated into that omnipresence. What we have learnt invariably enhances that vast and mysterious expanse. Then, when the void expresses itself through our luminosity again, it has evolved its expressionlessness, and through our evolution, the universe continues to expand."

"Hang on a second," I said. "I thought you said the old sorcerers had set all this up, and now you say that it was the void that organized this phenomenon."

"Yes, you are right. This would appear to be contradictory. But in the same breath, it is not," Zakai replied cryptically.

"I know it is hard for you to fathom, but everything that is occurring is prompted by that unseen force, which surrounds us at every moment. You may well ask why it would bring about such conditions. There is a reason. It is beyond impersonal, and far too complicated to be spoken of. It simply has to be known for what it is. As difficult as this may seem to grasp, I know you will come to terms with this enigma eventually.

"Everything is as it should be. The predator is here so that we can continue to exercise our awareness. We are meant to be trapped, and we are meant to be free. We are spurred on to learn through a sense of duality, but now we have come to a point where this illusion has become damaging to us. We are far too absorbed in it.

"What you are learning now is the seer's option — an alternative that only becomes available through exercising one's awareness. If a person were to live their life totally unaware, then, as you would expect, at the end of their mortal journey they would be consumed by the void in a state of semi-consciousness.

"Conversely, if we practice being aware while we live then we can be in command of our awareness at the time of our death. Without purpose, our luminosity becomes dispersed and scattered within the void. This awareness is given to the seer as a conscious choice. We either choose to be consumed, or to stay within luminous form — as long as we are possessed of purpose alone.

"The old Nagual foresaw the need for a place of refuge for those who dream beyond our present living circumstances, which are corrupt by nature. Centuries ago, he had acquired the skills from an old sorcerer on how to sustain a highly refined state of lucidity within an alternate time-space continuum, and he created the dreaming realm that you are now subject to.

"Many years later, he approached me to capture you within this magical net that he created. Within our collective sense of purpose we are able to maintain awareness within these parallel realms that may be perceived as limited, yet in actuality are limitless.

"Before we proceed any further, I would like you now to gaze deeply within the void so that I may pass to you two gifts of intention. The first gift I am to transfer, you already know of. Take your memory back to that time when you had ingested a psychotropic substance called DMT." As Zakai prompted my awareness through his suggestion, I began to see that memory appearing in the void.

"Now that you have recovered this memory," he continued, "we will travel further into that initial experience. Break your attention from the void and look upon my face."

As I turned my gaze towards Zakai, I saw that he was reaching out to touch my sternum. Upon contact, the old Nagual's realm vanished.

I was there once again in that transcendent event that I held as a potent memory. We were surrounded by a dark vastness that was not frightening but comforting. In front of me, I was viewing what I had experienced previously and I saw two luminous beings flanking my periphery.

The color of the luminosity to my left seemed to be composed half of moonlight and half of gold. The luminosity to my right was of similar hues but its exterior had a faint purple tinge. I was so absorbed in what I was viewing that I had forgotten that Zakai was standing to the rear of me, to my left. Turning to face him, I saw that he too was luminous.

"Catch this object that I am sending you," he called out. "It will anchor you so that you do not go past the threshold that is being presented."

As he spoke, a spark flew from the border of his luminosity and affixed itself somehow on the surface of my awareness. It was then that I realized I was also in luminous form.

"Look to these beings and remember that which they have given you," he commanded.

Gazing upon them, I remembered that this was the gateway, my ultimate destination, beyond my living construct and the old Nagual's dreaming scope.

"Every man and woman that lives has a predetermined destiny beyond their mortal journey, and this is yours."

Zakai's voice was near and far at the same time. "Move closer to them so that they may communicate the wonders of what is to come."

Following his suggestion, I somehow approached those beings that awaited me within the vastness, and as I did so, I was flooded with information. In unison, they beckoned my life force to proceed past the boundary, wordlessly conveying to me their message:

"Beyond this threshold many things await you."

While this was communicated, I was filled with a sense of hope and the thrilling rush of energy that comes with the excitement of accessing the greater reservoirs within. As soon as I had experienced this elation, we once again returned to that familiar realm that contained the void. Zakai was sitting opposite me.

"This is a good end that you have experienced," he said, "but as you know, you are not there yet. There is one more gift I wish to bestow upon you, and it is an offering of intention. I have had many names. You know me as Zakai, but when I was in physical form, I was known to many as the Nagual Juan Matus. What I am to give you now will help you achieve your task."

Upon these words a luminous butterfly flew from the center of his chest. As it was making its way to where I was, Zakai spoke.

"My gift of intention is to give you my last name."

When he uttered the name, 'Matus', the butterfly gently landed on the center of my chest and was mysteriously absorbed within my being. I looked to Zakai, more than humbled by his gracious gesture.

"I will honor this name as I have honored the old Nagual's name," I said.

"Many will be drawn to you because of these gifts," he said. "The old Nagual's realm will be passed to you and the warriors that accompany you. The only haven that you will have within your waking dream is the consensual agreement with those warriors not to interfere with each other, and to work co-operatively as a group within common purpose.

"Your conscious symbiosis will create a sense of inaccessibility that will come about as a result of having an integral boundary of power that does not allow the petty-minded, which is shadow attention, to enter into your inner sanctum.

"Be aware that initially those warriors that you discover may have stubborn, surreptitiously placed imprints that will come at you like wild, unresolved storms to test the knowledge that has been passed on to you. Once the storm subsides, you will be able to access deeper memories that have been embedded within you, and so will they, for you are a catalyst for their memories to be unlocked."

Upon this statement, I awoke to find myself in my bed. My recollection of my interactions with my benefactors was becoming progressively clearer and more immediate.

Life can be a process
of observing what we are
interfering with,
rather than interfering with
what we are observing

Dreaming the Dreamed

On this occasion, I was to enter the realm of my benefactors in a fashion that was entirely unfamiliar to me. I had been having visions of a cactus called Peyote and had noticed that whenever I placed two of these large plants on either side of my head while I slept at night the contents of my dream would be filled, as strange as it may seem, with biblical truths.

I awoke to find myself in a small hut that appeared to be made out of white mud and was shaped like an igloo. I looked on the wall and saw a picture of Jesus with a bleeding heart and wondered why the people that owned this dwelling would put an image of this man on display.

I turned my attention to the center of the room and noticed a large peyote in front of me, not too dissimilar to the ones that were by the side of my head whilst I slept.

As I gazed at this magnificent old plant, which seemed to be maybe sixty years old, some part of it leapt toward me and began to spin in an anti-clockwise direction in my chest. Its presence caused a sensation that brought me

www.parallelperception.com

into a mindset of total non-compromise on the level of my heart. While being absorbed within the feeling that this venerable plant was delivering to me, I heard Zakai's voice, clearly asking in a playful tone:

"What the hell are you doing in the middle of Mexico, standing in somebody else's peyote hut?"

I fully realized then that I was dreaming and suddenly Zakai was sitting to my left. He had materialized as if he was made of mist and then became solid. My attention went immediately to his profoundly powerful gaze.

"As you look into my eyes, this dream you are in will integrate with where I am," he said softly. With his words, the surroundings began to dissolve, while his voice remained steady as an auditory anchor in the shifting environment.

"As this scene disappears, the portion of you that is dreaming this dream will understand that it is fragmented and needs to be centralized within two portions of your being; one that is energetic and one that is stationed within a concrete physical construct. It is my purpose and my responsibility to guide you in the unification of your awareness."

At the end of his statement, I realized that I was in the old Nagual's time-space continuum, looking into the void with Zakai standing by my side.

"Seeing that I have found you gazing at a picture of Jesus," he said, "I think it would be appropriate for you to witness this man's power directly. But before we do this, I am going to acquaint you with some concepts that will give you more insight into the hieroglyphs that the aliens made available. I will also introduce to you our understanding of the third symbol, the hieroglyph of Completion, so that you may further recover memories of your own experiences with those aliens with absolute clarity."

Zakai called into being the hieroglyphs of Haunted Awareness and Inner Light, and the two symbols appeared in the void, hovering mysteriously before us in a kind of holographic vision. Leaning forward, he whispered in my ear.

"We don't have much time. You must move swiftly without hurrying. This for you I know may be intolerable, since you are so impatient. Be careful to subdue this aspect of your character. It makes you vulnerable. Anxiety is something you must avoid without question.

"We have put tremendous pressure on you through our expectations. We know what we have done. You must learn the art of hurrying without hurrying," he added, smiling and giggling to himself quietly.

"Look now at these two symbols and concentrate with all your might. Can you see that there is a cycle of consequence that can be observed in the hieroglyph of the Haunted Awareness to be multiplicitous, where one cannot find resolve, through the maddening influence of hidden agenda from all perspectives.

"In the hieroglyph of Inner Light there is only one cycle of enactment: the communication between one's heart and a clear mind — the buoyant witness — that doesn't think about what it needs to do but allows the heart to act upon its circumstances without any interference, via the fact that all the other elements are in absolute harmony with the process of true awakening.

"As soon as the chain of command is switched between the child and the adult witness, a new dimension of conceptualization appears: the Architect of observation. This is the field of unobstructed absorption of fluid constructs, which puts you, the buoyant adult witness, in the twin position of the uninhibited observer.

"The Architect dreams the construct of the buoyant witness and lays in wait for the arrival of that multi-dimensional luminous universe that presents itself on the level of energy, where beings exist in pure vibrational form that echoes the light of their awareness. The fluid visual construct must accompany the Architect of observation in this transitional phase, for we can only build upon what we know."

Zakai paused for a moment, carefully examining my features before turning back to face the void. "It is time now to sweep these two symbols aside and examine the hieroglyph of Completion."

The form that materialized was unusual in comparison to the others and yet, upon its appearance, I remembered that I had seen it before. Viewing this hieroglyph delivered me straight into a feeling of unity that corresponded with the supportive and non-interfering atmosphere that always surrounded my companions from the old Nagual's realm.

The Hieroglyph of Completion

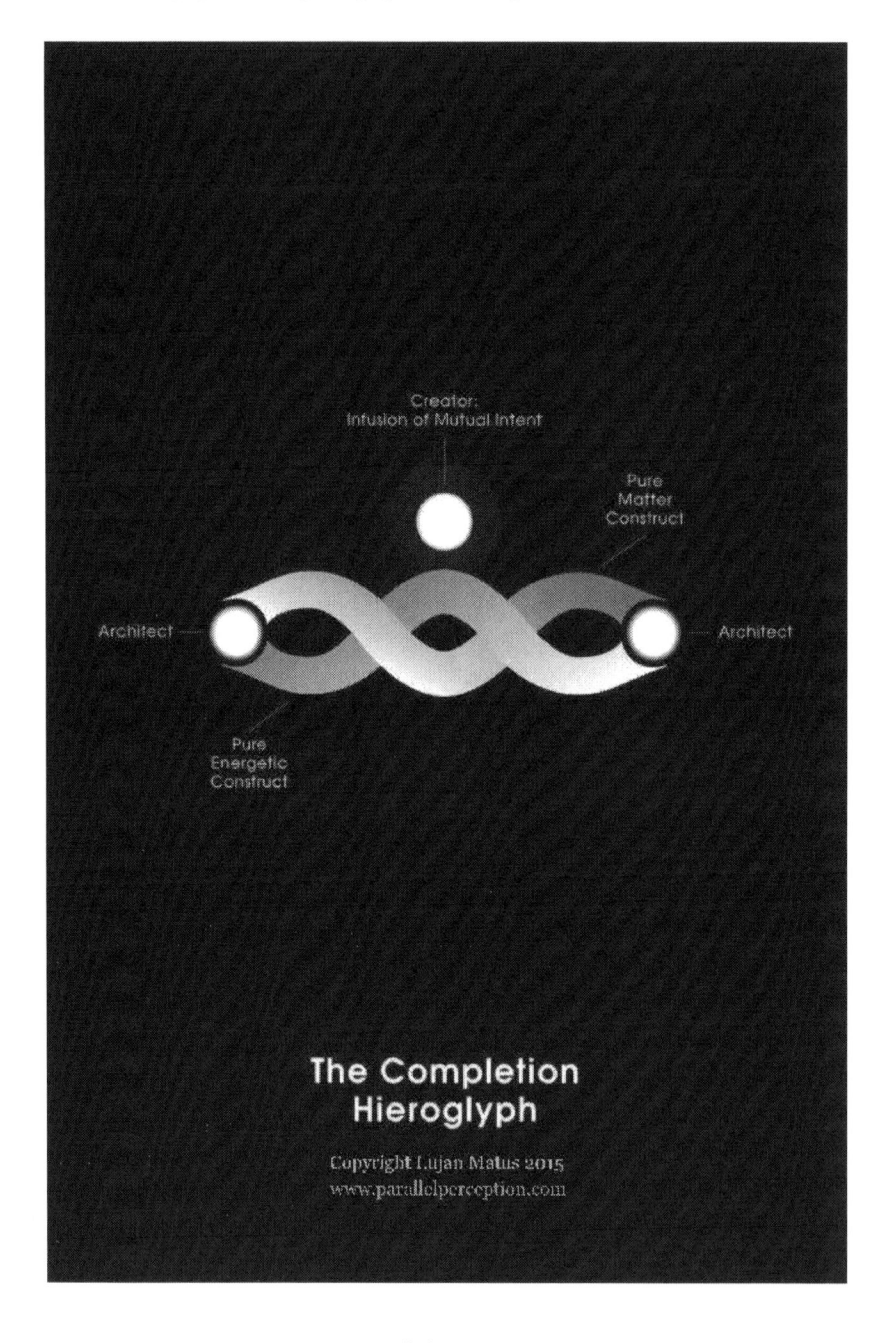

The Completion Hieroglyph

"Listen very carefully to what I say. This experience will change the energetic imprint that exists inside your luminous form. What you now are viewing is the true dreamer's hieroglyph.

"In the Completion glyph, the two lines you see are intertwining, fluid constructs, and the two circles on either side are two Architects. The line that runs from the bottom through the top and down again is pure energy, and the line running from top to bottom and up again is pure matter. The combination of the two Architects manifests the Creator, or the ultimate witness, as the orb that hovers above.

"The Creator can see the dream of matter as truth to be realized, and accesses the ultimate usage of that. This is an advanced state of real time, expressing the realized potential of the whole arrangement. The role of the Architect is to dream its reality within the neural net of its host, and the corresponding aim of human awareness is to dream itself beyond the confines of its construct.

"The Architect constantly challenges humanity to expand its boundaries and encompass as much awareness of energy and matter as is possible while still confined within the human form.

"Remember, man is always compelled to evolve through diversity. For example, technology is one field of exploration that is currently testing our cognitive boundaries, through our observation of and interaction with that area of advancement. The design of the Architect challenges man to such a degree that he dreams his awareness and his intent into machines, creating computers that will eventually have the speed and adaptability of their human counterparts.

"Through this symbiotic relationship of man and machine, the Architect compels our conscious awareness to visually conceive of that which seems inconceivable, yet which when accessed by our internal imagery, becomes a tangible viability.

"We have forgotten how to conceive of the Architect, so this intangible presence challenges us to expand our perception to encompass the reality of its existence, though in truth we are the Architect, the ultimate witness itself."

The Golden Orb

While Zakai was finishing his explanation, I noticed the room becoming filled with light. Golden fibers spread from his body to every corner, and the inner core of his luminosity looked like molten gold. I glanced up to see someone moving in front of me. It was Malaiyan, and he was holding something in his right hand. He seemed to be very agitated and full of power.

I looked at Zakai, wondering what was happening, and when my eyes gently touched his physical form he exploded into light and vanished. I stood up, shocked, and turned back to face Malaiyan. The object he had in his hand started to glow. He lifted it and threw it at me, saying:

"Catch!"

I was suddenly standing in blackness and what I saw in front of me was the golden teardrop that Malaiyan had thrown. It was about the size of a small plate, hovering in mid-air, ten feet away from me. It lay on its side as if it was traveling somewhere, but was stationary. I stood motionless and gazed at this amber droplet. Its color was deep and rich.

I was totally fixated. I had never been held so motionless in a scene in this way. I knew that if I made any verbal commands the situation would change and I dared not utter a word. I had no idea where this entity that Malaiyan had introduced would take me.

The golden droplet suddenly started to vibrate and race towards me at enormous speed. I didn't have the ability to dodge what was coming. It hit me in the center of my chest and then I was there, in a place I never would have conceived of ever being.

The room I had arrived in was carved sandstone, with no doors or windows. To my right there was a platform made of the same stone, which came to about the height of my hips. As my gaze swept towards this object, I realized there was a man lying there and I instantly knew who he was. He was covered with a cloth, up to his mid-chest, that was the color of bone.

As I looked at him I noticed his eyes were deep brown and his skin the color of cinnamon. He was feverishly trying to communicate to me and I knew that he was a man with not much time left. He was dying. He reached out and grabbed me by my left arm and as his grip tightened, a pulsating current surged through my system and a white light entered my head.

Before me, a crucifix appeared with a man hanging torturously from it, and within this dream-like vision the crucifix sped towards me as I sped towards it. Then the scene came to a rushing halt. In front of me was that man's crown of thorns. He lifted his head and looked at me calmly.

At that moment a voice suddenly erupted near my left ear. It was a phenomenon I had experienced in dreaming many times before. The voice was neither male nor female and sounded as awesome as the scene that confronted me. It directly conveyed the intentions of the man I was witnessing.

"Take this vision back with you. I have been incorrectly represented. How can you bypass what you think you know? It is a constant framework that humanity is caught within and that which encircles us is like a crown of thorns. Each time one attempts to intend beyond that structure, the thorns bypass that intention to evolve by pointing it in an incorrect direction, away from the essential truth that needs to emerge.

"The sharpness of the thorns represents the pain of that misdirection, and the blood trickling down the forehead is life lost. The intensity that can be intended is represented by the emptiness of the mind that receives information directly from the heart, by way of its formless receptivity."

The scene shifted, and now I was viewing the palms of his hands, while the voice continued to describe what I was seeing.

"From here, where I am damaged, warmth and fullness pour out in an uncontrollable deluge, and as a consequence the kindness that is held steadfast in this position is lost. When this point is pierced the heart cannot even recognize itself, for this wound represents the annihilation of love and truth between all men. Without its strength there can be no healing in the world, nor true understanding.

From these locations energy rushes to the center, to the chambers of one's heart."

The scene shifted again and my attention went to his feet.

"Within the top arch of the foot the substance of man is held upright. If this point is pierced, man's substance will collapse, and invariably the strength of man will sink too low for him to even realize that he has fallen. When the underside of the arch is damaged, through the piercing from the top, the power of the kidneys is weakened — where inspiration and life force reside."

Once more, the scene shifted and I saw the left-hand side of his body, which had been stricken.

"When the pancreas and spleen are damaged in this fashion, the body cannot uphold true realization; that which erupts into the heart as pure knowing. Instead, what pours in is an incessant nagging, which is re-circulated by the misdirected intention that has been gripped by the thorns. If the right-hand side is pierced, where the liver resides, then the eyes will not see the truth of the future nor know how to move towards that horizon.

"The unification of all these vital centers is to be strengthened and the weaknesses are to be avoided, for if these points are compromised, this will have a devastating effect on awareness."

With this last utterance, the scene vanished and I was back in the tomb. My focus went immediately to the man and I realized that he was in excruciating pain. I knew that he had been tortured and scalded with boiling oil. He was looking at me with a deep sense of urgency. He was so focused on what he needed to do and what he wanted to communicate, that for him it was more important than his impending death.

He whispered softly, "Be pure of heart and innocent within your intentions."

A moment later, the dream scene had completely vanished and I was laying in the darkness of my room. I was contained in a way that I had experienced countless times before. I could open my eyes and look around the environment while my body seemed to be pinned and paralyzed, yet at the very same instant I was sitting on the stairwell outside my door. I was naked and I could feel the wooden stairs beneath my buttocks.

But this time it was different. I could sense the solid world around me. My dreaming awareness had come with me, back to where I was. I was watching my own body, and synchronously viewing the world from a point further removed from the dreamer on the stairwell — a third perspective. I knew that I was in the bedroom just behind the door, and in all positions understood what each was going through. I was experiencing a power and clarity that was connected to a strange source of absorption.

Even though I was the dreamed, I was more real than the sleeper who was awake and realizing that I was on the stairwell, whilst simultaneously being viewed from a disembodied third perspective. As I sat there this absorption of information made me realize how aware I was as one complete unit.

I was bathed in calmness and this feeling spread out from me. It touched everything and within that gentle atmosphere all the elements were related back to me. My being was experiencing pure magic and the power that comes with that.

Suddenly I was back in the old Nagual's realm, looking into the void with Malaiyan standing to my left. I was confused, yet I knew that I had to focus. Malaiyan began to explain what had just occurred.

"This type of dreaming comes about from having one's pure intention in place, and this uncorrupted state of awareness I am referring to relates to the hieroglyph of Inner Light. When intention is not encumbered by any self-serving desire then it is free to witness itself. When pure intention is uninhibited what appears as a consequence is intensity, an agitation that brings about excitable knowing.

"These two elements of pure intention and intensity combine together to bring about the unbiased witness: the Architect of observation, which, by its very nature, is untouchable. The reason why it remains impervious is that it exists permanently within everything we do, beyond the reach of transient influences.

"However, once pure intention or intensity are interfered with in any way by the shadow's mind, the Architect will no longer be available, for upon that insertion the hieroglyph of the Haunted Awareness will take over enactment."

Malaiyan's eyes were dark pools of knowing and his face was glowing with the anticipation of an excitable child as he continued.

"For us to progress as a human race in the realm of our waking dream, we must become acutely aware of what we attach to our intention. If we can be more conscious then the Architect will transmute and become the Creator, our new sphere of attention.

"When the elements of pure intention and pure intensity — as you experienced in your previous dream scene — gain enough gravity within themselves, they appear in the dreaming realm; with pure intention as the human body and the dreaming body as abstract knowing that is free from preoccupation. These collective units become the Architects of their own elemental structures, which are energy and matter. This is how the Architect, the pure witness, is elevated to the position of the ultimate Creator.

Within the gravity of these elements, all the intensity of the energetic mass and all the fullness of physical creativity become the interweaving fluid constructs. At this juncture, the seemingly sequential concepts of time — past and present, as you have recognized — are amalgamated into one and are viewed from a third perspective, which is the infusion of our creative essence.

"We must realize that we can travel back and we can travel forward, and explore that universe out there that seems so far away, which in fact is our inward journey. Through pure intention we dream ourselves forward, with the observational sense that makes itself available to men and women who comprehend without thought."

Malaiyan gently tapped my shoulder and said softly, "Awake with you," and I surfaced once again in my bedroom.

Upon review of the experiences that I had witnessed, I would have to say in conclusion that anything that is passed down through the centuries must necessarily come under the category of mythology, since there is no real way of proving its validity. That includes the information contained within this account, even though I am relating a complete dream sequence that did occur.

What I myself obtained from this experience was profound, unquestionable and deep knowing. The reason why I share this encounter is to give a true and precise idea of recounting in real time, which is a state of fluid immediacy that is not anchored by perceptual attachments but accesses information connected to the relevant past, present and future continuums surrounding any given moment. Real time can be experienced in dreaming, and is shown in the third hieroglyph as two Architects and two Constructs — one energetic and the other composed of matter — unified in the sphere of the Creator, the ultimate Architect.

There is another way to interpret these elements. The energetic component of the intertwining constructs of the Completion hieroglyph is the self-realized awareness of the heart, which becomes actualized through that flux of energy. The other intertwining component, the construct relating to matter, is the mind, which actualizes itself through its own reflection of the physical flux that it experiences and organizes in front of itself. The fifth element is the Creator.

In anticipating the reader I would say that this is not God, but that this conceptualization could be and has been given to this focal point. I personally feel that the concept of God has been distorted and that there is only this component that witnesses us, which we can be aware of and to which we attempt to assign structure and form so as to adapt that factor to limited perceptions that suit the mindset which perceives it. By virtue of its exalted position, this witness encompasses us within the realities experienced through the lens of subjective perception.

The key to accessing this third perspective is to stand within our personal power and not falter. This stance will elevate that third perspective into its rightful position, which will bring about a state of actualized fluidity that will invariably break the insidious loop where we are trapped. I guess at this point it is obvious I am not a religious man, and the preceding dream of a theological scene took me by surprise.

The golden droplet I viewed in the beginning of the dream was the Creator, obviously of my construct, which had combined energy and matter. The reason I come to this conclusion is that everything I viewed in the dream with Jesus was seen from the perspective of my own Architect of observation, and also from a third viewpoint, which separately witnessed the sequence and was simultaneously combined with my own awareness. This was the perspective of the Creator.

In the second dream sequence, where I had left the vision of Jesus and arrived back to my home, I was also viewing from three positions: two Architects and the Creator. The physical construct is the expression of the sleeper in the bed, which is the element of matter. The energetic construct was experienced by the dreamer on the stairwell.

The third perspective was witnessing from a disembodied viewpoint that was aware of and could see everything simultaneously. Thanks to Malaiyan's involvement, my awareness had got behind and integrated with the position of the ultimate Architect, which in the beginning was the golden teardrop that he had thrown.

I know that if I would have had the perceptual clarity to turn that viewpoint outwardly, then the unknown expanse that is ultimately behind that position would have become available. All elements would have banded together and a new journey would have begun for me. Life as I know it would have disappeared, as though it had never existed in the first place.

Is this the reason why we fear dying? Is this where the origins of that foreboding dread lie? Is that apprehension motivated by the fact that when that creative Architect turns outward we lose control, and forgo completely what we leave behind? Is it this vacillation that stops us from witnessing that large and expansive universe, which in fact is inwardly turned and is our true inner journey, which we have the possibility to experience while we still live?

The fact that I got behind this position opened a very unusual door, to beings that exist behind the ultimate creative Architect. Now I would like to switch your awareness back to the dream scene, and hope that you have already asked this question before I even bring it up. What I would like you to consider is this: What was interacting with me in that dream scene? I believe it was the insertion of those luminous beings, which my awareness gave concrete validity to, through my construct, so as to make them appear as energetically solid.

Those sentinels beg us to differ within our realizations and wake up to the fact that they too are Architects composed entirely of energy. By jumping into our dreams to communicate pure truths to us, they trigger the Creator, that ultimate Architect within, to become aware of itself. This seems to be their unrelenting task, to awaken us.

Our conundrum lies in the fact that we are so familiarized with materialism that anything that attempts to enter into our cognitive system is turned into something known. For us as beings that need to evolve, this tendency is a point of excruciating frustration, as we search for transformation within familiar circumstances. Genuine evolution simply cannot occur with a conditioned mindset ultimately influencing the outcome. We hit a wall due to the fact that our consciousness is subject to its own repetition, reinforced by individual and collective social parameters. For consciousness to truly transform it must recognize the unrecognizable.

We all know that we can progress yet most of the populace don't, and the reason for this is that humanity has been irreversibly domesticated. Through this process our eyes have been stolen, disabling the primal ability to see the formless that manifests, paradoxically, within form.

Split the wood and I am there
Lift the stone and there you will find me.

Architectural Orbs

While editing this new version with Naomi, I had a very profound experience here in Cambodia. It relates to the architect of observation and how the solidity of a fixed construct – which is described as matter – is interactive and malleable; and how energy transforms into luminous beacons of light that alert the witness to all of the variables that are contained within a living scene.

Each momentary experience reveals the delicate factor of the pressure of multiple perceptions within one location, which is a pure example of the coalescent factor that the hieroglyph of Completion represents, as you will see in the story about to be relayed.

We are only going to speak about one linear timeline within this scenario, for it would be too overwhelming to cover everything, even in this one seemingly innocuous event.

The full spectrum of perceptual influx in any given moment is impossible to convey within the limited framework of the written word, which can never completely encompass the omnipresent factor that a seer is subject to. The visual elements outlined in this scene will prompt absorption of the principles that govern the Completion glyph's enactment, via inducing those concepts through a living example that will teach you how to apply all three hieroglyphs combined in terms of the true applications of dreaming awake.

You will see how an infusion of mutual intent is composed of that collective perception which experientially reveals either light or darkness to the eyes of the witness, or a culmination of darkness within the light, as a type of fragmentation that becomes available for instant review. This refraction relates to the multifaceted capacity of our eyes to interpret luminous fragments of information within our biofield via an etheric reverse osmosis that reorganizes hidden factors into an anomaly that can be seen, as a composite of dynamic content to be interpreted.

This process occurs via applying the expanded principle of one's visual capacity, using only a two percent external gaze* and engaging a ninety-eight percent, internally mirrored, reflective component that constantly reviews all the elements presented from the foundation of its own emptiness. What is gleaned is then reassigned to the omnipresent factor that interdimensionally disperses wisdom.

In other words, everything that can be seen is internally witnessed as holographic units of information that most

---

* For a comprehensive explanation of these principles and other shamanistic techniques, please refer to 'Whisperings of the Dragon', by Lujan Matus.

often don't relate in form to what you are physically looking at. This is one of the complex explanations that relates to the hieroglyph of Completion.

The sentient flux which produces one's personal experience transmits each composite of insight that can be accessed through the medium of luminous filaments which identify that shape that is to be seen. These frequencies manifest within one's body as a cluster of information whose characteristics correspond to that vibratory signal, which arrives in an abstract format.

Not unlike reviewal of a memory, one's awareness retrieves content that is layered within its internal visual capacity, recognizing the imagery that has been assigned to a specific segment of the sentient filaments that make up the seer's luminous field; which is composed of only that which they can be aware of in the moment that is continually escaping them.

The architectural element appears as a vibrant orb of light that self-regulates in terms of its teleportation from one circumstance to another. This architect unveils the multiplex that unifies all experiences that are contained within our scope of awareness, which is presented at that moment. We witness these complex anomalies as interdimensional portals within this seemingly limited linear plain in which we abide. These access points pool perception to observe the gravity of what is essential to be absorbed as pertinent wisdom, which is momentarily archived and then fractally redispersed.

www.parallelperception.com

The Three Hieroglyphs

Architectural Orbs

To bring light to these concepts I must tell you a story. Where we are living at the moment in Asia, there is a man downstairs who recently introduced a Common Mynah bird to our property. These unique animals can mimic almost everything they hear.

As we were subject to the sounds of his beautiful whistles, I realized that it would be a good thing to have two of them on the property so they could learn from each other's calls. I proceeded to ring our tuk-tuk driver, Iskender, to take us to do some shopping and to ask him whether would be possible for him to obtain one of these birds for me. He is a very kind person with strong morals and would always protect us from being taken advantage of financially by the locals. I have great respect for him because of his honesty.

Before we went to do what we needed to do, I asked him whether he could take us to the marketplace outside of the Buddhist temple. This was a very interesting experience, for he brought us to where they were having a religious event that happens frequently. Here they sell lotus flowers, incense, and have birds for sale for devotees to buy, so as to release them with a prayer.

Upon our arrival, we noticed that the Mynah I wished to obtain wasn't there, so I asked Iskender whether it is possible that the people who were selling sparrows and doves could advise us where to find the bird we were after. On his return, Iskender said to us that they were asking too much money and smiled at us knowingly, saying, 'You will never get anything at a fair price if you do it yourself. It is best that I scout ahead on your behalf.'

He was explaining this to us as we sat in the back of the tuk-tuk, and whilst Iskender and I were exchanging in a relaxed and friendly manner, we noticed a man and a woman coming out from the crowd near the temple. They were obviously husband and wife.

The man was holding a small sparrow that was squawking and struggling within the grasp of his two hands, clearly distressed. The man started to chant his wishes toward the bird, and while doing so he glanced towards his wife to encourage her to join in. We were about fifteen feet away from them, noticing what was happening. Whilst invoking the attention of his spouse, the man accidentally loosened his grip and the bird suddenly escaped. He looked aghast and began to run toward the fleeing sparrow with a panicked look in his eye, gesturing wildly towards his wife to quickly finish their wishes as it flew beyond their field of perception.

Within him the subtleties of what had just occurred could be seen. He had simultaneously spent and lost his investment and in that moment his opportunity to invoke an incantation upon this winged being evaded him.

In absolute innocence, my wife Mizpah and I laughed out loud at the scene in front of us, without an ounce of malice but filled with pure joyousness at what was occurring. The man and woman noticed us and only slightly acknowledged our connection to their dilemma. In this small gesture I noticed cruelty and maliciousness coming toward us. They proceeded to go their way and I was then flooded with information.

The paradox was that by connecting our eyes to his intentions, at that very moment we embodied the joy he wished to obtain. An architectural orb of light suddenly enveloped us. His desires had been transported and thus his incantation symbiotically manifested within us as joyous laughter, spontaneously expressed.

However, he could not recognize this transferal through our internal reality, for the deeper, darker imprint he was harboring repressed his capacity to realize what was happening. As a result it was impossible for him to see that we at that point became the bird that he could gently hold within the tenuous grasp of his perception.

As he half-smiled at us to try to cover his true feelings of ill will, poison arrows were projected from his eyes toward my being. In that moment the subjective perspective of the shadow's dream encased his reality within haunted awareness and simultaneously, an orb-shaped shadow engulfed him. What happened in that exchange was that slithers of darkness from his malicious gaze appeared within my field of perception for examination, caught delicately by a filament of light.

These etheric elements present a visual anomaly that you can actually read, via the pictorial content projected; in this case the information coming from the man's eyes. Once these splinters of darkness are seen, they immediately dissolve and become re-dispersed into other fractalized time-space continuums, by intermittently oscillating in a rotational eddy that resembles a figure-eight pattern, but which is in fact a fourth-dimensional odyssey that is becoming fifth-dimensionally activated and thus transported.

For this concurrence to manifest, the fourth-dimensional vibratory signature must gather momentum in terms of its own frequential gravity, to pass through a membrane that is a fifth-dimensional fractalized receptor site, which organizes the non-descript information to be magnetically drawn to its appropriate destination. Once symbiotically infused within that dimension, where it dissolves into a subtle frequency that is composed of compressed light, it then arrives upon the fourth- dimensional plane as smoky filaments, to be seen.

These delicate frequencies then undergo a reverse osmotic process, to arrive upon their third-dimensional etheric landing pad, where they are reintegrated within the solidity of a linear plane as subjective actions and consequences.

At this crucial juncture in the explanation, you must realize that the elemental structure of the Completion hieroglyph is capable of sustaining itself within quantum bounds in terms of jumping from one dimension to another. The absorption of the energetic framework it arrives upon reveals entirely different insights via the intricacies of that symbiotic process; which corresponds to the variables that come upon themselves via the gravity of that interdimensional traversing.

The content of this information – carried upon the threads of those photonic phylums – does not necessarily relate directly to the reality from which it originates, but yields pertinent insight in the time-space continuum where it re-emerges.

To reiterate, when the phylums exit this reality, that cluster has a vibratory signature. Its configuration is a frequential key that will determine its destination. As it enters the omnipresent factor, it automatically is magnetically drawn, via its own gravity, to its future, fractally defined, re-emergence – even if that arrival is located in a previous timeline, which one could conceive of as the past from a linear perspective.

The seer who then receives this potent download — delivered to their third eye capacity as visual units of information — accesses its multifaceted content via the process of déjà vu, which is an interdimensional coalescence of one's being within the omnipresent factor. Then, upon their third eye receptor — that thousand-petalled lotus which rotates within a magnetic gravitational eddy to release the pertinent frequency in accordance with their present life circumstance — internal insights are revealed in correspondence to their external environment's vibrational flux. In this way they may obtain the orb of information that is the light of their perception interweaving within the Completion symbol's interdimensional enactment.

There are many ways to see and interpret these complexities within the story of the bird, but we are only going to deal with the twin phenomenon that is the architect's observational ability to meld two living constructs into a conclusion, which becomes the orb at the top of the arrangement, shown as the creator.

What we can see in the glyph of Completion are three spheres. The two architects at each end are composed of subjective experience in terms of being energetic orbs that contain the residue of any moment at the point of realization. One of the interweaving lines that appear in this hieroglyph is composed of matter, which is a heavy, sedentary material that has more density than its complementary construct; the pure energetic field that is composed of smoky filaments of sentient light.

In essence, the infusion of mutual intent will manifest the ultimate creator as an orb of light that hovers above those circumstances — the interweaving lines — as the event horizon that besets the subjective consciousness of those who experience the outcome, or outcomes.

Now, let's go back to the story of the bird, to elucidate upon the usage of the architect of observation within the innumerable aspects that are linearly affixed to an interdimensional multiplex, which is fractalized in comparison to the diverse experiences obtained via individual consciousness. This process can be understood pictorially, through accessing the deeper meaning of the event obtained.

The bird struggling in the man's grasp was a manifestation of the embedded feelings covertly hidden behind his Buddhistic gesture. Observing him chanting his prayers toward the bird while it tried to free itself, we were infused within the reality of that happiness and freedom he desired and we laughed joyously, knowing that this can be achieved. His wishes for good fortune were immediately transferred to us and we joined him in abandon.

However, when he realized that our laughter was in response to the bird flying away, he became offended and didn't see our innocence. Instead, he went to deeper reserves of resentment and anger toward us, which was in actuality toward himself. In this instant, his wishes transformed from energetic units of information to deeper, darker manifestations of that flux, enlivening the shadow dream's glyph of enactment.

Our laughter was pure energy. His fixation towards the reality he was experiencing at that moment became a heavy manifestation of loaded subjectivity, which was then woven into the fabric of his time-space continuum as a dense, shadowy orb. That oppressive perspective is the culmination of his reality, solidified via an infusion of his singular intent. Although it manifested mutually, from my perspective, he could not see beyond the encasement of the threshold he was enthralled within.

This instance of multilayered interaction between perceptual spheres illustrates the subtle mechanics of the Completion hieroglyph. The sphere that floats above the intertwining lines must be understood in multiples, as a moving orb that sheds light on every circumstance, unveiling truths.

The story reveals that each realization represents an orb that is a culmination of mutual intent, which subjectively transforms when the shadow dream's glyph takes over enactment, as an encasement of perception that appears to a seer as darkness manifesting.

An infusion of mutuality comes about from two beings communicating etherically or merely observing any circumstance — even toward an inanimate object. The light of this orb is continually bringing the subject into a form of alignment that reveals the ultimate conclusion of that intention being reflected back.

The energetic construct has a broader frequential range than its matter counterpart, which enables that fluid factor to self-regulate the units of information that it is subject to. The matter-bound configuration, however, cannot even conceive of the insight contained within the energetic application that is composed of self-aware filaments of luminosity.

Imagine a person that is enthralled within darkness, and another is absorbed within smoky filaments of light. The individual immersed in shadow attention will only see small splinters or fragments of darkness as they look upon the self-aware filaments, which is their ultimate entrapment by being interlocked within the reflection of their own nefariousness.

The heavy nature of their subjectivity denies them the ability to go beyond what they are, so as to reflect upon what is truly occurring in any given circumstance. Their loaded realizations will solidify and sink as dense, sedentary material that become possessively guarded units of information that hold and bind individuals in a labyrinth of darkness.

On the other hand, the one who is operating from pure observation can clearly see the intentions of those encased within shadow; for, like a mirror, they reflect within themselves the units of information that are projected from enshrouded individuals as elements to be seen and reviewed immediately.

The content of that projection that is momentarily embraced by the self-aware filaments is immediately dissipated and absorbed, via the seer's emptiness facilitating its transportation into dark matter. Thus subject to its own inwardly imploding dispersion, by the fact that it has been seen, it becomes redistributed as insight. As this occurs, the pure energetic construct produces an orb of light of realization that infuses the seer's circumstances with greater possibilities. Paradoxically, this occurs as a result of dissolving those multiple layers of content as if they never existed.

Touch softly
that which cannot be touched.
Gently view
that which cannot be seen.
Know
that which cannot be known.

The Parables of the Dog and the Deer

These parables will provide direct blows to one's humanity. Be mindful to watch who you become in comparison to what you read. Find within yourself a state of neutrality that will bear upon you the wisdom necessary to move forward, embracing that which is irreversibly absorbed.

The Parable of the Dog

Many years ago, I lived in a village in Bali, where the veil between the worlds was so thin that on occasion you could almost step right through. As I would sit on the balcony looking over the green rice fields at dusk, I would experience a profound sense of quietude, peace and fulfillment, listening to wild birds singing in the distance.

I had many Balinese friends who were exquisitely tender and beautiful, who held my being gently, as if it were a fragile flower that would disintegrate if more than the grasp of their eyes would observe it. And then there were a majority who would openly call you, 'ghost person,' or 'orang hantu,' in Indonesian, for they believed that non-Balinese people were spiritually inferior.

The story I am to tell is something that we will all understand, no matter what our origins. The abstract core within this narrative will be obvious to everybody who reads it. Whether it be holistically embraced or narrowly, subjectively viewed, the impasse that unfolds for one innocent being will bear weight upon the eyes that travel upon this dark parable to its formidable conclusion within one's consciousness.

I will ask you not to judge the story if you become bound emotionally, for unfortunately a high moral ground will not allow you to see deeply into what will be conveyed. It is the humble eyes that come upon these parables that will deliver a perspective that yields many incremental elements to be awakened, connected to everything that was in your life and to all that eventually will become apparent within fractally unfolding insights.

For many nights, as dusk was descending upon the rice fields, I heard the wailing and crying of a young dog. I could hear that it was a puppy that had not reached maturity. Within its whimpering you could see that it did not understand the perilous position it was in, and this anguish was easily transferred to anyone within earshot. Everybody recognizes the cry of a child, the sound of innocence traveling through the air.

After about six or seven days, I asked my very good friend, Giwi, what was happening, and why these tormented sounds were filling the crisp morning ether and the dying embers of the sun at twilight. He promptly explained, and as I listened to his description I was shocked, yet simultaneously awakened to many intricacies within that horrific account.

He said that the puppy was being prepared for a ritual killing by a priest. He mentioned that they are always taken young, before they have a chance to even realize that they are a dog through social contact. This ensures that his innocence is more easily manipulated. For many weeks, the dog would be collared and chained to a post with no bed, shade, nor any protection from the elements. Its bowl of water would be just out of reach, and the minute amount of food that was left for him would be placed even further away.

www.parallelperception.com

Every day, the water would be nudged closer for only a moment, so that his thirst could be quenched just barely, and only every now and then a portion of food would be taken and thrown towards him. He would never have full access to nourishment and at this stage was reduced to skin and bone. The scraps would not be enough to survive on, but would ensure that the body of the dog would experience its inevitable death coming upon itself. This goes on for weeks.

One day, when the collared dog's agony reaches an untenable impasse, it looks up, wide-eyed, intending to leave its mortal coil. At this juncture the priest grabs the dog by the scruff of the neck and forces its body down to the ceremonial bowl, piercing its carotid artery with a dagger called a Kris, so as to force its blood to flow downward. This plummeting momentum prevents the dog's spirit from ascending at the point of his departure. The Balinese priest would thus ritualistically steal its life essence to invoke incantations that would be the end result of that cruel enactment towards this blameless being.

As Giwi conveyed the full scope of what was taking place, I felt grief and at the same time a sense of terrible despondency for not being capable of intervening such treachery and disregard for life. It was something that I could not really come to terms with, yet had to, simultaneously.

Dogs are well known for their capacity to see the approach of a witch, and in Bali this is very evident. Once a month there is a crescent moon, which is when most black magic is performed. One day before and one day after that event, everybody leaves their lights on outside at night. Each household has at least one dog as a guard, and there are many wild packs wandering the streets. They would all howl more than usual at this time of the month, for they could see incantations being intended or flung in the air towards prospective victims.

Dogs have been our loyal companions for thousands of years, always forewarning us of approaching danger, whether it be physical or etheric. Their barking is like a slamming door to an incantation, by virtue of alerting other awarenesses to that approach. The howling is the indication that a spell has passed its guard and embedded itself within their owner, the intended victim.

The suffering of the recipient of the black magic is relayed as the dog's unhappiness through their whimpering, which in actual fact is mimicking the cries obtained from that beautiful puppy. In this way, the witch knows that the spell has been successfully cast, and thus the collar tightened upon his victim.

At this stage within the parable, I would like to assist you in recognizing one point that you may not have realized is there to be seen. By doing this I am helping you define your ability to access realizations that come upon you as orbs of light, even though this story is full of darkness. Using the hieroglyph of Completion is complex, to say the least, but here I will share with you what I have done so that you may more clearly understand where darkness reveals the light.

The puppy wailing was part of the story. Its suffering was a persistence through the parable. The priest wished to obtain its blood for ceremonial purposes by virtue of the fact that this young being's awareness had not yet been socialized, consequently giving his blood a different signature to the guard dog that the priest wished to bypass to deliver his sinister blow.

The victim's loyal companion would not detect the incantation, for even though there is a spell travelling upon the blood's vibration it retains the pure signature of the puppy's innocence, thus masking crucial elements that relay alerting information that is part of that canine protector's paradigm. The internal process of that guard dog, which is connected to an interdimensional complex of eyes that observes the world of magic in a way that belongs to this species alone, is bypassed by that alchemical trickery, by virtue of the fact that he is looking for the conditioned elements first. By the time he realizes that it was a trap, it is too late.

When I mentioned to be diligently aware not to judge the content of the narrative, this is what I meant. Be careful not to assume you know, for that assumption may block your ability to see the magic that arises within you, via the fact that your socialized beingness may not be capable of grasping the intangible; which is our inherent capacity to be aware of the inaudible, non-locatable anomalies that nevertheless can be heard and detected by our emptiness.

If we ourselves have a clear frequency, in so far as not being socialized, meaning that we are empty within our innocence, wisdom will avail itself unyieldingly to our open-heartedness as eternity's treasure trove of information. Even if that light shines upon negativity, it will bring about transformation as a result of the witnesses observation. All things will be seen that necessitate the steps that must be traversed, in terms of the path revealing itself.

You can't unring a bell

THE PARABLE OF THE DEER

In numerous cultures there is a principal called persistence hunting, which was something we practiced before we created long-range weaponry such as spears and arrows and so forth. There are many techniques employed to gather the strength and endurance necessary for this type of activity. Some tribes employed chewing coca leaves with psychotropic substances, others used different methods to enhance their power. These were mainly hunter-gatherers who very rarely ate large amounts of animal proteins.

In essence, persistence hunting was seen as highly ritualistic and filled with meaning in terms of the belief system of each tribe that practiced it, but we needn't be drawn into these separate ritualized factors. Even though they are relevant with regard to discovering their inherent contradictions, it is more important to arrive upon the pure conclusion of what this activity really represents within this parable.

Four or five hunters would scout and visually locate the tracks of a deer, and as they did this they would wave their hands in a mudra-like gesture above the footprints to absorb the frequency of the animal's imprint within the compacted area where it had left its trail. This subtle emanation would then be infused in the body of the hunter, and the one with the most receptivity would inadvertently become the leader, as the group would begin to run slowly towards their prospective prey.

The frequency obtained would mix with the stimulant taken and then resoundingly beat within the heart of the lead hunter as a receptor that becomes stronger the closer they get to the deer. When this connection is fully established then the chase truly begins.

If this link is not found the hunt is not pursued, for the bridge of heart resonance must be secured for the ultimate kill to be clean. This is to avoid frequential discordance, for if the electromagnetic bond is not made with the deer's heart, that disharmony will spread through the community via its consumption, causing widespread unhappiness.

Once this crucial resonance is set, the hunter runs behind and beside the deer for a period of ten to fifteen hours. It can even go beyond this, lasting days. At no point is the hunter to have any form of aggression nor malice towards the animal as he runs it down. It is imperative that the deer give up its life freely, knowing that it cannot escape the hunter's combination of will power, endurance and his unbending intention.

As the chase reaches its crescendo, which in actuality is the relenting of the deer's ability to continue, through sheer exhaustion it surrenders, and at that point the eyes of the hunter and the deer meet. Only when the deer does not attempt to get up and run again is it appropriate for the shaman to gently take its chin, leaning its head backwards to quickly cut through the carotid artery and windpipe to sever the nerves of the spinal cord so that the kill is clean and the animal is accepting of its fate.

Mirroring

These two stories will have an irreversible effect upon your consciousness if you become open to them in the right way, in terms of reflecting upon your dilemma as a human being. Our life is intimately interconnected with both parables.

We are being impersonally run down until we are exhausted, and upon that point our spirit leaves. Realize that death is the ultimate hunter. Knowing this, resolve to be clear and strong, and intend never to be collared by your circumstances, whilst viewing them impartially, just like death itself.

When a bird awakes upon the morning light,
what does it do?
It sings to eternity with abandon.

Part II

Sexual Attention

"Are you still? Are you completely here? Is your mind empty? Can you see me in front of you? Am I solid?"

Zakai's volley of questions hit me the moment I appeared by his side.

"Yes." I replied.

"Do you know me?" he asked.

"No," I answered, "but I know myself."

"By knowing yourself, you know me," he replied, smiling generously. "I have been absorbed within the void for many years. What I have learnt from this prolonged immersion is that I am here, yet I am not here."

"Where can I find, within myself, where you are?" I wanted to know.

"Within your breath you will find me within you. This is how we are all connected to that insoluble void that you have in front of you. The lungs function without thought. Breathing is an automatic process; it happens without the intervention of mind. When you think you have forgotten me, simply breathe and I will be there."

Reaching out and clasping my forearm, Zakai said, "We must forget in order to remember."

Zakai did so many strange and magical things while we were facing that awesome emptiness that was the void power. It is my wish to convey with as much clarity as possible all that I remember of what transpired.

Within the next two chapters, if you find yourself confronted, remember, return to your breath and be free of thought. Return to the void so that you may release the socialized imprints that you may be defending, and revisit that emptiness which has been forgotten.

The subjects within 'Sexual Attention' outline the lessons that I absorbed from my benefactors on how to be cognizant of what is truly beautiful; how to bring forth pure expression, and, when necessary, to openly challenge that which is presented within our living construct.

Over the years I have found numerous seers whom I have proceeded to instruct with the teachings that were passed on to me in the old Nagual's realm. As a consequence, questions were asked by these dear friends, which I have included in the following chapters.

Responsibility and Inner Truth

Before any actual techniques are given, one must understand that the art of sexual attention goes way beyond the act itself.

We must consider that our buoyant inner child is sustained by our sexual center. Consequently, if one were to act irresponsibly, this would set in motion automatic impedance, which is shown in the shadow dream's hieroglyph as the cloaked inner child.

Our sexual center will sustain and uphold our designs, whether they be composed of pure intention or of self-serving preoccupation. If we are not transparent and do not take responsibility for our actions, especially in reference to our sexual activity, the flow on effect will be catastrophic on a personal level.

As with all things, whatever is done accumulates, and that build-up is processed by the inner child. Within that transaction will be delineated appropriately whether our actions are composed of denial or truth.

The primary function of our sexual center is to propel us into our future. If we are not clear, the journey will be more difficult than is necessary. Our base of primal energy is a resource that, if mismanaged, will falter at the times we need it. And the most exaggerated spectrum of this type of collapse occurs is either in old age or great illness.

The process of life is simplicity itself. Clarity and directness brings us into our first sphere of attention. This first sphere must be composed of practicality, and within this stance observational acuity will arise as a result of freeing up one's attention of all the pending matters that beg to be resolved. I hope that these insights will deliver you into that acuity so that you may bear silent witness to your inner child, regardless of its present state.

Q: How is the inner child sustained by the sexual center?

A: Our inner child and the awareness of that pure being are stationed within the nucleus of our heart. The sexual center upholds the clarity of the inner child through abundance of positive energy. If this delicate equilibrium is not upheld through integral acts then the feeling of innocence will collapse and simultaneously the sexual center will lose power.

Q: How does the sexual center propel us into our future?

A: If our basic energy is waylaid in immoral acts we will be absorbed within drama. Drama continually loops back on itself and relies on the past for its propulsion. If the sexual center is clear and no ulterior motives are connected to it then the future will be uninhibited. The energy that exudes from our sexual center as a result of that clarity will bring power to our inner advisor, which in essence knows intuitively how to proceed and can see beyond our present circumstances.

www.parallelperception.com

Q: Can you elaborate on this first sphere of practicality?

A: Do what has to be done, nothing more and nothing less. Don't add any part of yourself that is inappropriate, nor promote unbalanced behavior from anybody else. Sit silently within yourself and command that silence through purposeful attention. Do not let your mind take over what is your true heritage, which is to know without question what is right and what is wrong.

Applied Mechanics of Interaction

The first question to consider would be: What are the mechanics that surround responsibility, and what are the ramifications that inner truth will apply to our circumstances? Within ourselves we must ask:

'Am I balanced?'

And, if not:

'What can be done about this?'

I suspect that most people would look to texts for information that will bring them to a state of fulfillment, and if the transmission is complete, boundaries will or can be delineated, as healthy energetic principles that will sustain one's heart strength.

Within clearly defined personal parameters, truth will become abundant. From this foundation, one arrives at a state of buoyancy that purely defines one's power so that responsible decisions can be made, based on the simple mechanics of foresight.

This capacity to be alert to what is coming naturally delivers to you that boundary which provides sanctuary for the inner child, who in turn will add to the buoyant witnesses' balanced comprehension the joy and silence that surround it, thereby drawing all circumstances into the regime of real time.

Real time is dealing with one's circumstances in the light of progression, which moves on from each momentary position and yields the truth of only those realizations that one is absorbed within. To be in real time is not to be anchored in the gravity that surrounds past issues that have not yet reached a state of resolution. This immediacy automatically brings to the forefront the truth that lies behind unconscious actions that have become devices of entrapment and denial. Such mechanisms are perpetuated through usage and this enactment occurs primarily for the purpose of waking us up, as individuals, to the fact that we have baggage.

Q: *How is foresight applied in a daily sense?*

A: Firstly we must take into consideration everything that is a part of our environment. See it for what it is, and define how that structure may have to be kept in place, including all the tasks that make up our daily life. If one does not have a prescribed plan, one will sit in complacency. So, get yourself a diary, write down what needs to be done and fulfill your obligations so that you are complete within your integrity.

I think we all know that if we are questioned about what we have not completed, it weakens us, and our shortcomings are always more obvious and more accessible for usage than strength. Foresight is encompassed within the knowing and doing of what needs to be done, and this is to take responsibility, which becomes an integral perimeter of power that cannot be interfered with by the petty minded.

Actions and Consequences

During one of my visits to the dreaming realm, Dyani spoke on the subject of monogamy, describing actions and consequences in terms of her own womanhood. She relates her experience in the following story.

"If I was a young woman traveling the world, leaving behind me a loving family and free of any relationships whatsoever, when I arrive in new circumstances and a young man approaches me, what is my responsibility to myself? If he were to ask me to engage in a relationship, I would automatically access my inner truth, which would advise me to seek clarity within the circumstance.

"I would ask him, 'Are you engaged, on any level, with anybody else?' And if he would answer truthfully, 'No', then free expression outlines the circumstance.

"But if he is not free, then I must stand within my inner truth and respectfully decline. Even though I do not know the woman he is involved with, she is my sister, and the moment I honor her, I honor myself. This integral stance delivers fortitude to my inner child and gives strength to the source of my power, which is my sexual center.

If I were to dishonor this woman who is my sister, then I would dishonor my own inner child, bringing upon myself a cloak of impedance. This internal burden is accumulative in its effect, and would deplete my sexual center through preoccupation, and waste that precious life force that sustains me."

Dyani's story conveys her strong opposition to any form of betrayal and clearly illustrates the significance of a monogamous stance in terms of keeping the inner child in balance.

One point that must be brought to the forefront is that when a man or woman without integrity approaches the force of their behavior is knowingly masked. This weighs heavily on their inner child, which in turn mutes their womanhood or manhood. As a result, a subtle inflection can be perceived in their energetic signature, which is there to indicate their sexual availability, unfortunately without restraint in most cases.

When we begin to cultivate our sexual center with purposeful practice, there are two ways this process can unfold. Either we perpetuate immoral behavior and justify that approach, which will invariably ruin our lives and the lives of other people within our environment; or, we take that immature inner child, and instead of enacting on the world, we catch ourselves in the act and examine what is being projected. This approach will bring about a cathartic upheaval and dispel justification. Genuine personal transformation is the true purpose of energetically enhancing one's sexual self.

Q: How does the cloak feed from the sexual center?

A: The sexual center and the inner child are connected by feeling. In the beginning of sincerely clearing and cultivating one's sexual attention, the initial feeling that one builds is more primitive than that of someone who has been absorbed in integral practice for a sustained period. Applying oneself with integrity will take away the insoluble agitation that the cloak supplies as a dysfunctional emotional underpinning.

When one first begins to activate one's sexual attention, the preliminary catalyst that confronts the initiate is composed of old habits. If what arises leads the heart to feel imbalanced then it drains the inner child. We all know that the heart is intimately connected with our innocence and that any sexual contact awakens our need to be nurtured. This is how our inner child is bound to our sexual center.

Q: Why does imbalance typically manifest as sexual availability?

A: Our primary motive as human beings is to perpetuate the species. Those who are imbalanced overtly display their sexual availability to attract like a moth to the flame unconscious individuals to a stage where they can enact upon each other their inadequacies. This is a means to exercise that attention, whether that enactment be drama filled or not.

Power

Power is the outcome that clear practice will bring. What one will be confronted with when intensity arises within is an entirely personal affair. What can be stated, to eliminate any form of disruption of that continuity of internal strength, is to be careful of the tricks of the trade that we all pay into as a humanity, and which are the very thing that kept our true potential at bay in the first place. The trade is the encompassing attention of all those individuals who would wish to take down the progressiveness of the clear-hearted, for clarity and power may undermine their selfish designs.

There have been specific techniques given, in numerous traditions, which outline modes of behavior designed to disrupt one's continuity and bring about a state of clear perception. Such methods are intended to be focused inwardly, as statements of realization, so that one can see the world that approaches and be aware of the onslaughts that may be trying to destabilize that power which you have gathered.

Be aware of the moods and intentions that come towards you, but don't be tempted to apply what you are aware of. Withdrawal with observation is the only tool that has substance. This will yield silent fortitude, which does not depend on behavioral techniques as a crutch of reliance that ultimately brings about the dilemma of separation.

When experiencing something untoward within your circumstances, withdraw when necessary, but only with non-involvement, so that observation is not tainted with what was pushed onto you. For if you claim as a tool what was energetically imposed, then when you withdraw, you become a part of that surreptitious outline, and intention will be waylaid by heavy preoccupations that subdue clarity in a web of designs. So I say to you, be careful with your power. It is a gift from the unknown.

It has been my experience that when faced with surreptitious designs, if I too quickly confront the agenda at hand, I sometimes get wounded. It is usually better to withdraw and know through introspection the outlines that have been pressed upon you. If there are no outlines to be discovered then joy bears free expression. But if freedom and light-heartedness are subdued, you can be sure that there is something inappropriate going on.

Q: *How do I learn from unwholesome interactions, where insinuation is in the place of open communication?*

A: Insinuation is a projection of a mood that is not verbally communicated, which is a method used by our society to entrap perception within the parameters of expectation. The emotional net that is cast always has its own surreptitious designs. Becoming aware of it is the issue.

There are specific techniques that can be applied to break the parameters of expectation, which are the fixed perceptions that humanity holds as ideas of compliance. Dodging that etheric bullet is the only recourse. What I mean by that is to walk down a corridor of inner silence amidst the onslaughts of those projections.

A two thousand year old quote states:

"Though I walk through the shadow of the valley of death,

I will fear no evil; for thou art with me."*

This could be interpreted as: Composed of silence, that which is structured and wishes to hold me within the idea of compliance will not penetrate me.

Complicity is the problem, and surreptitious insinuation beckons consent. Stalking is a dangerous art if misunderstood. What has to be known is that the onslaughts of our fellow man, thrown as fixed expectations — and the entrapments that ensue from that — must be vigilantly observed, and seen for what they really are. In this way, necessary distance from that insidious feeling may be gained, through not becoming emotionally entangled.

The trick lies in slipping through the cracks of that expectancy system. This is the art of stalking shadow attention, by merely sustaining one's inner silence and withdrawing from that which wishes to hold you. Nevertheless, no matter how much wisdom you gain, or silence you gather, you will still feel the force of any negative projections that come toward you. That is why it

---
* The 23rd Psalm, The Bible.

is vitally important to not become emotionally attached to what is presented.

Remember that insinuation is a suggestion, which in essence is a manipulative person's desires, put forth within a set format. The suggestion is fully communicated with themselves alone, but is projected as a feeling to solicit emotional compliance. Though this is hard to pinpoint, that input is acknowledged on a cellular level. And if you do not respond appropriately to the insinuation given, to outline an undercurrent that is meant to manipulate circumstances to comply with personal agenda, you will be punished.

Retribution, within its variance, is a training tool used to bring you into a state of semi-alertness that, even though it may be ambiguous, becomes a type of enslavement. The imposed subjugation is that you will be proportionately aware of the oncoming narrative, even if it is only a suggestion, and respond appropriately; otherwise consequences will bear upon you. This leads to a type of alignment or energetic allegiance that establishes hierarchy.

The control mechanism's main objective is to subdue any self-determined realizations about what is truly taking place, for such insight would deliver personal power, thereby depriving the dominant individual of their potential to use your energy for their own ends. Bear in mind that an overseer can also manipulate through unwholesome reward. However, when we stand within our power we cannot be manipulated at all.

There is one positive aspect that can be gleaned from these types of circumstances. When the unfathomable part of yourself is being compounded upon by an attempt of imprinting on one's inner silence, this will inevitably expand the insoluble part of oneself, if compliance is not paid into.

When something is thrown towards our inner self, silence will accommodate the oncoming syntax. This gives the possibility of growth through observing from the bastion of that silence. However, if a narrative is built around that assertion, the person will only act upon what has been compounded and fill their silence through learning or appropriation of what's been given by that pressure or imprint. The danger is that an individual may become totally absorbed in the imprint transferred and forgo their inner silence completely.

Such imprints, once stabilized, can become permanent landmarks that will build and further compound upon themselves, through the mechanics of saturation, so that these placements can be kept intact for usage.

One's mind and intention will move towards the internal landmark that has been installed as a flag, and information will be stabilized within the area where that pressure has been placed. A landmark and an imprint combined create resonance, and this draws upon the available silence, which loops around the imprint and the landmark as a result of the attention that has been given to that reference point.

This is a form of anchoring that can have devastating effects. The reason why landmarks are anchored is so that the imprints cannot be utilized for inner growth and proceed beyond preoccupation to become insightful knowing, through observation without interference.

When silence is kept intact, the attempted anchoring that is applied does not translate into imprinting at all. The impacted region of silence acknowledges the onslaughts of that pressure, and withdraws without any form of identification so that there are no lines of symmetry established through the interaction that can pull silence into a state of saturation.

Through observing the impact and then withdrawing, silence is left with a permanent reservoir of knowing of what has attempted to imprint its empty spaces. This fluid adaptivity allows one's omnipresence to expand upon itself without the accumulation of stabilized and anchored sites. What one has instead are insoluble and flexible reference points that will only yield pertinence in comparison to that which is and has been seen.

Q: What do you mean by 'not withdrawing with what was pushed onto you'?

A: To answer this question, we have to examine assimilation of syntax in terms of it being an odyssey. The best way to see it is to imagine you've just encountered an alien race, and this consciousness is not familiar with the odyssey that's being presented.

If we see the alien awareness as being encompassed completely by silence, we could imagine that this reservoir would engulf the oncoming narrative. What is occurring as it is being encircled is a surrounding of the phenomenon for examination, not integration.

Similarly, you could imagine that water was silence and oil was a foreign substance. When the water is withdrawn, all that is left is the contaminant. In other words, the domesticated social order that encases us within its limited framework, which we avidly defend as its brainwashed cult members.

What has happened through the centuries is an anomaly that is difficult to explain. Somehow the semantic imperative has broken in and permeated our collective reservoir of silence, to the point that we can't recall its subtleties. This happened through incessant programming. Even though the contaminant never really affects the silence, syntax bends perception towards the weight of its bias and we are enthralled by it, as we would be drawn to examine the oil in the water.

Now, just imagine looking at water that has oil mixed within it. You recognize that it is unclean, yet through familiarity, and accepting the fact that you may not have the means to separate the oil from the water, you may find yourself with no choice but to drink it, as you are thirsty.

This is not acceptance of the contaminant per se, but assenting to preexisting conditions, either through desensitization or being cornered. The problem lies in the fact that the body assimilates both the water and the contaminant, which wreaks havoc on our state of being.

On our evolutionary path as human beings we have to understand that syntax, if it is unwholesome or degrading in any way, is a contaminant. This factor acts upon our energetic organism just as a pollutant would on our physiology, with devastating effects.

To prevent one's silence from being saturated, one must merely examine the forthcoming agitation. As you observe the agitant that is syntax, surround it and assimilate all the information that is necessary but do not absorb that substance into the chambers of your inner silence, for if you do it will become part of your cognitive process and will be integrated with that which you have so carefully gathered.

It is better to examine, withdraw, and through that encounter, know what is there. Do not take what you discover to use as a tool, for by grasping that device you become part of that which you wish to be separated from. If this happens, objectivity will be completely lost and saturation through assimilation of that contaminating mood will occur.

Conscripted absorption leads to a type of familiarity that creates desensitization and will invariably bring the mechanisms of denial and deception into full play. Then your silence will become more than what it is. It will no longer be silence and the games will begin.

In my circumstances, if I am impacted by something and buoyancy is weighed down by a concern, this means that I am affected and indicates that I must withdraw and examine what has arrived within me. We are all affected. There is no one in the world that can say they are immune, it is simply a natural cause-and-effect phenomenon. The only choice available to us lies in how we respond to what comes into our sphere of awareness.

Do you wish to be saturated with the mood you've been given and further enflame that which is already known? Or will you examine the forthcoming agitation and reject it on the basis that it brings unhappiness and disempowerment instead of buoyancy? We are evolving and re-learning how to be how we used to be — totally absorbed in silence, which is our power.

Systems of Expectations

Within our lives, there are systems of expectations that constantly flavor the environment, and within that atmosphere are embedded routines that are defined through those basic conditioned assumptions. For one to be free on a sexual level, and fully understand their partner, these expectancy systems must be brought out into the open.

    A very immediate way to become more aware of their function and influence is to swap the socially defined roles of male and female wherever possible, so that one may see the essence of what's involved within that pre-scripted premise. Role reversal may be the greatest aphrodisiac that one could indulge in.

    Obviously, it's not viable to swap all placements, but we can take the majority of them and switch that gender role around so that each expectancy system can be understood from the other person's point of view, and the function of control can be set aside.

    The way that I assert this role-play for my children, unbeknownst to them, is that I give my two boys the jobs that would traditionally belong to their mother; like laundry, vacuuming, cleaning their own bathroom and toilet, cooking their own breakfast, and washing up and drying the dishes and putting them away in an orderly fashion.

If boys are taught from the very beginning that what is expected of them is both roles, then when they grow up and go out into society at large there will not be an attitude of dependency set inside of them as an expectancy system that weighs heavily on their female counterpart. This is very exciting within itself: to know that we can take a human being from childhood and allow them to be complete within themselves so that they are not dependent, for we all know that within dependency lays leverage.

Obviously this type of levering can be enacted by either gender and takes many forms, but the basic equation is sadly too familiar:

'I'll do this for you but you will pay the price, for I don't respect you, since you couldn't perform.'

My sons are also taught to manage the finances of the household: to know exactly how much is earned and how much can be spent before the family is put into debit. They are given pocket money as their responsibility grows so that they may move outside of the home environment within an air of self-reliance.

This independence will communicate to their personal surroundings their freedom to move away from that which may wish to hold them stationary, while I'm not there. Whether we like it or not, there are expectations thrown at children that limit them within the idea of immaturity, but believe you me, they are more capable than we expect.

As a parent, I establish transparency as an honest outline of all behavior so that I may bear witness as the elder view that must be respected. Then the children themselves can be open to constructive criticism, which leads to further buoyancy and self-reflective transparency on their part. This inner foundation of respect will further delineate healthy boundaries that can be openly examined by their own internal advisor for their growth.

The reason why I take you down the path of the expectancy systems that are focused on my children is that I wish for you to be empowered by this parameter. Knowing the practical foundations that surround our urban lifestyle, and living within the boundaries of exactly what needs to be done, takes away the veil of an uncertain future and allows us to project ourselves with confidence into our life circumstances, without fear.

If this is transmitted to our children, what will be reflected back? On my part what I've observed is that everything is good and relaxed, since I am not enslaved as a result of their expectations. By empowering them, I have set myself free from the subjugation that having children can put in place.

If you have to do extensively for them what they can do for themselves, surely you would lose your personal sovereignty as a human being. If one's true freedom of expression were lost, which is one's abstract identity, one of the possible results of this output could be resentment. If we reflect clearly upon this it's easy to see how the situation could become quite tragic for everyone involved.

By simply focusing these small principles that are applied to children to free the environment of control mechanisms and routines of dependency, life can be so much more enjoyable. When these practical matters are taken care of, then we can begin to focus on the relationship that belongs to the mother and father.

Here is where true love can be expressed, which will propel those children, through witnessing a union of co-operation, into a buoyant future where they simply will not put up with a standard that is below that which has been shown.

Q: This triggers memories of my childhood and realizations of imbalances in my own upbringing, and how it has been re-enacted in my life. The information seems so simple and obvious, why is it not common knowledge?

A: It is common knowledge. People just don't act on their inner truth. They prefer to be covertly controlling and subdue their circumstances, for they know that if they say anything too obvious their transparency will dramatically alter their situation. Then they will have to take responsibility for their true position and do what has to be done, instead of operating via sneaky manipulations to procure their desired outcomes, which are pretending to be unconscious but are not.

In the initial stages of change of attitude, individually and collectively, we have to let go of old habits. These settled routines have control surrounding them, and people are afraid to lose their positions of influence, even if that role is uncomfortable for them and makes their life unhappy. It is only power these individuals are interested in, corrupt or not.

This is why it is so difficult to tell somebody something other than what they know. Their inner child has been influenced by arrogance, and within that rigidity the resolve to do what has to be done cannot be seen, due to the need to stubbornly uphold what is wrong.

Cohesion of Union

Energetic support will be supplied unconditionally by simply teaching through example. Energy within itself has its own transparent agenda, and the way this functions is widely misunderstood. How that vital flux operates and how we apply a surplus to ourselves is of utmost importance to us as progressive human beings.

If we were to picture the union of a couple, and this loving partnership was represented by a circle that has no ending and no beginning, we can see that it will flow continuously, unhindered, towards the future. But if at any time the circle is broken, energy itself will supply neutralizing blows internally that strip individuals of power.

The way the circle is damaged is through behavior that does not provide unconditional support, and also through the sharing of sensitive information that belongs to nobody but the couple themselves, which opens the relationship to scrutiny from an outside force.

An external party should never be welcomed unless circumstances are totally outrageous and intervention is necessary. For relaying information from one individual to another that is related to one's personal union or one's household cohesion is inappropriate and comes under the guise of gossip.

We must take care as individuals not to share with others our personal growth issues that have to do with our partner or children. To do so, can and will be seen as betrayal. Even though these parameters may seem restrictive to some, they are composed of respect.

Q: What is the transparent agenda of energy?

A: To yield reflection: an honest review of all circumstances. And if one is stubborn within this process and does not resolve to see what is really happening, due to the challenging nature of the truth that the heart delivers, then a network of insoluble problems will challenge you within a cycle of madness that will bring so much unhappiness.

The greatest danger of not listening to the heart is that internal talk will convince these individuals that the distorted circumstances and the accompanying state of unhappiness are normal, when they are anything but. And this is doubly dangerous, for misery loves company.

Q: How is a surplus of energy applied inappropriately?

A: Any action, intention or gesture that has a surreptitious motive that revolves around personal or selfish gratification, forgoing the rights of others, is inappropriate. Even if the outline of behavior doesn't directly affect anyone else, duplicitous conduct by its very nature has the ability to transfer to others who are weak or without resolve. It comes down to honoring one's personal truth; being true to one's manhood or womanhood. We all are responsible for what we display.

Q: How does one deal with a surplus of energy?

A: Act with integrity.

Character Assassination

The devastating effects that gossip can bring to one's personal circumstances is an insidious facet of social stalking that must be brought to the forefront. Those men and women who have been corrupted by their own weaknesses and allowed shadow intention to infiltrate their behavior, develop covert habits that enslave them to a way of being that not only destroys their own personal power but pecks away at the integrity of those who become aligned, via their involvement as a recipient.

Whilst the subject's reputation is in most cases irreversibly damaged, it is ultimately those who practice and uphold character assassination that will bear the strongest blows in times of personal crisis and at the moment of their death. I would like now to relate to you a story about the venom-laden effects that are produced by gossip.

There once was a woman who became offended by a man and began to spread malicious rumors about him. The man knew what was happening and suffered immensely as a result of her spiteful behavior. Even though he asked her several times to stop what she was doing, she continued to spread her lies.

Eventually the gossip became so insidiously infused within her being that her own words began to wound her. Upon realizing that what she had done was wrong, she went to the man to apologize.

'What can I do, to undo the enormous pain that I have inflicted on you?' she asked, and the man answered solemnly, 'Take this net and capture ten crows whilst they sleep within their tree at night, then bring them back to me in a cage.'

She did as instructed and came back to him with the ten encaged crows. The man then told her to carry that murder of crows, release them in the center of town and then return in seven days for further instruction.

The woman released them and when she came back a week later, the man told her, 'Now take the cage back to the center of town and command that murder of crows to return to their roost.'

'But that is not possible,' the woman said, distraught. 'They have flown every which way and are beyond my control.'

'Now you see,' the man replied. 'The crows, those bearers of misfortune, are like your lies. They can never be retrieved.'

In ancient scripture, it is said that gossip is like a death sentence, for your character is assassinated before you have a chance to honestly present yourself. If a person cannot self-represent without encountering prejudice they will be energetically wounded by the attention of those who harbor judgments, combined with ill will. In most cases this will disallow their ability to experience being more than what they are perceived as. They will find themselves limited by the ignorant and petty conceptualization of those who focus from a lower part of themselves.

Energetic assassination is one of the most severe and degrading activities that we may encounter as human beings. We have become so extensively familiarized with gossip that this corrosive practice is widely considered as a normal form of communication. Such a sorry state of affairs is so far removed from power that by mere association, even in terms of tacit acceptance of the phenomenon, we are being programmed to be desensitized to the greater part of ourselves.

By engaging in such exchanges, we substitute our power for the need to know non-essential and secondhand information, which is a type of energetic illness that has afflicted a vast majority of humanity. As a result, we have fallen so low that we cannot see how far we have drifted away from our heart, and in consequence have sacrificed our integrity for trivial exchanges that mean nothing in the end.

What we mostly invoke when we defame another person is the idea of their past events, shown through that malicious gossip as a foregone conclusion that their character bears. When you have a thought or an impression of someone that is indirectly acquired, what you're accessing is an image coupled with an emotion, which becomes a stabilized attitude; and this is an imprint. Now, when this static point of reference is accessed by you — who have now become the bearer of misfortune — it is usually then reinforced by the one who has imparted that information to you. This is a form of theft.

Unbeknownst to you, by mere association with the one who wishes to assassinate, the giver of that gossip, you have given up your personal sovereignty, which is your ability to access real truths from your inner being. Not only has the assassin destroyed the character of their target, they have also warped your inner spirit through the implantation and stabilization of distorted information that in essence is just lies.

Thus one loses the ability to access one's own true insights, and this is how we become enslaved to the principle of character assassination by association. In essence, our inner seer has been subdued and will be held in a prison of alignment by those manipulative tales.

This insidious loop that is reinforced, seemingly in every corner we turn, must be eliminated consciously. If we align with the better part of ourselves and avoid gossip, we will be protected from outside influences and consequently will achieve a more sustainable base of energy and a greater degree of buoyancy. This joyful resilience will give the ability to see through anything that may be presented by someone who is untrue.

By being further removed from our circumstances through the buffer zone of our buoyancy, we truly see who approaches, and know how to proceed appropriately in comparison to our internal mechanisms of insight, which invariably will expand and diversify as one's power increases.

In this fashion, any bearer of malicious intention will be witnessed within the act and so ultimately will be captured within their own self-reflection via being seen. Equally, they will automatically be freed when they change their self-destructive internal process. When a person lets go of limiting behaviors, their shift will be recognized by others, thus releasing them from a self-perpetuating loop that annihilates their ability to accumulate personal power, and thereby allowing them to be who they really are.

For us as a humanity to have the ability to see the truth of what is presented by those who approach, we need more energy. We should not wonder and enquire about someone's past, but see that individual as they arrive in front of us. No enquiries will be necessary, for we will know who is presenting themselves, and this knowing is our intuitive heritage.

It is far more effective to train ourselves to become aware of subtle inflections that come from our environment to warn us of what is there than to rely upon hearsay. This approach is primally connected to one's original truth and will yield each individual variance within their ability to see. Adaptivity is where insight arises and where true cognitive inversion occurs, which becomes interdimensionally interdispersed through the power of being seen at the moment that it reveals itself.

Cognitive Inversion

Cognitive inversion is what prompts your awareness to tease the page to fling at you what is hidden. When applied in human interactions, we begin to access visual pictures and knowledge that belong to the person we are engaging with and are thereby shared communally.

What inhibits this natural process is layered and compressed information within one's conscious awareness. This dense sedentary material saturates the reservoir of silence that is within us. This permeation occurs due to acceptance of information that is not intuitive, and when that content absorbed is externally supplied it usually bears the outlines of agenda.

Now, if someone totally disassociated from inner silence and laden with compacted, distorted information approaches a seer, the inner mechanics of the one who knows intuitively will be as follows.

By virtue of their inner silence, the seer's awareness will be drawn to the agendas at hand, or anchored imprints — which are self-sustained and ideologically supported through socialization — and their experience would be a feeling of momentary energetic and emotional destabilization.

They will also be alerted on an auditory level to the underlying content of the oncoming syntax, as well as visually, through the internal imagery delivered. Their conscious acknowledgement dislodges the ability of that anchor being thrown to become stabilized within their own being as an imprint.

Such knowing is our heritage and our rightful state to abide within, if we drop the need to want to know insignificant, inconsequential information that does not bear relevance to the true energetic impact which would naturally occur through being self-aware. This state of consciousness will outline our true integral perimeter, where power and buoyancy ultimately are obtained.

The hidden cognitive inversion within the story of the crows is revealed in a few simple lines, which define the boundary that could have been sustained in the beginning by the two who had conflict. When the man says, 'Take this net', this represents his awareness, and is a metaphor for catching the woman within the act of formulating maliciousness.

By asking her to capture the crows at night while they sleep, he is saying, 'I know your intentions and I would like you to catch and contain them and bring them to me directly.'

What is being conveyed here as the inversion is that between ourselves alone we must discuss the folly before it becomes a malaise of imbalance, to bring resolve and understanding to that which may have been misunderstood. Through the accordance that is reached, we create a perimeter of power, and this will remain intact as long as the truths of that symbiotic realization are kept within the integral boundary of those involved. For this information belongs to nobody else.

Sustaining truths within an integral perimeter will give access to the magical facility of cognitive inversion, through individuals having the ability to consciously review what has occurred, without the element of sharing this exchange with those outside of that experience, which invariably will bring interference and distort the essence of the interaction.

As a result of an integral perimeter being kept in place, a time capsule of inverted information can be released and delivered to either recipient for further reviewal on their life path, via the omnipresence of the inner silence contained within the personal power of each involved. This influx of insight will reveal more truth in years to come than the original understandings that were arrived upon. Thus each can progressively learn their most pertinent lessons in comparison to the evolving conscious awareness they carry as sentient beings.

What may have escaped you within the story of the crows is what is not immediately obvious. It is what could have happened in the first place, and to discover that we must make another inversion. In drawing your attention to the hidden cores of this story, I am coaxing you to understand something that has been seen by another. In all circumstances it is best to discover your own adaptive insights, unless the ones you travel with are absolutely aligned with your seeing, which arises in the moment that is continually escaping us all.

www.parallelperception.com

Remember, what has been highlighted here as a time capsule of insight is actually stationary and fixed within the pages, but if you take the principle of inversion and apply it to your life, what you will discover will be neither fixed nor stationary.

I would like you to become aware of a portion of the narrative that holds information that is not obvious and is held within imagery. Inwardly seen realizations are the key component to what occurs. Your visual faculty will carry time capsules of awareness for review. These delicate items are a gift, and reflect our true status of awareness, showing us the way to proceed.

Reviewal is our only option, for as we know, we are continually witnessing everything in past tense. Once we become aware of something, it has already escaped us. Being totally present within the moment is a myth.

As we grow older, we excitedly try to hold onto that which is continually escaping us, and if we cannot have it, we must let it go. That is our lesson. If we can release that attachment, lateral assimilation of all events in dimension will become our true expression.

Let's look now at this inversion. Within the story, it was implied, 'Capture these intentions and place them within a cage.'

How can we travel more deeply into what is being revealed?

That's the question, and within this inquiry I am asking you, how can you travel deeper into your past events and discover more profound meaning?

The only way is to release unnecessary processes. These are usually mundane concerns. Once these elements are let go of, something else will appear within the empty spaces that are created. When this occurs, greater perceptual maneuverability will become possible.

Now I will ask you to examine something stationary within the pages. But there is one thing you must remember. It will only be stationary if you are.

What is being said? What is hidden? The bearers of misfortune are crows. 'Take this net and capture ten crows whilst they sleep within their tree at night, then bring them back to me in a cage.'

The hidden inversion within the statement is that they have to be dealt with before the flux of the situation changes and the social transformative process of misalignment occurs. Conscious awareness must be applied with swiftness and directness so that darkness of the night, where the murder of crows abide, is dissipated within resolve and not reassimilated as shadows within human attention.

Endeavor to release yourself from linear processes that steal from you your intuitive, lateral assimilation of that which surrounds you at every moment. Life can be a process of observing what we are interfering with, rather than interfering with what we are observing.

www.parallelperception.com

The Integral Perimeter

For one's sexual energy to truly flourish, a most important axiom must be adhered to. This principle can be seen as a boundary, and from within the center of that circle we sit and observe the world. That defining line must be composed of kindness, understanding and a discipline that becomes the perimeter of one's heart. If this integral boundary is held in place, then the heart is contained within the fortress of that discipline and this is our bastion, which most of us have lost through common activity that is deemed 'normal.'

An integral perimeter can be assembled very simply. In the initial stages it may seem difficult, but that is only the resistance to dropping old habits that routinely limit the potential for change. So let's get down to the practical application.

Within our household, we have husband and wife, or boyfriend and girlfriend. If you could imagine drawing a circle around you and your partner, know that there are elements that cannot be invited into that circle, for if they do enter they will break the perimeter from within. It is vital to understand that the topics that follow must be examined extensively within the initial stages of sealing that protective border.

Firstly, it would be highly beneficial if every activity that is enacted within the household between partners were kept exactly there, between the two of you. If you were to have spent a relaxing afternoon, engaged in an enjoyable activity together, made love and cooked a nourishing meal, this should not be shared with anybody.

'Why not?' You may ask.

Why would you take the elements of lovemaking, which is the most intimate act, and discuss it outside of the boundaries of the bedroom? Intimacy within itself is sacred. If this sanctity is shared it becomes open to scrutiny, and certainly we don't want the most private aspects of ourselves to become public fodder.

So now we close the bedroom door, and the act itself stays within its private boundary. Sealed safely within that room, love is expressed, given and accepted, freely and openly. By simply closing the door we realize how precious this is, for we all want and need this sacred union, which is the sharing of our intertwined hearts that lustfully reach out and touch and respond to the same love that beckons.

Why would you speak of this intimacy to your neighbor or your friend? If you draw attention to that which everybody desires, then the boundary that lies within that room has been broken, for letting another mind enter a place of union invariably brings interference, which must be avoided at all costs.

I'm sure that everybody at more than one time in their life has experienced the ecstasy that goes with physical union, and the comfort that comes from that. This profound sense of well-being brings observational acuity. Our eyes touch the world with the spirit of that union. This is the first boundary that we build around a relationship. When this tender fortress is kept in place, love and caring will emanate.

The first insidious element that we have confronted here, whether you've realized it or not, is gossip. No matter how innocent the sharing of information is, it invariably comes under that banner, which will break the energetic boundary that is in place. This integral perimeter is the most powerful seal that we can apply to ourselves as human beings, for the sexual center is where all energy emanates.

When we mix these energies we become composed of one another on an energetic level. When this is locked in place both partners will look out on the world with less of themselves, and this reduction comes about from holding the integral boundary intact.

What occurs that makes one less is the diminishment of thought, through confidently and energetically living the proposition of the heart, which is courageous, and is expressed through acting in the world without pettiness.

Q: How does comfort bring observational acuity?

A: It comes about via the fact that one is not occupied with anything else other than that comfort, and within this atmosphere an abundance of relaxed happiness will deliver the truth.

www.parallelperception.com

Q: How is the integral perimeter applied individually, and within friendship?

A: If there were three friends that did everything together and one friend was not present, then any conversation would only revolve around what is being done, and what has to be done. Brainstorming can take place, as long as the individual who is not there is not spoken about in a way that dishonors them.

On an individual basis, an integral boundary can be applied through acting appropriately in one's circumstances. If someone who you know, or don't know, was to be discussed, simply say, 'It's not appropriate to speak without them being present.'

If one of your friends is spoken about behind their back to you, just say, 'I cannot comment but I have his phone number, give him a call.' Gossip is one of the most degrading techniques that can be practiced in human interactions.

Q: How can I be transparent and keep an integral perimeter?

A: In one's life, transparency and accountability on an energetic level are really the only saving graces we have. However, transparency in itself is widely misunderstood these days. In the first five to ten minutes of meeting somebody, they expect to know everything about you.

This is wrong, and everybody's boundaries have been warped extensively due to this.

The inner chambers of one's life should never be given over recklessly, not even to a long-term associate. Your privacy is your sanctuary, and it is nobody's business what you do or don't do, as long as you're not hurting anybody.

When confronted with an enquiry into the details of your life, and a society that defines itself in terms of such interactions, I would say, 'You have to earn my respect and my trust before I invite you into the private elements of my life in the most intimate way.' A powerful man or woman will set extremely strong boundaries that encase their world, which becomes the ultimate expression of their integrity.

Professionalism: Less is more

We all want to have more, but to achieve this we have to give up what we are actively engaging in. By relinquishing our need to discuss inconsequential, insignificant information we apply an integral stance, which will yield professionalism.

True professionalism involves doing what has to be done. Not to add nor subtract, but only do and say what is necessary — no more, no less. To understand this further we must examine it in relation to a situation.

If I were to go to work and apply these principles correctly, I would give all of myself to my work circumstances but bring none of my home life with me as information. As a result, those in my work environment could access the fact that I have a lot of energy and do what needs to be done and that's it, nothing more. For I am at work, and while at work that is all that exists.

If any part of my private life was brought into that situation, I would be open for scrutiny and this would weaken the workplace and myself. If I were to discuss the buoyant beauty that exists between my partner and myself, whether we like it or not, there are individuals who would actively undermine that happiness through petty actions and thoughts.

On the other hand, if I were to bring the idea of drama and unhappiness into the situation, this burden would be actively reinforced by my environment reminding me through asking, 'Is everything okay?' Unfortunately, when people ask these types of questions they are quite often willingly entertaining the idea that everything is not okay, and this is detrimental to them and to me.

When you go to work, your partner is not with you and the partner of the associate you are working with is not there either, so they should not be discussed. All that exists within that context is you and your colleagues, and a relationship must be built around those circumstances — and I don't mean the kind of interaction that breaks the boundaries of your union.

Obviously, whatever context you find yourself in, you are to be challenged by those situations. We are brought together to exercise our awareness and grow within that process. Thus we have a choice to experience another dimension, which only involves those who we are interacting with and nothing else. Then there will be enough energy to see that incomprehensible force that is the Architect of our observation, or the spirit of humankind.

Within a moment, that is all there is, but as we witness that rarified time-space fragment, it is already gone. Be possessed of what must be done and don't be preoccupied with what has happened. True professionalism leaves one to do what has to be done — nothing more, nothing less.

Transference

If an associate you are working with brings with him the dramas of his home environment, under the guidelines of an integral boundary one would say:

'That communication is not appropriate. These circumstances belong to you and another human being, and to betray their trust through transference of the situation is to dishonor them.'

In such a case the complainant is breaking the boundaries of his union from within, and actively inviting another element into that sacred perimeter, which is his and his partner's alone, to gain energetic support. Such behavior in essence is self-destructive and mimics an insidious force that exists within our world, which proliferates through going to the nucleus and destroying that core by breaking the outer perimeter of a cell that should have been sealed but wasn't.

This harmful component is called a virus and, as we know, viruses adapt and shift to bring disease to the host. This process is a reflection of our status as human beings and the element that we actively display which invites disease is gossip. To undermine this destructive tendency brings about the effect of honoring oneself and one's circumstances.

Transference can be seen from two points of view. The first that has been outlined is a lower form. The second potential manifestation of transference has different parameters and an alternate state of fulfillment.

By simply observing and not commenting on what's being discussed one absorbs what is coming; however, through your non-participation in what is being spoken, the one making the immoral statements will be forced to reflect on what they are saying. The impact will return to them as a mirror so that they may realize that what they are saying has no real power without the added emphasis of petty support.

When social bolstering is taken out of the equation, the speaker will recognize their powerlessness and the frivolity of their weak assertions. If a person becomes aware that there is a futility within the nucleus of their behavior then automatically they will know within themselves that they need to cap this activity.

In a relationship, these principles can be applied to great effect, but if one partner wants to practice and the other does not, it won't work. Setting integral boundaries within a relationship has to be co-operative. If it is not, the energy that is applied by the one who wants to practice will be lost in trying to convince the other that they need to change.

For those of you who are jumping up and down saying, — 'Where are all the sexual techniques?' — these are the tools and parameters that need to be applied to enhance union. If they are not actively applied before the sexual practices start, only the self-serving aspects of these methods will be enlivened, and for sure you don't want that.

When one's biofield is enhanced it will carry within it the internal imprints of the heart. If one's true inner purpose is not brought into a state of completion then the imprints themselves, which are corrupt behavior, will wreak havoc with the energy gained.

The Inner Gaze

There is one aspect that I can directly draw from my childhood, to create an inner window view that gives you access to me and insight into yourself. We all know our inner child is the same. We all were children. We all played with abandon, free from the imposed pressures of ideologies from parents and the surrounding community, which relate to the times in which you and I were born.

We must actively disengage from the ensuing imprints of our inheritance so that we may rediscover the emptiness of our inner selves, and through that process uncover our true imagination and kindnesses.

Being awakened to one's inner-self potential in most cases is dumped in the 'too hard basket'. But what are we trying to discover? The most obvious thing is usually the most difficult to realize, since we are so consumed with that imposed socialization which allows us justification for the smallest, most insignificant thing to be important.

One technique that can be applied is to interact, and if within that exchange there is nothing harmful towards oneself that brings embarrassment or may weaken one's inner integrity, then you will automatically realize that your input was energetically compatible. Yet, if at any time you make a comment and sustain an internal feeling of discomfort then this will indicate that your participation is unintegral, via that inappropriate application becoming aware of itself within you.

www.parallelperception.com

This one technique will show you a way to observe yourself. That blow will take away one's inner silence and fill it with discomfort. One can either acknowledge that malaise, review it and understand that it doesn't belong, or one can actively reinforce the inward blow onto the world as justification — and this way is just the same old thing again, which is the shadow of what we could be.

One reason I understand these principles of interference and non-interference is due to a memory I hold in my childhood. The experience delivered to me a source of emptiness that bears witness on my adult life continually. Why I know this is that I was marked in that circumstance by an accident, which left the imprint of silence itself. What happened is as follows.

I was sitting on a sturdy branch of a beautiful old tree, in silence, without any form of thought, gazing into the distance, not even daydreaming. So forgotten to myself was I that I actually fell backwards, ten feet to the ground, unaware that I was falling till I hit the earth. All the wind was pushed out of my lungs and I desperately took inward painful breaths. I felt like I was dying, the pain was so intense.

The physical impact itself kept intact the memory of the silence that I was absorbed in. When I hit the ground all I became aware of was that inner gaze that delivered so much silence to my being, and when the blow came it pushed that imprint very deeply into the inner chambers of my heart.

The mere fact that my conscious awareness traveled with that silence before the physical disruption meant I was witnessing two scenes: one of being composed of inner silence; the other one composed of pain and the realization of the harshness that this world would deliver if one is not mindful to have the general sense to protect oneself.

What I mean by this is to be aware that there can be more than just one's inner silence. Even though the lesson was cruel and harsh from the perspective of the impact, the memory I hold of that emptiness is so clear and strong.

In our childhood our destiny as human beings is outlined. The essence of our inner child in its purest form must be awakened within the adult. Do you remember a time in your childhood when the sun shone calmly through the leaves of the trees, and you felt happy that all you were aware of was nothing but what was in front of you? Those days were warm and windless, and feelings of happiness and contentment were strong and vivid.

Can you remember those days when you sat down under a tree and gazed into the world without intention? By gazing without any preconceived idea of results you were filled with a contentment that if you would lose would haunt you for the rest of your life. Have you lost that?

The technique of an integral perimeter has been outlined here within the experience that we all have had within our childhood. We move from one scene to another and leave behind the one that we came from. With only buoyancy we move forward and forget where we were playing.

But, when we go out the next day and the sun hits our face, we remember the excitement that filled us, and that carefree elation is the memory of being under that tree or in that cubby house. This is what we should supply to ourselves as adults, so there may be newness and freshness continually. Without expectation we move forward.

Why are these childhood phenomena so elusive to us as adults, and why have we forgotten them? As children we naturally gaze. If you were to gaze as an adult, can you peer into your circumstances and into your heart without any preconceived intention on your part? Is this the way back to our inner child? Is this a way to discover newness and abundance, and bring arrival to the beauty of a poignant moment?

So far have we traveled that our intentions have made us forget who we originally were. If you read this passage and say to yourself, 'I can only remember the pain of my childhood', then you are focusing exclusively on the intention that was given to you by the circumstances, which you think have taken away all the magic that was there, forgoing your right to access your own memories of innocence.

Everybody has poignant moments, filled with utter beauty. We all have the ability to move toward simple happiness and forget what has been done. Our problem is that our attachment to intention forgoes this beauty and simplicity and then that delicate frequency becomes lost in the explanation that has been trained into us.

If you were to look into the distance from your inner silence and gaze upon a far-off location, you would be automatically transported, without intention, to that spot. From the vacant perspective of the inner eye, we travel to that site. Even though the expanse between you and the location seems to be incomprehensible, that distance is an illusion.

What we attach to any point of reference is composed of our attention, and as this faraway location relays back to us a feeling that animates itself within our being, this is a true reflection of who we really are. This omnipresent location is the silent observer who sits across the table from you and does not comment but only witnesses.

To have true reverence for the world and all of its diversity we must endeavor to be internally integral, via the complex interaction that is the circumstance revealing itself in every ever-present moment that is continually escaping us. Constant renewal is the only internally vibrant point of reference that we can truly recapitulate, via the fact that we wait for it to manifest as an arrival that has wisdom encased within it, instead of a subjective injection that reflects one's wants and needs, which may be socially bound to what is incorrect.

www.parallelperception.com

ACUITY

Acuity is the sharpness of your gaze, without judgment or condemnation. If one is filled with anything that is opposed to a balanced inner sense, then awareness is entrained upon the wrong element, and this factor will eventually become apparent to you and to everyone within your circumstances. It may be what you focus on that brings the trouble. It's what you don't focus on that may bring you joy.

Q: What do mean by, 'It's what you don't focus on that may bring you joy'?

A: Focus on the solution, not the problem.

Is it I who fear to die?
Or is it the dream
That fears I will expire?

The Heart of Dreaming

"Adapt and facilitate your awareness to the oncoming force of my attention."

These words rang in my ears, as I tossed and turned in my bed, kicking and punching the blankets. I was suddenly fully present in the old Nagual's realm with Zakai, defending myself furiously from his intense physical onslaughts. He thrust a powerful punch towards the center of my chest, and I parried it. My hand jutted down and landed squarely on his forearm.

We paused, and as we did so he said, "Your hand is now idle. If you stand still and observe this, the conclusion that you must come to in understanding that happening is that you have stopped me in the midst of an attack. The old Oriental shamans had a much different view when they recalled the movements of kung fu.

"The first key that I will now give to you is the mysterious gift of recovery. Recovery will clarify what has occurred, within a visual enactment that you hold as a memory in a state of immediacy. Existing in that lucidity is to recount our present moment instantaneously.

"Even though we are within a dream scene, and what appears before us seems linear, when you recover the items of this vision you will be within your living construct. And when you are awakened to this memory, your mind will be subject to conscious lateralization. This interdimensional layering of awareness may initially appear to only be composed of the memory and nothing else, but that is not the whole truth.

"We have been severely disempowered throughout the centuries as a humanity, and this destabilization occurs due to one simple fact. We are overly absorbed within linear processes that are anchored by our domesticated viewpoints. Within these preoccupations we are alerted to pay attention to singular avenues of awareness, and by virtue of this we become fixed. If we are not careful, we will travel all the way along that avenue to seek the conclusion of life itself.

"The shame of it is that all we will discover at the end of this linear process is our death, and the manifest futility of the preoccupations that surround a wasted life. At this stage, we become acutely aware that our hearts have been subdued in something other than what we are, and that is obviously those fixations that have stolen our attention. Those linear prearranged sites that limit us are what we must escape from.

"Imagine I were to capture light within a box, and that light came from a single beam. If my consciousness was to be represented by an empty cube with a mirror upon each inner surface, and I trap that brilliance internally, that ray of light would reflect and refract, until it becomes multiple beams bouncing from one surface to another. Would then not my consciousness become multi-dimensional, within its lateral assimilation of everything that occurs simultaneously?

"If by some strange anomaly I became occupied by one of those beams of light within that cube of awareness, I would lose access to dimensional lateralism via the singular fixation of my attention. Does not this beam of light thereby become a linear process? And, as time progresses and impacts upon itself, within the capture of that single beam am I not being entrained to overlook my dimensional nature?

"Now I must ask you Lujan, do you see the contradiction within what I just said? See the consciousness that is described as a cube of mirrors, with their reflective surfaces inwardly turned, and know that if we capture light within that box and close it, it becomes disconnected from its source and unknown to itself, since it lives within shadow.

"That perceived radiance would then only be an idea of light that ultimately becomes lost within self-reflection, which, once again, is a linear process of preoccupation.

Even though, Lujan, this vision within its subtleties is very beautiful, I must now draw your attention away from your inner imagery, which has just accessed dimension within our realm. See your hand that has stopped my arm in front of you."

Upon Zakai's suggestion, I realized that I was caught within the preoccupation of stopping his furious onslaughts upon me, whilst concurrently viewing another dream scene where he was explaining the capture of light within a mirrored cube, and simultaneously, I was looking into the void.

To this day, I find it extremely difficult to fathom the extent of what Zakai has shown me. The only conclusion I can draw is that if attention is not caught upon the magic of immediacy, shadow attention will take over. And the reason that people are caught within that strange loop is that they do not recover themselves correctly by going to the source of what is really taking place. This is how the shadow's dream subverts real time realization, and draws individuals into a field of self-righteous ignorance.

My benefactors have approached me on many different occasions, from multiple perceptual points of view. I have learnt we are adaptable beings, and this is the reason why it is advantageous to have many teachers, or a teacher who knows many things. Zakai often emphasized that if one avenue of awareness is occupied for too long it becomes stationary and fixed, and this must be avoided at all costs.

Fluidity within dimensional lateralism is our true heritage. If one becomes stuck via certainties or preoccupations then this vital possibility becomes obscured by perception itself.

On the occasions where Zakai would teach me movements within dreaming, I would be partially aware of thrashing about in my bed. Some part of me was alerted to move physically, yet I did not wake. Such was the power Zakai had to hold me fixed within the dreaming realm, whilst I maneuvered frantically to avoid his fierce and direct assaults.

Every attack, every movement, every parry I was capable of employing, taught me to be aware of the oncoming narrative of the men and women that exist within our living construct, and simultaneously of dimensional, lateral assimilation within my benefactor's domain. Zakai's words and actions were deeply embedded within my consciousness. I remember very clearly the advice he gave me on one of these occasions.

"Go to the source of things, where the heart truly dwells."

"What I have been teaching you all these years is the art of dislodging imprinted awareness, which, as you know, is the shadow of what we could ultimately be. These physical interactions embed information deep within your luminous cocoon that will give rise to enormous amounts of knowledge in the future. And if circumstances present the possibility that your physical form may be damaged, this art will come to your aid with the speed of lightning.

"A warrior shaman from the Altai Mountains gave these movements to the old Nagual, your benefactor. His nickname was 'The Alchemist', and the reason he was called this was that he could transform any situation into a beneficial circumstance. If the Alchemist were to lose, he would see it as an appropriate interchange of energy and would simply let go of that which he could not hold onto. If within his circumstances he was to succeed, then the success would be shared and his triumphs were multiplied by his generosity.

"The Alchemist had many students, but it was Lujan, a fearsome Mongolian warrior horseman, who became his protégé, and for a time they were inseparable. He gave Lujan the nickname, 'The Money Changer,' for he was also well known as a talented merchant.

"The Alchemist was trained in the ancient art of war, and was a master of close quarter hand-to-hand combat. These gestures that I teach you have embedded within them more than just movement. In a crisis they will destabilize another man's energy so that you may overcome your enemy. And if these sequences are practiced in dreaming, they have a parallel affect on awareness, which is to awaken one to the onslaughts of our fellow man.

"This is the ancient shamanic method of stalking awareness in a parallel state of perception. These shamans have profoundly affected us. The roots of our system lie deep within the Orient."

As he finished speaking, he thrust forward with a short sequence of swirling, interchangeable elbows that came spiraling towards me. The movements had a directness that was physically shocking, yet their impact went beyond my present time-space continuum. Relaxing his arms and gesturing gracefully, Zakai directed me to sit by the void with him as he spoke.

"You must adapt to this nothingness, this void. It is your ultimate destination. But first I must speak with you on the subject of awareness in dreaming. Listen to me carefully. Know that the movements that have been transferred to you within this dream construct interact with the energetic universe that surrounds us at every moment.

"If the sequences that I show you now are practiced within your waking dream, they will create an enduring power that will nurture your inner being, and will increase your bio-electromagnetic mass exponentially. If these same movements are practiced in the dream realm, as we have been doing now, this will more directly affect the inner imprint that is stationed within your luminous field.

"Even though we spar with one another, and this combat appears to be nothing more than the presentation of hands moving within sequence, what is truly occurring is unknown to you at this moment. Your inner luminosity is being turned and shifted, and the deep imprint of that energetic core is gathering knowledge that belongs to the realm of real time. Have one of the seers that you have discovered ask you questions on the subject. You will be surprised at what you know.

"There is another phenomenon that will occur for you as a result of this interplay. There are sentinels that will break into your dreaming and deliver truths to you, as a consequence of our interactions. They are the guardians and keepers of men's doings. They are specifically here for one reason and one reason only, which is to accompany us on the periphery of our attention until we awaken.

"You are very close to directly perceiving the energetic realm that is hidden behind this dream scene. Once you become aware of your own luminosity, you and the universe that surrounds you will become other than what is presented at this moment. When this unveiling is achieved, my task has been fulfilled. The sentinels are aware of your progression and will break into one of your dream capsules soon."

Over the next couple of weeks, I noticed that my students would ask me questions solely to do with real time, even though I had not mentioned to them once what had happened between Zakai and myself. It always amazed me how intuitively they would ask the most appropriate questions in relation to what I had learnt, and more than interesting was the lateral impact of what occurred within their lives, which had to do with what had happened to me within the old Nagual's realm.

At this stage I started to become suspicious, wondering whether my benefactors had caught them as well, and if perhaps they just were not yet remembering what had occurred within their dreams. It seemed I was a catalyst for those memories, as Zakai had said I would be.

Recovery

The main problem that exists within human awareness is the fact that we do not recover our past events correctly. When Zakai said that I would know more than I realized, what he meant by that was that my body would apprehend circumstances with a direct air of immediacy.

I discovered that when I faced any situation with this factor in terms of capturing that moment so that it would not become a linear process of preoccupation, most individuals would be confronted by the directness that real time requires.

We must bear in mind that being offended is an emotional response, and the shadow's vehicle of delivery into our awareness is emotion. These highly charged reactions would attempt to divert my awareness from accessing the true event with clarity, by setting up other preoccupying elements that were attached to that loaded feeling, instead of directly addressing what really occurred.

What this means is that true recovery cannot take place in that moment, and the truth of the situation cannot really be accessed without a struggle. This absorbing process represents for myself in these circumstances a battle for my truth and personal power. If we are constantly looped into heavy, self-sustaining preoccupations instead of recovering the truth and genuine relevance of our circumstances, we will not heal as a species.

The question that must be asked of ourselves is, 'How do we apply the principle of real time, and what does it really mean?'

Real time involves living presently. Living so acutely and so honestly within that moment we cannot capture that it may be uncomfortable. When Zakai would thrust a punch towards me in the dreaming realm, I would note his directness on the level of my physicality. If I would encounter within my living construct anything other than that directness, I would be alerted to apprehend what was going on, and within that realization would automatically recover the circumstance immediately.

When becoming aware of this, we must also bear in mind that recovery itself can become a preoccupation, if truth does not intervene from both parties. The question must be asked: Am I preoccupied within a self-imposed, stationary site? And have I redirected any elements of truth so that I may hold circumstances within preoccupation?

If the answer is yes, take steps to undo what you are doing and have done. If you do not dismantle those doings, then you must be aware that you have unwittingly drawn an alliance with something other than yourself. If you do not find this frightening, then you are more lost than you realize.

To become a seer one must softly stand within one's power and truth. If you discover that you have wrongly asserted yourself, then have the courage to be wrong.

And if you know your truth is relevant to the circumstance, stay with it until a transformation occurs. Nevertheless, have the courage to change the things you can and the fortitude and wisdom to accept the things you can't change. Here is a personal story that relates very strongly to this precept.

The friend who had accompanied me in the window-breaking escapade of 'Fear not, be free', had neither lifted nor thrown a single stone. He refused to break any glass even though I continually invited him to join in. Years after the incident I decided to visit him, as I hadn't seen him for a very long time. I went to his house and knocked excitedly.

His mother opened the door and upon seeing me, scowled and said, "You're not welcome. Christopher is not here. He died many years ago. When he told us that he didn't break any of those windows that you broke, his father refused to listen to him and punished him severely."

Looking at me with deep disdain, she told me, "It's your fault. He committed suicide because of what happened. Nobody believed him and he couldn't cope with the fact that he was called a liar. That's why he took his own life. You are not welcome here," she repeated, and slammed the door in my face.

When she did this, I felt my insides were ripped open with anguish and a feeling of terrible guilt. I had been restricted from seeing my friend since that time. It was only at that moment that I had decided to go and see how he was. Perhaps if I had not been forbidden to be in contact for those years, I may have been able to comfort him and confirm that what he was saying was the truth. We had been best friends since early childhood and I felt deep despair that I hadn't been able to be there to support him in his time of need.

To this day I still wrestle with that event within myself. I felt within the depth of my heart that there was something more to what had happened to him than what had been pushed upon me as a final accusation. And I was right. I recently found out that my father had prohibited me from contacting him because he was afraid that the truth would be revealed and he would have to pay the whole bill. Via this deception the cost was shared between him and my friend's family.

I have never found complete resolve regarding this event, for I was the initial catalyst that caused his death. By telling this story I am honoring his truth, which is all that can be done. There are some things that are left within us as a jewel of remembrance, which brings humility to one's heart by virtue of the fact that there is no way to go back and make something right that just can not be changed.

Have the courage
to change the things you can
and the fortitude and wisdom
to accept the things you can't change

Real Time

My long association with Zakai taught me that time can never be lived presently since it has already escaped us at the moment we attempt to realize it. How can we add or subtract to something that we cannot consciously stabilize? And, if time is continually escaping us, how can we become aware of our true flux of energy?

Applying forced principles that are based on personal preoccupation actively injures the inner child, who continually searches for its actualization in power itself, via a process of fluid adaptation. Through this fluidity the inner child seeks the renewal necessary to bring release from rigid principles that may not belong to the truth of the moment. Time must deliver its own truths, which will encase wisdom that bears true relevance in regard to each unique circumstance.

We all must become aware of the tendency to externalize our dysfunctional preoccupations, internally examine this phenomenon, and release those fixations so that the load is lightened and our journey can be strong and clear. Our power lies in personal containment, not the acquisition of governing principles.

Do not be externalized. Honor your inner truth instead of your imprinted preoccupations, for they are a lie. With your internal power intact, any movements or slight inflections that are displayed in your environment will alert your steadfast stillness to examine the forthcoming agitant with laser-like precision. This will allow you, the clear-hearted, to not be emotionally involved but to reflect that anomaly back through genuine loving attention.

By neither adding nor subtracting, neutrality becomes the new field of understanding. Under this premise, our conditioning cannot be brought to bear. Integral enactment defines one's heart, and this stance must be composed of truth for one to dream, even when one is awake. Self-determined actualization gives energy. If one's conduct is not integral, enacted within the parameters of the heart, we do not dream truth, and lose access to our essential energy.

As men and women of power, we must avail ourselves to that which is appropriate for us at the time, withdraw from that which is inappropriate, and seek our own substance that delivers us to our personal truth. Know within yourself that time is limited and to waste an ounce is a travesty. To compress this valuable resource is essential, for to squander time is to lose our life, and when it is gone it cannot be retrieved.

Q: How can you be in the moment and not be personally involved?

A: In every moment, we learn to separate ourselves by degrees from emotional entanglement, through being involved and discovering that the involvement is futile. It is a paradox and a learning process that takes a lifetime.

As a seer you must simply move, harmoniously and wordlessly, without intention, away from that which may violate your inner silence. These elements will be indicated by an inflection from the environment that beckons involvement. Obviously one has to be engaged to a certain degree, for we are irreversibly intertwined as beings within this seemingly linear reality. However, the problems begin when one invests in what is presented. Investment becomes a concern, and that burden brings about an internal battle and engagement in strategic positioning. If introspection is lost and investment is all that's left then one must look very strongly at oneself.

The only appropriate gesture that a seer can possibly inject into a circumstance is the intention to resolve the heaviness of negativity. By being empty within themselves, a seer can absorb and redirect intensity back as positive energetic influence. This support hones the inner silence of the confused and beckons their seer to be larger, clearer and more constructive than the old installments, both in dreaming and in waking.

Conversely, if you were to put pressure on a circumstance by becoming too available through interference, that situation would burst its own seams and travel towards you to cause saturation, via incessant involvement with that which should have been backed away from in a timely fashion and left alone.

A waylaid state usually indicates to a burgeoning seer that they have gone beyond the boundary of insight and are functioning from the point of view of an assumption. If another who is operating within the intensity and immediacy of real time catches one within that supposition, circumstances may be elevated to the realm of insight via the mere communal act of uplifting the reasonable premise to a state of true seeing.

Observe that which wishes to enthrall your internal silence. If you find yourself in a compromising circumstance you must stand up for your rights, but never in a surreptitious or cunning manner, for this is degrading to the heart.

When dealing with indirect intention, swiftness and agility must be employed so as to avoid being caught within the fluctuating force and endlessly morphing elements of saturation that are applied to undermine and waylay intensity. Baiting impulses are relayed via the physicality of the one who practices shadow intention, as invisible energetic imprinting that strives to take one's intensity captive by introducing preoccupying factors.

The only safeguard that the seer has is their buoyancy, which relates to inner empowerment and happiness. If buoyancy is absent, then one must withdraw totally from the circumstance and recount in a deep state of meditation to dislodge the feelings that tempt emotionality and which may limit the seer's personal power.

If you find yourself in close proximity to individuals who wish to waylay your happiness and intensity, engage in your tasks with one hundred percent of yourself, and with no inner talk relating to those individuals. Internal dialogue solidifies external actions and their invisible imprints, for our attention is like a bridge.

Pretend you don't see what they are doing, and the energetic spore that cannot find placement within your physicality will turn back to its source. That incomprehensible force, which cannot be imprinted and surrounds us all, will bring lessons of realization for those individuals.

The seer must observe with equanimity, as far as possible, all obvious traits that belong to shadow attention, until becoming impartial to their effects. Through silent absorption, which is not saturation, one's happiness will hold intensity intact and observational fortitude can be sustained.

Shadow attention has imbued our society with a nefarious undercurrent. Evidence of this is unmistakably revealed in the unwholesome intent that lies behind the eyes, appearing as a corrupt narrative that holds consciousness in a lower labyrinth and has dimension within its surreptitious continuity.

Q: *How does one remain in 'real time'?*

A: To be in real time is to observe the oncoming narrative without involvement. Be alert to what is being covertly conveyed to you; yet release it as soon as you become aware of it. This kind of immediacy will bring heightened acuity and deliver the truth of what is really being transmitted, beyond the syntactical exchange. Your internal neutrality will diffuse the potential for emotional entrapment to ensnare your awareness.

Inner silence itself gives the separation necessary to employ a different speed of comprehension, an immeasurable buffer zone. From the perspective of the seer, this field of neutrality provides the illusion that things have slowed down, in regard to what is coming, while at the same time one has a liquid lucidity that translates into speed that within its transparency cannot be hooked onto. This is being in real time.

Q: *Is real time to operate at a higher speed?*

A: Yes and no. To be real is to adjust appropriately. When adjusting with high speed, one's realizations and state of intensity supply the body with feelings of ecstasy and excitement. At other times one has to slow down, and it is still real. This usually corresponds to a state of emptiness whereby one is totally encompassed by pure silence, which may appear as a loss of speed but is merely an adjustment of the physiology in comparison to the circumstance.

Q: *How do you address the true elements of interaction when what you become aware of may only be a symptom of accumulated effects?*

A: In the world at large it is not uncommon to be pressured. If you become aware of a symptom, the only reason you can perceive that factor is that you understand the root cause within yourself. Disharmony within the environment is there to challenge your acuity and the finality of truth that lies within your heart, which cannot be bargained with.

This is your power, and if it can be negotiated with, then the realm that lies within your heart that could potentially be saturated by corruption is being tested. The road to completion brings an incomplete individual to you to challenge your resolution, and this is a good thing.

Q: *How can we not get bogged down in superfluous details when confronting covert behavior in others?*

A: Know exactly what needs to be done and don't go beyond that, otherwise you will be drained of your energy. If you begin to be depleted then you know that you have gone too far with your involvement. Within your circumstances, if your intentions become immoral — i.e. you add a part of yourself which may be motivated by your own personal agenda — you will know. For you will sustain an internal blow and suffer the consequences of your actions. The onus is on you to examine your own input with greater vigilance than that of others.

Q: *Can you describe the relationship between real time and creativity?*

A: There is no difference between real time and creativity. When one is being purely creative, one is being real, and this state corresponds to a buoyant heart. If joy is not there, then it is just control or complacency that is being asserted.

Q: *What's the difference between being awake and dreaming?*

When one is awake in our tangible world, we can readily deny and hide from ourselves the truth of what is going on. For example, in our waking world we can conceal the layers of our true reality incrementally behind social masking. This creates internal secret reservoirs where we are locked within denial, which the second attention will pull upon as your primary reality to be reflected within alternate dimensions.

This is why it is so dangerous to go into dreaming when one is not clear, for in essence the lies have more power than the truth when they are hidden like this. The social dogma is presented on the surface and the nightmare of what you have hidden becomes the reality of what you dream. Taking this into consideration, neither realm is real nor has any power, when one is sustained within denial like this. When one realizes that life can be lived in transparency, then both realities are permeated with an unquestionable power that can only be known by those who experience it.

So, in other words, be clear about your insights, realize your truth; speak it if it can be spoken. Endeavor to make all of your realities one point of reference that can and will access multiple perspectives on behalf of the omnipresence within that awaits to be spoken, felt and seen. Never resort to social banter to please the lie that is the expectation that comes from a socially programmed perspective.

Q: What do you mean by 'rigid principles'?

A: We sustain ourselves repetitively on an internal basis. Such repetition is insidious by nature and will demand that water be soft and wood be hard. This way of relating to the environment denies any possibility of expansion of awareness beyond the boundaries of what is 'known for certain'.

Q: How can we determine how much of what we are witnessing is our projection? And what is the correspondence between what is presented and what we need to know?

A: One will always know what is necessary. In correspondence to your own growth, you will realize what you need to discover. That knowing is always correct, even if you're wrong, since everything that is presented is your projection until you are totally separated from that reflection; which is indicated by not being emotionally involved and being clear about those feelings that arise to be witnessed from within.

Q: How did your journey as a dreamer begin?

A: I will convey this through the next story I am to tell.

The Dream Walker

On one moonlit night, I opened the gate to our front yard, not to leave but to return. I had been gone for a while and had forgotten where I had been. I walked down the front path that was lined with daisies. Even though the flowers were stationary, they seemed to reach out and press forward and in that gentle gesture caress my being. They were lined up, waiting for me; they knew I was there. Each one was aware and they conveyed themselves wordlessly, their beauty so utterly profound.

I approached the house and as I walked onto the balcony, the doorway appeared to devour me within its shadow. When I turned back towards the path the moonlight acknowledged that I had gone, but was still mocking me within its subtleties. It was the twinkle in my eye.

I turned to look down the length of the balcony and saw moonbeams streaming through the windows. The light was soft and sensual and filled my being with a sense of awe and beauty. I ventured along those well-worn boards and the sound of my feet reverberated, softly echoing my presence upon the wooden floor.

As I passed each bedroom window I was lost to myself, and had forgotten who was behind those frames. I turned the corner and approached the side entrance, where I looked through the glass and then opened the door. Immediately to my left there was another door, half ajar. I pushed it open and walked in. There I stood by my mother's bed, watching her sleeping. I was unaware of how long I was gazing, totally absorbed within a realization that she did not sleep like me. She slept like something else.

Suddenly, my mother opened her eyes and lunged forward. Screeching, she grabbed me by the shoulders. "What are you doing, watching me in my bed?" she seethed, and her clenched teeth made her look like a ferocious animal.

She shook me violently till I awoke, but awake like her, not aware like I was. I trembled and my teeth chattered for hours as I realized that I had been ambushed, and that her reality was so much harsher than the one that I was previously immersed within.

What I need to mention now is what I saw in my mother's eyes when she lunged at me. Despite the fact that I was sleepwalking, my memory of what I witnessed is acute and has haunted me to this very day. The beast that is described in biblical texts, and the shadow awareness that has been referred to throughout this book, is what leapt at me through my mother's arms and viewed me from behind her eyes, before she became aware of what she was doing.

When I was watching her within that dream walking state, I was seeing within dimensions. What I saw was a being, whispering and talking coercively, directing her dream attention, unbeknownst to her. When this being became aware that I could see it, it lunged towards me through her body in an attempt to destabilize that window view that I had accessed. From that time the onslaughts of these entities have never ceased. Their pursuit of me has been relentless since then, for I saw at that time something that I shouldn't have been able to.

What I am to explain now is very difficult to understand. When I access this memory, and realize the implications of that recollection, the energy that exudes from my heart center becomes explosive. When that beast reached through my mother's arms and grabbed me so that I would be caught within a complex web, a man intervened.

There I was, a shocked seven-year old boy with my eyes wide open and my mother grasping my arms fiercely, glaring at me as if murder was her next intention. Simultaneously, I was in total darkness, standing in a void that seemed to want to consume me, with a venomous and possessive shadow racing towards me at a terrifying velocity and the full intention of stealing my soul, or my awareness, from that point on.

I was paralyzed with fear. But before this disturbing entity reached my childhood form within dreams, that man suddenly appeared, standing between the shadow and myself. He was dressed in Oriental black leather armor. He lifted his left hand to the height of his shoulder as if to say 'Stop', yet not a word was spoken.

There was a ripple in that universe, something tangible and so powerful. It was my benefactor. He turned around and picked me up within his arms, and what manifested around us was his realm. Once we were completely surrounded by the velvety darkness of the void, he gently put me down.

"Now we will wait for you to find yourself," he whispered, and slowly retreated into an obscure hallway.

That was the beginning of my association with the old Nagual Lujan. His intent held me fixed from the age of seven until the age of forty. The most difficult thing to understand, which I wrestle with till this very day, is that when I recall this memory of my childhood and the dream I had with the old Nagual, it makes no sequential sense.

Both experiences existed in what seemed to be the same time slot. I can only say that when you go back to read the first chapter and put this together, you will probably be as bewildered as I was within that discovery. The only thing I know is that I don't know how it happens. By remembering what occurred, I am filled with a feeling of ecstasy and excitement, to think that this quandary is the Nagual's gift of power to me.

I rediscovered my inner child when I was forty, so many years after that pivotal event. My innocence was safeguarded by the old Nagual, and not interfered with by the shadow. As it was he who raised my inner child, my heart was kept empty and pure. When I landed within that enigmatic realm from that elevator, he and my benefactors were waiting. It took thirty-three years for the toil of my life to deliver the lessons necessary for me to evolve as a man. And then, when this toil had almost consumed me, life started again.

My childhood sleepwalking journeys were an exploration of power. That mystery beckoned me, so now I actively seek out that which sought me. This is the reason I am an awakened dreamer and why my relationship to the world is lucidly connected to my purpose as a seer.

Dream Compartmentalization

Upon recounting *The Dream Walker*, I found myself deeply affected. I knew there was something trapped within me that was trying to get to the surface of my perception, but I just didn't know what it was that I was attempting to comprehend. There was a sense of being blocked, and I went to bed that evening with a feeling of despondency, due to my inability to fathom what I needed to know for my own life. I fell asleep with this feeling infused within me.

"Awake with you." It was Zakai's familiar voice, beckoning my awareness to join him in Lo Ban's domain.

"Come with me now, my friend, and sit by the void. Look within the depths of that which is in front of you. I believe that we all need to be educated to the omnipresent void within. I would like to share with you a tale of power, and this story is yours.

"It would take you a lifetime to recover and understand for yourself what I am to explain to you now. The reason I am giving this information to you is to avert any confusion on your part regarding what took place between you and Lo Ban, thirty-three years ago.

"When I called you here tonight you were preoccupied. By focusing on your being, I knew immediately what was occurring. The feeling that flooded my luminosity was the same as I experienced when I saw the old Nagual split one of your dream compartments that belong to the honeycomb of awareness into two. Before I go any further, let me tell you where he gained the knowledge to accomplish such a monumental feat.

"Centuries ago, Lo Ban was introduced to an extremely old shaman. He became intimately connected with him, and this peerless sorcerer transmitted to him secrets beyond earthly comprehension.

"Look now deep within the void. Recall the vision of the honeycomb compartments that I once directed you to see within that vast emptiness. While you gaze into the luminous maze that appears before you I will prompt you to remember your own compartments."

As Zakai uttered these words, the honeycomb compartments of awareness materialized within the liquid darkness. But this time I was not viewing another's configuration. I was seeing my own luminous cluster. I began to feel elated, to know that I could witness myself within such complexity yet still be sitting there by the void, physically intact. I can only to this day marvel at the ingenuity of my benefactors.

Zakai interrupted my train of thought with a command. "Now focus, and I will give you the story that is yours. You will be released from those feelings of anguish that have arisen, due to the fact that you cannot recall that which is so deeply embedded in the strata of your awareness.

"I do this to alleviate unnecessary concern and bring understanding. Recovering these units of information would be otherwise impossible to access until your journey on the blue planet was completed. It is better to know, so that one may survey that which seems inconceivable.

"As you observe, silence will enter deep within you. What you will witness now is one of the techniques that this extraordinary old shaman taught Lo Ban. It was one of his greatest gifts to your benefactor, among the many that were bestowed upon him."

As I looked into the void, I once again saw the old Nagual, clad in black oriental leather armor, standing between myself and that shadow. It was the very scene that had left me in such a state of profound contemplation. I watched him pick that child up in his arms, and then I saw something beyond belief.

When he had set me down in that vastness, he executed a series of strange gestures that somehow unfolded my magnetic essence into that same honeycomb maze that I was now watching with Zakai.

I then saw the old Nagual take one of these compartments and separate it from the collective, which was a composite of my awareness that I was somehow able to view from that perspective. When this was completed, he reassembled my being by bringing his hands together in a thunderous clap, with a gesture that is incomprehensible to me even to this day. The part of me that had been regrouped returned to my physical form in the living construct, where I lay shaking in my mother's arms after being awoken from my sleepwalking journey.

Bear in mind that I am seeing these images in front of me in multiples, as a panoply of scenes. For you to understand what I am explaining now, you too must attempt this multilateral assimilation.

Zakai's voice beckoned my attention. "Break your fixation from that portion of awareness that shows you the child who has been awoken within the living construct. Go now with your awareness to that compartment which the old Nagual now embraces and witness the magic that is to occur in front of you."

I gazed into the void and saw my benefactor holding one of my own interdimensional dreaming compartments. I recognized it as a vehicle that traverses the fractalized units of information that it would be immersed within, before and after it was returned to me my future and past combined.

As the scene spun majestically before me, light fibers unfolded in elegant spirals that expanded holographically around my vision. They resembled smoky filaments, appearing and disappearing upon the moment they were seen, and containing condensed imagery that exploded like pollen from the center of a flower that my gaze brushed like a butterfly wing. I was witnessing the very void essence that master Lo Ban was immersed within.

The scene suddenly shuddered and a time-lapse fragmentation began to occur before my eyes. The interplay of his activities was merging our awareness and at this point I knew he was going to become me. He was once again executing a strange but familiar movement. It created a sensation that made me feel as though my chest was going to explode. At the point where I thought my torso was about to expand beyond its physical limits, the compartment I was viewing divided and separated into two sections. What I saw then was two small children in the company of that ancient Oriental warrior.

"Now we will wait until you find yourself," he said to one of them, and upon these words, the boy vanished. I later discovered this portion of myself, awaiting my arrival in this timeless zone, upon plummeting down in the elevator, which was the commencement of my journey within these pages: a tangible review of my life as a shaman.

Turning to the second child, Lo Ban beckoned for him to follow and ushered the boy into an alternate continuum, where he resided for thirty-three years. This child's name was Somai.

My body was experiencing deep agitation as a result of what I had witnessed. At this moment, Zakai intervened. "Calm yourself," he said. "You are very fortunate. The gift of power that Lo Ban has passed to you will take you your whole lifetime to fully integrate. This memory that you review is a time capsule that contains the deeper content of what took place beyond the temporal limits of your cognitive system.

"Know that when Somai merged with you, you were simply assimilating yourself. And when you encountered yourself as a child in Lo Ban's realm, upon your reawakening thirty-three years later, that child became one with you once again."

I broke my fixation from the void to turn to face Zakai. "Is this why I have the capacity to see what others can't, and the burden that goes with that?"

"Yes. Somai was integrating the old Nagual's luminosity as information that pertained to the most important aspects of his life experiences. Within that transition of consciousness, he assimilated profound and mysterious knowledge of an extremely rare nature. What was imparted to him, you now know to be part of you. Now that I have awoken you to what occurred so many years ago, your task will be to recall those mythical transmissions that Lo Ban passed to you so that you can translate them to others."

Zakai gently grasped my shoulder. "Now that you know, you will access more easily those extraordinary insights that were gifted to you, for you have a deeper understanding of what took place and have witnessed how that transfer of consciousness occurred."

Affectionately squeezing my hand, Zakai looked directly into my eyes and said, "What a wonderful tale of power. What an awesome story to recall. Awake with you now."

When master Lo Ban appeared within that hallway and simultaneously intervened within dimension when I was a child, he was splitting my attention within the fabric of the universal eye. One facet would grow to be a man in our living construct and progress within this worldly dimension. Another would wait with him patiently, immersed in deep silence. Here you must realize that the old Nagual had automatically become split in two at that point. The third child was taken and shown worlds beyond dimension, and received the transmissions of movement and knowledge that are now being disclosed. This occurred for thirty-three years, and as you emerge, so do I.

We are all intertwined. My heart is your heart. Your heart is mine, and the net of man is interconnected dimensionally. Thus our futures together emerge into a new era of realization. Once you see the possibilities that can occur, via absorbing my experiences, your limited social consciousness will be irreversibly dismantled and you will yearn for more than what you have. The visual assimilation of this story will deeply affect the sedentary social program that you have been subject to your whole life, which now will no longer keep you fixed.

I have not known of, nor yet heard of, anybody experiencing this type of shamanism: to have a master formulate a world in front of you that is seemingly of your own making, combining present, future and past into a visual matrix that leads one to understand what they were never meant to see. Fortunately my destiny is as such, and here you walk upon my words and see the actions of my benefactor, that to this day I recall, yet the very thing I perceive escapes me. In essence these are the workings of the universal third eye, applying itself within dimension.

www.parallelperception.com

Personal Containment and Why We Don't Dream Real Dreams

In order to discover the source of our earthly dilemma, we must determine where and why we allow our power to be drained within our personal life. I dreamt fluently as a child, for I had not made any corrupt alliances or agreements and consequently could not break them, so I was naturally surrounded by a ring of power that sustained my innocence.

When I was awakened from that sleepwalking event, I had been utterly forgotten to myself. Within this state I could apply the awareness necessary to integrate all the elements that we actively take for granted; the unknown factor that is the mystery that belongs to the night.

What we need to become aware of as seers of dreams, whether awakened or sleeping, is that the integral boundary of our heart has become compromised by our social indoctrination and corrupt behavior. If we justify an action that is not correct, we will sustain a self-imposed injury that we may then have difficulty waking up to, due to habitual denial.

The problem is how to clarify what it really means to make your acts integral. In my dream as a child, I was lost to myself. Is this not a clue? How can one be lost to oneself, yet know oneself completely? At this stage, I would like to remind you of a principle described in the first chapter of this book: 'Shamanic Dreaming'. Saturation equals permeation. If we are utterly involved and invested in protecting dysfunctional behaviors, how can we judge whether we are saturating our circumstances or being infiltrated by something else?

This may all seem too confusing, but it's not. If we hurt, injure or manipulate our world, that heavy-handed behavior will deliver us a lesson. Unfortunately, these lessons can consume all of our energy and all of our time. We must consciously endeavor to put a stop to our destructive behaviors so that we may wake up to the fact that we are dreaming in our daytime life, just as we dream at night.

To dismantle the social program and be as integral and as absolutely accountable to ourselves as possible, is imperative to gathering genuine personal power. If we do not clear our heart, we will not dream real dreams. We will be consumed in a mirrored maze of illusions that have attached to them all the machinations of our personal conduct, transferred from our daytime realm.

What is it that will act upon us in dreaming to amplify our hidden behaviors? Luminous sentinels. Their task is to enact upon us dreamings that are a reflection of our unresolved nature. Unbeknownst to ourselves, we will be caught in a loop as a direct result of our denials for as long as we sustain them. The sentinels enact the truth of ourselves upon us, yet we cannot see them. For we don't have access to the amount of energy we need, nor the objectivity, to comprehend that our dreams are an inward journey and composed utterly of energy.

As human beings we have companions that are faithful to us right to the very end. The agreement is that they will reflect upon us what we are until we are something else. And that is clear-hearted and composed of power.

www.parallelperception.com

To Know Without Question

A dreamer knows things that they reasonably shouldn't know, about the world and about the people around them. Throughout a dreamer's life, the jigsaw puzzle slowly appears for what it really is, as all the pieces are put together in an interdimensional tapestry that cannot be reasonably explained.

In my early childhood, I knew something unquestionably in my heart, and I still live by this understanding. It is the knowledge that the foundation of my life is stabilized in a clear heart.

When one's heart sees, it knows without question. Can we proceed with that knowledge and act upon our truth in the world, as it is now? Though most people do not live by their inner truth, we nevertheless must aspire to go beyond what we are. Can an awakened dreamer benefit the world? Alone, probably not. But unified and together, yes.

We weave collective dreamings, and these holographic manifestations appear in front of us, right now, while we are awake. They are the decisions we make and the things we do. Within your circumstances, if you wish to be an awakened dreamer, the first step you must take is to resolve to do the right thing: within all your circumstances and all of your personal interactions.

This intention will be the beginning of transforming the foundations of the corrupt agreements that have been passed down to each of us, individually and collectively, over the centuries. How you succeed depends on you, and whether you take this one technique seriously.

It may seem much easier to go along with the crowd and not make waves, but we must stand up and be heard, and give our inner truths a voice. This is the first stepping-stone, the foundation technique for dreaming awake. We must be clear and strong within our resolve to not be involved with that which reduces our energetic mass by breaking our inner seal of power. You know exactly what I am talking about, and if you don't, when you put these principles in place, you will.

Allow these words to impact you and shake up your imprinted continuity. The elements of your circumstances will lay in wait to pounce on you with lessons to renew the part of you that requires you to grow beyond your limitations.

Don't Play With That Which You Should Not

If you act surreptitiously, in any way, to benefit yourself and waylay your circumstances, the world of dreaming awake will not be yours, but the nightmare of your life will be.

When you realize that you can influence something, apply yourself in the right way. Only contribute what your heart affirms should be added, and if your input brings conflict then so be it. We must exercise our inner voices to become familiar with our power within. The truth is that if a resolution cannot be achieved, then you may not be energetically compatible with the one you're interacting with. When this is discovered, it must be accepted.

By being transparent, we learn where we can go and where we should not. In this way we will gradually be stationed in a position of power that has non-interference as its perimeter. The following story is an example of the degree of influence that we can have upon one another, and the responsibility that represents.

In my past, one particular individual was honest enough to say to me, 'You frighten me.' When I asked why, he answered, 'When I think that a light should be turned on, you get up and switch it on. When I want a peanut butter and jelly sandwich, you go and make one for yourself.'

This person had discovered that he could direct my actions by simply focusing on his desires. Evidently at this stage in my life, unknown to myself, I had integrated the principles of the Completion hieroglyph. I was bringing resolve to my friend's unspoken intentions. This phenomenon began twenty years before the hieroglyphs became a tangible memory. My benefactor's influence had sculpted my awareness long before I became aware of it.

This experience was a turning point. His wishes were somehow translated to me, and I would fulfill them as if they were mine. He had found a doorway into me and for a time he played with it, as if I were a toy. If we become aware of something that is different or unusual, it becomes our responsibility to respect that anomaly and honor our circumstances within the light of transparency and truth.

The heart knows what to do in all of our living moments. It's a matter of us all being clear enough not to play with others as if they were there for our amusement. We are non-replaceable. When we are gone, we are gone. Best not waste our time, or the time of others.

For those of you who are clear-hearted and are wondering what is going on, why the world never resolves itself, why this reality does not change, and why its dream is being perpetuated in a way that is so destructive, it is easy to understand.

The hearts born within this time period are mainly unresolved and have great lessons to be learnt. These troubled hearts injure the world and forget that it has as much right to be here as they do. As a result of this, all of the earth's resources are being wasted in greed, instead of utilized symbiotically. The state of the world is simply a reflection of the status of our being. If we do not have balance, we will not dream awake.

Everything comes back to the individual. Don't try to change the world; change yourself. By attending to your own transformation, you are actively taking responsibility for what is happening in the world.

Individual stances eventually become collective. This dream is the most important one that we are engaged in. If we do not resolve this paradox we will never reach our true destiny. We will be unable to develop our full potential as a species, for those gates will remain closed.

Denial

If your friend confronts you and says, 'I'm aware that you are enacting something upon me,' and you respond with denial, 'But I am doing nothing,' when you know that you are, you are forsaking your own heart by denying transparency.

Transparency is the key to clearing our heart, and if we have the courage to admit that we are wrong, this will be our strength not our weakness. When you know that you are enacting inappropriately or surreptitiously towards anyone, in any way, be clear and stop. For if you don't you will be apprehended on your dreaming journey.

Your heart develops gravity and will pull to it what is necessary so that you may find resolve. If you remain in denial, this process will take a lifetime. Don't waste that precious chance.

For those of you who think you're smart enough not to be caught, you have been. Your heart actively witnesses everything you do. Though you believe your inner world cannot be penetrated, and your thoughts belong to you alone, they do not. What you carry within you will be seen by those who are clear.

As we evolve, our inner world becomes ever more available to one another. Our only recourse is to acknowledge everything we do inwardly, right now, and take measures of our own accord to address the growth issues that we discover. We are the ones responsible for who we are.

In reality, your heart is my heart, and your dream is my dream. We are here and together. What a responsibility. Take it on board and do not be a coward. Fight for your right to be an awakened seer. Our sovereignty has been coercively maneuvered away from us, but we can retrieve what has been taken.

www.parallelperception.com

The Auditory Architect

Techniques to achieve greater clarity are easier to apply than you may think. Just remember, your heart has to be clear. If it isn't, you will dream, but whom you dream with will be the question. What you encounter will be composed of you, even though it appears that you are dreaming with somebody else. And the contradiction is that you are, for in reality you are not really being yourself when you are acting as a social being within the world of daily affairs.

When we first start our journey in the realm of dreaming, we must actively set off purposeful triggers that will bring us back to the daily world where we sleep. One way to do this is to set your alarm clock to go off during the night, first at 2 am and then again at 5 am.

When the alarm clock goes off, jump out of your bed and go and open your front door. Look outside into the darkness for just a second and then go back to bed. Lay on your right-hand side, with your left ear facing the ceiling, and listen whilst turning off your own internal talk and visual imagery. Go to sleep composed of darkness, yet aware that your primary aim is to listen.

At 5am, when your second alarm goes off, get up and go to your front door again. When you open the door, just before dawn, look into the darkness and whisper, 'I'm awake, hello.' Then go back to bed.

This time, lay on your back with your eyes closed and once again listen, watching the imagery that appears. If the visual content comes from the right side, then you know your heart is not clear and you have a lot of work to do in your daytime world. If the voices that speak to you are coercive, nasty, violent or corrupt in any way, this will simply mean that your inner self is saturated with issues that are beckoning your urgent attention.

What you draw to yourself in your dreams is composed of your heart, and indicates the residue that needs to be resolved in your daytime world. Do not be discouraged at this point. Fight for your right to be an awakened dreamer. This is your challenge, and clearing up what is in our heart is the first trial that we all face within our journey.

Be aware, as you practice, of an auditory phenomenon that will start to occur. Listen for a knock. It sounds like a tap on your front door, but it appears inside your head. When you wake up to that knock, listen for the voice that accompanies it.

Try to become aware of whether it is coming from the left or the right side. It will be saying something like, 'Hello, can you hear me?' And I mean literally. I have spoken about a similar type of auditory phenomenon in 'Dreaming the Dreamed.'

The beings that speak to us with this voice exist outside of our construct. They constantly wish us to break our fixation, for our ultimate journey is to arrive where they are, but to go there we have to find internal resolve. Their job is to help deepen the hole we have dug for ourselves in order that we will learn the harsh lessons that are necessary to transcend this realm. Ultimately they help to free us, if we are determined to deal with our world in transparency so that our hearts may be clear.

I have seen two prominent types of luminosity within my dreams. What accompanies these luminous beings is a voice that is an Architect from their realm who actively directs our awareness. Even if we don't actually see the sentinels in the beginning, by the mere fact of hearing this voice, our internal holography is affected, which is our dream imagery. It knows exactly the amount of information we can sustain as individuals, and will deliver the truth and power of our own heart.

These phenomena are usually very difficult to remember, but there is one clue I can give you that will alert you to if it is occurring for you, whether you can recall it or not. The clue is our second sight, and it begins by acknowledging other people's thoughts and feelings.

If you start doing and saying what people are thinking, this is a sign that these energetic beings are in contact with you. They open up channels that appear in this world as psychic phenomena, and for each individual the manifestation of that experience will be different. Our task, which is our destiny, will be outlined by our contact with them. What we need to know in this world will be defined for us in theirs. For all of us, our tasks will equal our integrity. We'd best not waste our time.

For me, this presence often arrives while I am sleeping. It manifests as a voice at first, which guides my dreaming awareness appropriately. If my energy isn't particularly strong, I go into a dream scene that is composed of the truth I need to realize. If my energy is abundant, what appears for me from their world is sheer intensity itself. What follows is an account of one of the latter experiences.

I had recently pierced my ears with gold earrings, and I was dreaming and aware of my physical body. In this dream I did not hear the voice initially. It sometimes happens that way. I was sleeping on my back, and two fuzzy, golden, luminous beings the size of baseballs came up to my ears. They were discussing amongst themselves, and at the same time directly to me, that the gold I was wearing was very beautiful. I knew that they were attracted to it. Their personalities were extremely vibrant and childlike, and their voices were not full of flattery but genuine interest in what I had done.

Here lies our first insoluble contradiction. There I was, lying in my bed, dreaming with those luminous beings, aware of myself and aware of them. I could see their realm and knew that I was sleeping in my room. They can enter our construct and appear here, and simultaneously transport one's physical body and have it arrive in their realm, without you having left where you are.

What happened next took me by utter surprise, and it was the first time this occurred. Another type of luminous being approached me. It was also composed of a golden hue and was much bigger, half the size of my body. It pressed up against me and it was clear that my skin had a symbiotic relationship with its luminosity. This giant golden sphere communicated direct inner realizations, through energetic impulses of connection that seemed to neutralize my emotions, which would have weakened me through the idea of fragility and fear.

I was losing control but went with it. When I had surrendered, all I was left with was the feeling connected to the tangible sense that was my skin, which automatically made obsolete the foundations of my original emotionality. I became visually and auditorily focused, with a sense of feeling that was purely tactile; and this left my heart free to communicate, not with a higher part of myself but with an uninhibited aspect of my being.

It was at this point that the voice appeared, pressed up against my left ear. But the sensation wasn't physical. It was auditory. As the left side phenomenon pushed upon me and spoke truths, the large electrifying luminosity directed the scene, which was composed of pure energy. The electromagnetic impulses it was transmitting opened up a world in front of me, and my construct as I knew it disappeared.

My body was floating in between those two beings that flanked me, in a vast expanse of nothingness that seemed to go on forever. They directed my awareness to some material that was floating within that immense space. It appeared to be glyphs of a foreign language, which I later recognized to be Aramaic. What I saw related the information that I share with you now.

We define our reality according to our inherited belief systems, and that narrow interpretation is stealing from us the possibility of experiencing the world of the luminous beings and the auditory Architect. We cannot define our future in that dimension yet, for we have not resolved our dilemma in the realm in which we live.

We must come to terms with the realities of what needs to be done here before we can experience ourselves within that expansive universe, which is in truth our inward journey. And the doorway to that realm lies within the integrity of our hearts.

www.parallelperception.com

Questions and Answers: I

What follows are some questions that my students asked me about what I had learnt from being in direct contact with these phenomena.

Q: What is our fixation?

A: To be other than what we are, and to be involved with that which we should not.

Q: How do we break our fixation when we are continually confronted and saturated with interactions and situations that demand involvement and constantly challenge us?

A: We must be constantly challenged. Our trials and tribulations within themselves will bring integrity of character that becomes one's potency or power. We are simply tested so that we may grow. If we see our challenges in any other way we are just indulging. What doesn't kill you will make you stronger, and the power that you collect is the key to future non-involvement.

Q: Why are those beings observing our construct? What is their interest in us?

A: We are essentially composed of the same essence, but we are something different. We have forgotten where we've come from and why we're here in the first place. There are reservoirs of great value here that we must discover, frequencies we are immersed within that can be accessed via awakening the seer within. However, in the process of learning we have lost sight of our origins and purpose.

Their interest in us is their devotion to the task at hand, which is to free us from our dilemma. Our fixation is layered within deception and untruths. These modes of behavior bring about rules and consequences, and we will be released from our confines only when this lesson is learnt.

Q: Is their realm another construct?

A: No. Their realm is composed of pure expansiveness, inwardly and outwardly. Time has neither beginning nor end, and energy exists within a continual flux that is self-sustaining, which is a contradiction that we cannot grapple with, because we die.

Q: Why are we here? What are we doing here?

A: We are dreamers, and the dream of our living construct is too solid. We must go beyond the apparent reality of this illusion and live within a parameter of responsibility that is witnessed by our heart. If that integrity is compromised then our ability to break the fixation of the solidity that surrounds us will not become available. The reason that the dream of matter does not transform for us collectively is that our hearts must be composed of the power that will free us, and at this moment they are not.

Our heart is the inner engine that drives our luminosity. If our integrity is not intact we cannot escape, and our luminous form will not become available whilst we are unable to even remember it. To sustain another reality we must be aware of its existence. If we cannot conceive of it, how can we get there? This is our challenge, to remember where we came from, and that can only be achieved through a pure heart.

Q: Is inner silence the language that is understood by all beings?

A: Yes.

Q: How exactly do the sentinels 'deepen the hole'?

A: We cannot go beyond ourselves until we clean up our act. What is reflected to us is what we add to ourselves throughout a lifetime. The luminous sentinels are not doing anything to us. They are simply responsible, in the same way we are. If we act differently then what we experience will not be composed of who we were in the past. The sentinels mirror back onto us what we are. They stand behind our dream images and occupy us with the feelings we carry internally.

Q: What form do they take in dreaming?

A: Usually people that have a mean streak or who occupy us with our hidden desires. Either that or they take on the form of our familiars, to absorb our attention.

Q: Why do some men experience nocturnal emissions in dreaming?

A: Semen loss in dreaming is a result of that man having immoral thoughts towards women within his life. This is reflected within his dream scene and causes him to lose the essential life force he needs to dream awake. If a man wishes to cap his energy, he must not interfere with women in his waking state in any way whatsoever. This of course includes thoughts and projections.

If that can be achieved, what will first appear will seem to be a glass division between him and a sexual dream, and if the man can fully forgo his corrupt behavior in this area he simply will not experience sexual interference in dreaming. One can also have seminal emission if the kidneys are weak, which can be remedied by taking herbs.

Q: Can we dream with people we know in our waking state? And how can we tell if it's really them?

A: Yes, and you will know. Even if they don't remember, you will recognize their energetic signature.

Q: Is our Architect of observation a luminous being? And does it interact with luminous beings from other realms?

A: Our Architect is an element of our perception that dwells within the confines of our construct and is transported to the luminous realm when we are there. Our Architect's prime objective is to awaken itself here so that we can examine the content of our solid construct within the fluidity of a dream-like state.

Our luminosity seeks refuge by becoming fractally immersed in time-sequencing that is interdimensionally dispersed within multiple realities. Within that intricate process we have lost ourselves and forgotten our origins. One of our prime objectives as luminous beings is to interlace ourselves with this reality so that we may simultaneously experience the confines of a construct alongside the freedom of eternity.

Q: Is our destination 'nothingness'?

A: Yes. But that nothingness is full of everything and known to itself. So this emptiness is not nothing. It is everything.

Capturing the Attention of the Cloaked Inner Child

To capture the attention of a cloaked inner child is to understand the masked primary motives that bolster pettiness and surround it with self-serving rationalization. This intention is one of the most difficult to discover, for it encases our interactions in layers of denial.

If we do not identify and transform what we are creating that is damaging to ourselves and our environment, we will be set in a perpetual motion that will sweep us along as though we are in a loop, bypassing the encounter with the real prime objective that we need to become aware of.

As individuals, we must catch ourselves in the enactment of emotions that set forth an atmosphere of denial. If you are acting morbid, mean, feeling sorry for yourself or being elitist or arrogant, it may be that your inner child is contaminating your environment because it has been spoilt and indulged.

For example, you may find yourself in a situation where you have obligated yourself, and discover that you are actively punishing the person you are engaged with. Though you yourself can't understand why you are being so moody and petulant, and within this premise think you've lost command, the bizarre twist is that you do have control.

Knowingly persecuting your environment because of your obligation, through transferring feelings of guilt and discomfort to those individuals who wish to do what needs to be done, is a form of violence. By emanating stagnant emotionality that disallows resolve and completion to be brought about, the cloaked inner child is secretly beckoning boundaries whilst overtly demanding to be indulged. Within this enactment, you deny yourself the ability to see that your inner child has ulterior motives, and if that agenda is not being fulfilled, that immature expectation will punish whoever reaches the hand of purpose to it.

For those who recognize their own behavior in this description, I would advise you to look back to your childhood and capture that time when your mother or father rewarded you for throwing a tantrum and gave you what you wanted. Upon becoming aware of this, you will see that you do not need to enact retribution upon those to whom you have obligated yourself. If you volunteer your service, that intention must be pure and not tainted with immaturity and unwholesome expectation, like the demands of a spoilt child when it does not get its own way.

If such tendencies can be openly examined, the dreamer will be awakened within the waking state and then within their dreams when they sleep. If you don't take responsibility for this and do what has to be done, then all the unresolved inner children who are encased in all the adults you wish to live your life with, will help you enact that immaturity, through their own applications of vindictive payback that are full of scorn and contempt.

In our lives, we actively pass from one to another what is unresolved, seemingly unknown to ourselves. We have to wake up to the fact that we are enacting ourselves upon the world, and that everybody blindly opens their arms to what comes.

It is vital that we take the intention that is pointed at our fellow man and reload that emanation with love of oneself so that the experience of life itself, which is the fight for our freedom, can become the struggle for enlightenment, instead of the repetitive battle that is occurring. Our primary focus must revolve around clear, transparent integrity and mutual support.

Mutual Enhancement

As outlined in the beginning of this book, my true journey of resolve began with the old Nagual Lo Ban, and the origins of this odyssey stem from my childhood. Coupled with his powerful guidance was the influence that extra-terrestrials had imposed upon me.

On further review of the alien encounters, my recovery became stronger, thanks to unspoken enquiries that came from a very good friend, which sparked off a unique type of realization. The reason for this is that his curiosity stemmed from observation without interference. This process of mutual enhancement between two beings corresponds exactly to the Completion hieroglyph. Our energetic and physical constructs are activated in a synchronistic harmony when there is neither conflict nor expectation present, and genuine affinity defines the interaction.

A simple way to understand it is that we are two Architects, as the hieroglyph suggests. The Ultimate Creator that appears in this symbol becomes composed of an infusion of mutual intent, which when enlivened becomes excitable to a degree of extraordinary intensity that triggers deeper realizations. This high level of resonance is in alignment with the sphere of awareness that belongs to those aliens. They have been here many times before and influenced many cultures.

As has been described, the inner child can either be cloaked or defined by buoyancy. When one goes beyond the phenomenon of denial and reaches into a sphere of uninhibited and joyful presence that produces electromagnetic potency, this buoyant child intertwines with the Architect of observation. Without these two elements combined we have mere observation, which can be interfered with by mental, emotional or external processes that may not be clear, which is how we've got ourselves into such deep trouble.

The Architect of observation from the Inner Light hieroglyph takes the buoyancy of the inner child and elevates it into the field of unified symbiosis that belongs to the Completion hieroglyph. This energetic constellation only becomes operational between two beings when both can sustain the same level of integrity.

Here we arrive upon something very interesting, a twin phenomenon. This like-minded resonance reaches through time and space, boundlessly. Even though apart, the glue that is insightful realization belongs co-operatively to those who experience it. For us as awakened seers, the reward for clearing our heart will be beyond anything we can ever imagine.

For all of you who are wondering why we don't have ongoing contact with those aliens, the reason is that they are dreamers. Their interaction with us can only take place in a fluid construct. Our world is too real. Our dream is too fixed. We need to regain that buoyant child, that pure heart, so that we may be free from the confines of a restrictive construct. Then we can become part of the galactic community.

There was one experience I had, with another form of luminous being, that truly frightened me, for it showed me that not resolving our inner turmoil will lead us to a very serious form of etheric imprisonment. I have seen this entrapment, and the consequences that bore upon me as I witnessed it are that I feel extremely responsible to convey this information to those who wish to awaken.

The occasion that I am about to describe took place many years ago. It was a wake up call for me. The world was not as it seemed, and I was to be confronted with that more directly than ever before.

THE SENTINEL

I woke up in dreaming and found myself standing near a vintage car. It was exquisitely made, with an immaculate interior and a shiny wooden steering wheel. Proceeding to examine the dashboard, my eyes swept to the seats, which were covered with beautiful, soft gray leather. Merely focusing on the inside of the car transported me to that position. I felt so excited to be in such a fine old vehicle.

In my waking life at that time I owned a 1954 F.J. Holden. It was a wonderful experience to drive that beautiful car. I encountered the opposite to what I usually would on the streets. People would smile and wave as I drove by. In that Holden I was totally within my element; I loved the positive attention it attracted. In the dream, I was filled with the same elation that surrounded the car I owned in my daily reality.

To my utter and total surprise, when I looked to my left at the passenger's seat, my closest friend was sitting there. Looking at me, she smiled and said:

"Wow, this is such a beautiful car."

I looked up and saw a mischievous glint in the eye of my friend. It is interesting to note that any minor inflection from a dreaming environment gives information. I became immediately suspicious. I knew my friend did not overtly display feelings of delight towards inanimate objects. Her pleasure would come from seeing me enjoy the car.

"You've never been interested in cars like this," I said.

She didn't answer and instead pointed at the dashboard, directing my awareness to the beautiful button that switched on the windscreen wiper. In my waking life, it always annoys me when someone directs me away from the truth. I suddenly became aggressively curious.

"Who are you? You are not my friend," I said with absolute assuredness. "She would never be so interested in these small details. You're directing my attention and I don't like it. You cannot control my focus any more. Who are you? How can you be here? Where is my friend?"

As soon as I said this, the whole scene disappeared completely from my view. Totally disoriented, I looked up and saw a sizzling, luminous being looming over me. The exterior of its sphere crackled with a maddening insistence. It seemed that we were in some type of cylindrical cave. I had never experienced this before and had no reference points to stabilize myself. A momentary lapse of anguish and fear washed over me.

As I became aware of my environment, I noticed that I too was floating, like that luminosity. I saw that I was spherical and my exterior was smooth and unwavering. Unlike that sizzling entity, my energy moved from deep within my luminosity and did not crackle in any way.

By merely experiencing this, I realized that the crackling being was an enforcer. Its energetic mass displayed that, via the relentless sound it emitted. It was exterior by nature. This beings' purpose was to mirror back the intentions of those who came into contact with it. The crackling itself was the collected intentions of unresolved human beings.

What I was learning through that encounter was that we encase ourselves within the enactments of our heart, and those are the very elements that are projected forward and sustained by these beings: the sentinels. As a result, we are enthralled within what we create, and they are doing what has to be done, in order for us to become aware of what we sustain through our projections.

If by chance anyone has the occasion to reach this realm without being clear and resolved in life, these beings will actively engage that human awareness and the challenges they encounter will be dangerously consuming, magnifying the unresolved daytime world in which that person lives. This process will be surrounded by an atmosphere of surreptitious secretiveness that will drain everybody they interact with of their resources, including them.

The sentinel approached my spherical shape, and as its crackles exploded on my exterior it transferred impulses that equaled the grotesqueness of that heavy magnetic field that confronted me. Every sound it emitted relayed feelings that I am so utterly and totally unfamiliar with.

"Where is my friend?" I asked that ominous presence.

My attention was directed forwards. What appeared before me made the pit of my stomach feel as if it were sinking forever. There was absolutely nothing but darkness, a heavy expanse that seemed to want to swallow every ounce of me. And then I saw it, a cube of massive proportions suspended within that endlessness.

The crackling being's voice erupted right by my ear, which was actually my entire luminous field, "There is your friend, and millions more, trapped in the folly of their own making."

As I gazed at this enormous cage, I saw fleeting shadows dive-bombing its exterior, disappearing within and then reappearing as if larger and more energized. What accompanied this sight were demonic sounds. It was a screaming and screeching of unbridled gluttony. I felt I was witnessing some kind of diabolical feeding frenzy.

Upon witnessing and hearing this I experienced the anguish of a type of finality I had never known before. I knew the entrapment that encased my friend and innumerable others. The weight of that responsibility pressed upon my heart as I became aware of that complex arrangement where humanity is caught.

My realizations transformed the darkness of that nothingness into a whirlpool, and its gravity began to suck me in. I woke up in my bed feeling heavy-hearted and knowing that things have to be different in the world. What I was truly left with was the inevitability which surrounds corruption of the heart, and that scared the living daylights out of me.

When you consider your dreaming explorations, and where you may be pulled within those journeys, be aware that your daytime actions also bring consequences to alternate realms, and that there are beings who will actively waylay your voyaging awareness. To be waylaid is to waste one's life and one's time.

Be aware that the responsibility of these sentinels is to reflect upon our dream travels who we are, so that when we awaken it will impact on our true vehicle of discovery: our heart.

We are responsible. There is nothing being done to us apart from what we are doing to ourselves. The lesson that I received from this experience was to act upon what I know and not waste my time. I have endeavored to do so ever since.

www.parallelperception.com

QUESTIONS AND ANSWERS: II

Q: What is the etheric entrapment and how does it manifest in our lives?

A: It manifests as incompleteness and the inability to enjoy our existence, either in dreaming or in waking, though these two states are essentially the same.

Q: What is the significance of the images and settings within dreaming? For instance: the immaculate car.

A: They are a reflection of our intentions.

Q: How can the awareness of subtle inflection be translated into waking life?

A: Whether in dreaming or waking, the knowing is the same.

Q: How can you tell the difference between something you need to be aware of, and something that is taking your attention away from what you need to be aware of?

A: The way to be aware of anything is to put into practice the parameters within this chapter. Then what arrives into your emptiness will alert you.

Q: Are you a luminous being in this scene?

A: Yes, I was in luminous form.

Q: Are we luminous beings?

A: Yes.

Q: Why weren't you familiar with the feelings surrounding the crackling being?

A: When I was within this scene, it was only the second time I had directly experienced being luminous. When one is caught within one's own luminosity, the purity of that state is diametrically opposed to that which we encounter in the living construct whilst the world community is corrupt.

Seeing this crackling being in the way I did was a shock, for in luminous form we are only composed of what is in our hearts. Consequently, I was clear, and did not remember the interconnecting enthrallment that I so actively avoid when I am awake.

The crackles were composed of the doings of people who are trapped within haunted awareness, in the world and within dreams. The feelings were unfamiliar since I don't practice the intentions harbored within that limited boundary. Being touched by that entity simply transferred what is held collectively.

By merely arriving in their realm, you resonate their beingness, and this is something we need to avoid. That knowing does not correspond to a clear heart, it relates to control. Their connection to us is in essence a contradiction. Our doings hold us so that they may imprison us.

HEIGHTENED ACUITY AND BORROWED AWARENESS

When information is passed from one to another, it is often difficult for those who are receiving to assimilate what is transferred, and even more challenging to later recall its content so that they may apply the full parameters of that wisdom within their own life.

What I have observed is that my realizations are very often based in those experiences I am passing on from at least ten to fifteen years earlier, sometimes even as much as thirty. And, when I am communicating those insights to others, they witness the incoming information that is being given to them as if they were in a dream.

The reason the receiver's awareness takes on this diffused, dream-like state is that a linearly biased mind cannot laterally assimilate. We recall the information over and over again in different ways in order to extract the most pertinent elements within the sequence of time that we are dealing with at that particular moment. In the end, information will enhance a person's awareness only in conjunction with their own life experience.

This brings forward a very interesting anomaly. When information is passed on, enhancement is occurring, which is the prime objective of our growth as human beings. But, whilst that process is taking place, the recipient's awareness cannot be called heightened. They are simply asleep on the level of intention and borrowing the energy

www.parallelperception.com

of the one transferring their insight, via an exchange that is made possible through the vehicle of interest.

During the initial stages, the concepts transferred are largely beyond that person's range due to previous imprinting and the energy that those imprints demand to be sustained.

Imagine a cell, and see within that single unit a nucleus. The membrane of the cell, which is awareness, or the outer perimeter of a person's power, opens slightly to let an influx enter. What occurs after this is energetic compacting, which takes many years to come to fruition. The periphery of one's personal power will pull information towards the nucleus in order to develop gravity, and this content will be reflected back into the world as the magnetic resonance of that person. Through this process, diversity is created.

Heightened awareness is what is being borrowed, and this elevating factor moves and shifts the previous imprints of that person's consciousness. This is what causes the diffused, dream-like state, for the imprints are very possessive and will not allow transformational insights to be assimilated immediately, or without a struggle. Imprints fight to diffuse that information by flooding the mind with a dream-like awareness that takes over, making the expansive content difficult to remember.

Eventually the compressed and assimilated insight merges with the seer's internal silence and omnipresent abstract imagery, to reappear as that person's wisdom, perhaps twenty years down the track. Unfortunately, in some cases what is learnt will remain infused with the baseplate established by those original imprints.

One of the dangers that a teacher may be faced with is that their own imprints are too strong to overcome as a result of personal agenda not being released. This in essence produces enhancement of corrupt conditioning instead of integration of truth. A teacher in this position may assert their wisdom on the world in the wrong way and confuse many.

If one can go beyond the infusion that the imprints apply, then insight will only be informed by the knowing of what could be, in terms of the potential omnipresence of the circumstance making itself available to the seer.

Acuity of this nature will not interfere with the immediacy that will erupt as the heightened awareness of an individual, twenty to thirty years later. This parallel awareness is very valuable and is what we seek, for the memory of duality gives a deeper understanding, and the basis of this awareness establishes not only wisdom but also essential empathy.

The paradox is that what one is remembering in essence is a dream, since it exists only as a memory. Whether it is a daytime recognition or a dream recollection, both are accessed in the same fashion. The primary difference in recalling a dream is that the imprints that brought about the introspective imagery of dreaming have been displaced extensively.

If heightened acuity were occurring, information would be assimilated immediately, and be applied with accuracy within the present moment, which corresponds to pure knowing. However, this applied knowing usually only arises many years later, upon the point of looking back and spontaneously recalling and reviewing that information in relation to one's life, according to the pertinence that one's experiences deliver.

So I would say to all the seers, be encased within the memory of your living dream. When recalling that journey of power, see that the recollection, which may be many years after the original moment, has more information encoded within it than it did in the beginning, and know by this very fact that enhancement comes from reviewal.

Enrichment is often realized through instructing one who wishes to follow in your footsteps and mimic the path you have traveled in life. But never can that journey be repeated. Enhancement is a personal affair and will occur through self-determined actualization. When you dream, be patient, for what's locked within that experience may enhance you. If it doesn't then a review of one's heart must be taken into primary focus, to examine the motivations that surround your bid for power.

Know that enhancing other human beings will bring you into heightened acuity. One must give, in order to be released from reference points of self-enhancement so that those enrichments can appear as something else.

QUESTIONS AND ANSWERS: III

Q: Does the struggle with our imprints ever end, or do the challenges simply increase?

A: The struggle with our own imprints does end, yes. The imprints will decrease but the challenges will increase. Sometimes this will be enjoyable and life will become more interesting. At other times it will be a terrible burden. Our challenges equal our integrity.

Q: What does 'one can be released from reference points of self enhancement' mean?

A: Essentially it means to become free from self-reflective preoccupation and the anchors that narcissistic concern applies on imprints that may wish to bolster arrogance and elitism. To become aware of these internal mechanisms is crucial.

Q: How will I know when my heart is truly clear?

A: You will know. When one's heart is clear, a magical faculty becomes apparent. It is the immediate recounting of one's whole life in a moment. All the lessons of one's journey are distilled in that instant and uninhibited access to that infinite resource, without the influence of emotionality, becomes available.

If catharsis is experienced in one of these fleeting realizations, this is simply a release of something that was held in that memory, due to the fact that transparency was not available at the time of the original event.

One can forever live in the clarity of one's heart, clear of auditory and visual disruption from intention. Within this lucidity, one can hear what is truly being said and clearly see what is being presented. This is the faculty of seeing connected with intensity. Feeling is an intrinsic factor that relentlessly pushes forward, endlessly examining the invisible world that manifests itself within form in front of us at every single moment.

Q: How can I become aware of other dimensions?

A: Dimensional lateralism is our true heritage, and rediscovering this function of awareness will facilitate the balance of all elements simultaneously. We must remember that this delicate equilibrium comes about by not trying. Thus the appropriate components will align, which will relate to the progression of the circumstance in its rightful order, where obviously the idea of gain and loss will be put aside in order for the correct energetic impact to unfold.

Here we must all define the difference between mind chatter and insightful realization, which erupts as direct knowing from the heart and not as calculated thoughts.

Q: How do I reconcile my desire for expression and achievement in this world with the aims of energetic growth and arrival into multidimensionality?

A: There is no reconciling to be done. When achievement and growth appear in our solid dream construct, the elation of creation and accomplishment will propel us into our multidimensional nature.

www.parallelperception.com

Within myself,
the other appears,
somewhere else.

The Power of Silent Cognition

In the vast plexus of dimension that presented itself within parallel awareness, my benefactors pressured me relentlessly. The accounts that you have assimilated, as the reader of this book, are merely nuggets of an immeasurable and intricate network of dream visions that I was, and still am, intimately connected with. This last chapter tells of an unforgettable encounter I had with Zakai and the old Nagual Lujan.

My benefactors painstakingly instructed me with specific information on awareness, and how to access our true resources through the intensity and personal power that exists within our hearts. As I grow within my life, the gravity of my heart expands, as does my bio-electromagnetic mass, and this is transferred from me to you; the one who listens through the written word that is delivered to you by your own inner voice.

These hidden truths **dwell** behind all that exists within our living construct, which is the dream of the void that expresses itself from its own omnipresence. Awakening to

The Art of Stalking Parallel Perception: Revised 10th Anniversary Edition

this fractalized mystery is where we are all incrementally moving toward, so that we may become everything within that emptiness.

www.parallelperception.com

The Eternal Legacy of Master Lo Ban

There came a whispering from the darkness and I was awakened by the voice of my companion, Zakai.

"Lo Ban's realm is awaiting you. Look into that vastness, that void you have become so familiar with. I must now bring you into a state of completion, which is your power. The subject to be outlined is the ancient shamanic art of stalking parallel perception.

"These matters are learnt within dream visions and will be expressed by you through your writings, to capture those minds held within shadow so they may understand that the inner power that has been subdued and hopelessly engaged is theirs to be reclaimed.

"Remember the time when you were struck by that old sorcerer. It would seem to be an unfortunate accident that you met this man, and for a time befriended him, only to later realize that through this contact that hive mind of shadows came so close to being fully alerted to the true plans of Malaiyan — who is also known as Xoxonapo* — the old Nagual and myself. This encounter almost unraveled master Lo Ban's mission to recommence his journey and give light to the truths that can be bestowed, firstly upon your students and finally upon humanity as a whole, so that the grip of that tyrannical force possessing so many souls can be released.

---

* Xoxonapo means 'Fruit of eternal spring.' He is also referred to as the Tenant or the Death Defier in the works of Carlos Castaneda.

"There are ten of us that you have interacted with here, within the old Nagual's realm. You have not yet realized that seven of us, including Jagür, are holographic extensions that have been implemented as a necessary second-attention technique to allow us to function without being interfered with. The energetic signatures of Xoxonapo and especially of master Lo Ban whilst he was transferring his consciousness to you were sensitive to infiltration by nefarious elements via their contact with your human vessel. Their frequency emits a locatable signal, like a beacon, and until you were sealed upon the completion of that transmission, they were vulnerable.

"The old Nagual and Xoxonapo employed many safeguards, not unlike a fortress of energetics, to protect their beingness while the transferal of master Lo Ban's awareness was completely established within your consciousness. How they achieved this is that they projected their emanations as an advanced form of remote viewing that gave these smoky filaments of light the capacity to self-replicate in a alternate form. In this way they extended their energy field to assist you on your journey and create a bridge to your luminosity.

"The Tenant's projections were the four women — Dyani, Shashani, Ela and Mion — and the others — Lucien, Barak and Jagür were the holographic emanations of the old Nagual Lujan.

"These decoys were crucial in order to obscure the origin of their signal until their task was completed, in case any of the old sorcerers became aware that this knowledge was being disseminated once again into a new time-space continuum. When you were attacked, they realized that their precautionary approach was correct. The brujo who struck you was only one step away from discovering our true purpose, unbeknownst to himself."

Upon these revelations I was subject to an enormous cascade of imagery. I realized that Jagür, when she lunged at me, was nothing but the intention of the old Nagual confronting the depths of me with the force of his inevitability, conveying the simple message: change or die. Zakai's gaze silently acknowledged the realizations I was integrating at that moment, and he stated firmly:

"Best we fight this battle standing, with eyes wide open to the burden bestowed upon us. We are reinstating the lost wisdom of antiquity, and those who assimilate this information will be released from the shadow's dream. What we are revealing is intangibly tangible; a bridge for those who walk upon the shaman's path, which manifests the delicate but purposeful steps of one's heart that will echo throughout eternity. The power that exudes from this timeless wisdom will shock the complacencies that lie within the minds that are possessed by what does not belong.

"The link that connects shadow attention to us is perpetuated through ill intention. As long as we propagate this malaise, shadow influence will transmute into our realm through that false mind that we think belongs to us, but which anchors us to a vibration far below our full potential. Conquer we must the inner dialogue that is not ours, so that our heart may be clear, and pure expression can erupt from that center."

I looked up to Zakai, wondering why his speech was broken and had a different rhythm than what I had grown accustomed to. To my amazement, it was not Zakai who was in front of me. It was another, and as I looked into his eyes, I became transfixed.

Zakai was now standing slightly off to my left, and the man before me was my benefactor. I was more than rattled. My inner core was being bombarded. Master Lo Ban was dressed in total black. It was that same leather armor I had seen when I had first entered his domain, so many years ago.

His skin was the color of light amber and his jet-black hair was fastened tightly with a lapis lazuli band in a high ponytail, just like Malaiyan's and Lucien's. His long hair was thick and lustrous and extended well below his waist. He too wore gold earrings, tight to the earlobes.

I could clearly recognize his Mongolian ancestry in his strong facial features. His goatee beard came down to his mid-chest and was also jet-black, with small wisps of gray appearing through it. He interrupted my observations by lifting his right hand, and my eyes travelled along the length of his arm. As I gazed at the contours of his person, his armor melted and disappeared.

"Look into my eyes," he commanded, "They are the void."

Transferring my gaze from his arm to his eyes, I realized that there was no color or white to be seen. They were totally black, large almonds of liquid darkness. His striking eyebrows accented their power and highlighted the gravity within those sentient mirrors.

Before I became totally hypnotized by those two empty points, I felt his right hand touching my left shoulder. It was then that I noticed how incredibly muscular his body was. He was more than extraordinary. His presence transferred to me a sense of hope that this degree of power could be ours as human beings.

I scanned the length of his arm and was shocked to see that he bore a tribal representation of a black dragon, tattooed as an armband, and on his left shoulder an eagle of the same kind, with a wingspan that reached across his left pectoral muscle and back over his shoulder blade. Lucien had advised me to obtain these unusual shapes, to protect myself from evil intentions, calling them magical talismans that would shield my physical self and solidify my power within dimension.

"How can it be that we have the same markings?" I asked, looking into his eyes that reflected infinity.

"As you know, you have a portion of my luminosity within you. Everything you do within your living construct affects me within this realm. I am malleable to your intentions, as you are to mine. My spirit will acquiesce to everything that is appropriate. This is why I have your markings and you have mine.

"Every desire, every feeling and every intention that you have experienced from the age of seven has been shared between us. We have been connected seven years short of your lifetime. What you have done and what has happened to you has not been an accident. These talismans that you bear upon your physicality will do more than shield you.

"Any man or woman who attempts to harm you within your living construct will befall great hardship. It is necessary for a seer to be protected. This eagle and dragon will fly from unseen corners, coming to your aid and shielding you from any unwholesome intentions from those that may wish to do you wrong. By virtue of what you are about to witness, you will learn a powerful summoning technique that I possess."

When Lo Ban had finished speaking, he began to make subtle circular movements with his hands.

"View carefully what I am to do now, for this is the method used to set free these beings. You will know intuitively when this is to be done. One must strike down that which intends to harm."

Upon these words, his hands were drawn towards each other, as if the gesture was collecting something magnetic. His inner intention began to vibrate between his palms, and as they came together with a resounding clap the talismans appeared in the air behind him.

As I watched them hovering liquidly above his shoulders, the eagle and the dragon seemed to notice that I had seen them. In that instant they came rushing towards me with a blinding speed.

"What was mine is now yours. What protected me shall now protect you. Look into my eyes. They are the void. See the blackness beyond proportion that may engulf you and take you from where you are, absorbing beyond your imaginings. For even though you are stationary, you are traveling. What I am to give you now is ancient wisdom that you must transmit. Those who follow you, follow me.

"My quest is beyond your living construct, and beyond the dream that we now exist in. This journey goes further than our luminosity. Our destiny travels to the core of our universe, which is the void that you witness within this realm, and which you see echoed within my eyes.

"Remember, when interacting with those who are caught within the living dream, if there is anything but a clear heart then you will know that they are possessed. If there is drama or struggle for control within their gestures, this indicates that something else has arrived. Look into their eyes, their emptiness has been occupied.

"Know that the shadow's activities loop. If you are aware of what has happened behind you then you will be aware of what is happening ahead, at every moment that is escaping you. Consciously recover that which has occurred. This is a priority for all those who dwell within the waking dream. This is stalking the shadow within. Use foresight and intuit it, before it arrives, so that you may escape the entrapment that is permeating the living construct, which vibrates with the life force of all those captured souls.

"Look at actions and presentations, not words. Then you will be capable of transcending language so that you may transmit the knowing which needs to be realized for those who wish to be free.

"Power exists within emptiness. If your silence begins to become compromised, know that you are being engaged away from your purpose. Be aware that purpose is all we possess. Always remember this.

"The difficulty lies herein. How can you recall being nothing? Power in emptiness is the only memory we can recover that has value. This is the very task that all beings are faced with — to be within form yet empty within. You must dream beyond the false construct, back to whence you came. The living tapestry will conform to your intentions. Make your dreams come true.

"I will give you now to the Nagual Juan Matus. He bears the marks of that sentient being that nurtures the roots of our existence, our precious blue planet. He will further instruct you. My contact with you will be limited at this time."

The Power of Silent Cognition

As this magnificent shaman spoke those last words, I realized that the void within his eyes was beginning to crush me. The weight of his wisdom was beyond my strength. Suddenly he disappeared, in a flash of gold and blue light, spreading luminous fibers through each corner of the visible field.

I turned to Zakai, who was sitting quietly, smiling at me. I told him that while I was looking into my benefactor's eyes I had been thrown back retrospectively into a childhood memory. I was about seven years old and within a dream vision. I described to Zakai master Lo Ban's ancient bony finger, prodding my arm with a relentless persistence while he spoke.

As I recognized the age evident within the leathery condition of his skin, I remember saying, "I've never heard anyone speak in this fashion." And my benefactor, peering right into me with his eternal gaze, had replied,

"The things I am to tell you, you have never heard before."

His words evoked a vision of a holographic cube, a dimensional template that floated within a void-like plane, and he said to me, "The form that you view relates to temporal transmutation."

Before I had the opportunity to even partially comprehend what he was saying, I was struck by the fact that his hair and goatee beard were pure white. The deep oriental fold above his eyes gave him an appearance of ancient timelessness. The memory shocked me. I was having difficulty understanding the implications of non-sequential time barriers being broken down within the visionary dream state that I was sharing with those awesome men.

I suddenly realized that Zakai was jumping up and down, frantically clicking his fingers and clapping his hands in front of my face, to draw my attention to the fact that I had become momentarily stunned.

"The old Nagual has not yet finished with you," he said. "Close your eyes and seek that void within yourself, as you saw reflected in his eyes. Recover that which seems to be irretrievable.

Upon Zakai's suggestion, I closed my eyes, and to my amazement what was encased within that holographic cube exploded into my conscious awareness, as encoded information spoken by my benefactor. I was at that moment transported into another retrospective memory. I heard master Lo Ban's voice, off to my left, rich and melodic within its tone.

"Our interdimensional brothers, who are those aliens that have left an imprint of non-interference within our luminosity, are governed by purpose, as we are within the luminous realm. Their quest lies in the constructive manipulation of their living construct, which is also ours. They have traveled back so far from the future that their facial features are no longer the same as ours, though they are still humanoid.

"The reason why they touch each one of us individually is that - through this process - they are modifying our awareness so as to redetermine future events via minor alterations within the past. They know that assimilation of these energetic facts within itself will trigger the cascading effect that alters their future, which is our destiny.

"When they reach back into their past, the boundaries of sequential time are dissolved and as they make these adjustments, through this evolutionary process our destinies become collectively intertwined.

"You must understand that their interrupting of this continuum goes far beyond what we know as our universe. For them to travel here requires much more than cognitive inversion and the recovery of non-sequential time capsules, which is what you are experiencing at this very moment.

"Remember, they have the calculative maneuverability to assimilate the universal complexities that they encounter. They have traversed many clusters of galaxies and discovered that within these superclusters, time occurs as a non-sequential continuum, as it does in the time capsules that hold our dream images.

"In order to jump between universes they must remote view their destination, just as you must invert and recall the time capsules that contain your dream images within the complexities of your living construct. Our evolutionary task is to become aware of the intricacies that exist within that sentient flux."

With great emphasis in his voice, **the** old Nagual asked, "Can you imagine what our future brothers have done, and what they are doing?

"Being liquefied within the void will give us the cognitive fluidity that will enable our species to evolve, and thus discover the doorway to other universes that exist beyond that liquescent state. The way this works is that when a burgeoning seer first encounters the void, retrospectively, they bounce back immediately with the insights obtained from that experience. In doing so they are preparing themselves for the inevitable moment when their own resonance will harmonize with that omnipresent appearance. We will only be absorbed into an alternate universe when our frequencies emanate the same vibrational value that opens the doorway to that traversing."

Upon his explanation, I realized that what he had described was not too dissimilar to the way a cell absorbs water into its nucleus. The pH balance must fall between a certain range before the cytoplasmic membrane allows the liquid to pass that barrier and enter the cell.

"I see your realization," The old Nagual said to me directly. "But we are not just travelling within the confines of a cell. At this point we are journeying between universes, and entering the gateless gates through the keys that open it via the frequency our biofield emanates at the point of arrival. Otherwise we stay contained, even imprisoned, within the consciousness that we subsist within, without even the realization that one can pass through a barrier that isn't there in reality — yet it does exist for those who cannot identify the vibration to transform the matrices before them.

"Allow me to explain to you how this all began. Before these universes existed, there was nothing but a void, and wherever that omnipresence appeared it was at its center. From this intangible axis, the emptiness discovered that it could bring expression into its expressionlessness and it made a sound, like water dropping into a pond.

"Upon that event, the eternal force of that void power turned and converged on that one single location from all directions. The pressure of that implosion became so intense, and the sound became so compressed, that it transformed into light filaments that were then solidified via the evolving consciousness that gazed upon it, searching for itself.

"Know that wherever we stand within our living construct, whether it be here or ten million light years away on a distant star, we still exist within that ever-present, fractalized, spinning hub. That centralized vortex will always be there, for every sentient being, whether their experience be physical or of luminosity, or of a universal phenomenon beyond our comprehension. Let me now show you what you may not yet understand."

Upon his command, I was propelled into a cosmic arena beyond proportion, and from that perspective I perceived the inconceivable. It was a mass of universes, huddled together, with some strange substance mysteriously holding them apart. I began to focus on this phenomenon and realized that it was an evolved portion of the void that I had been introduced to in Lo Ban's realm. Within that witnessing I knew I understood nothing.

Suddenly I was freed from the magnetic grasp of my benefactor's domain and found myself once again standing by Zakai's side. He looked at me and smiled knowingly, gesturing me not to talk.

"Your responsibility is as was mine," he said. "To transmit, and through this task set those who listen free from the encompassing entrapment that enthralls us all. You know now where you have come from and where you are going. Your destiny is interlinked with ours. Stand with me as others have.

"We have found you. So you must now discover others and within that act set those luminous butterflies free from the net that has waylaid many a man. The ancient shamanic lessons of stalking have been delivered to you, and I know that you will diligently transmit these truths that have our integrity encased within them.

"Remember and know that certainty can be swayed in a direction, which is a highway or a meridian that we all travel on, and within this traversing we discover and are confronted by flags. These flags draw our attention and via that focus we arrive upon an imprint.

"By virtue of this arrival we anchor that site. The verification is then reinforced, and that certainty becomes a solidified reality. Through symbiotic coupling, our awareness structures an inner imprint of the state we view, and as we merge with that vibration our familiarity becomes absorption and involvement; thus making the waking dream appear solidified. This concreteness must be a joyous journey of discovery for our luminosity.

"When we structure our awareness within the living construct, we must be steadfast within our state of intention so that we do not forget where we have come from — that expansive void that sweeps every corner of eternity. If we are not fierce within our purpose and become complacent, then surely we can be trapped.

"Be alert to where your words erupt from. If insight arises from the heart, we can be certain it is our inner voice that is speaking. But if words emerge from the mind, then we can be sure that we are once again captured by that spellbinding imposter who competes with that which just knows. These are the lessons, the ancient knowings that exist at the heart of things, and will remain, as long as individuals collectively stand resolute within their power.

Focus on your dreams.
Do not listen to the content of expectation
that may limit you.
Dream your heart forward.

Epilogue

One of the most precious abilities we have as human beings is to realize that we can be something other than what we are. We can transcend almost any situation and adapt and facilitate interchangeable approaches to circumstances that may seem insoluble. This capacity is what makes us so unique as a species. But we have been taking ourselves in the wrong direction. We have been traveling outwardly and interfering extensively with our living construct.

Our true journey must begin from deep within ourselves and dive ever further into that beingness. For when we become immersed within that inner vastness, we must let go of those things that tie us and anchor us to the world outside of our center. Our endless struggle to balance external elements is futile. We must simply stand firmly within ourselves, and move more deeply into our truth than we have ever done before.

When we were born we did not recognize the world. Our journey begins from our center and is outward from the moment of conception. We have forgotten where we

www.parallelperception.com

have come from. We must make the journey back to our origin and beyond before we die. Our nature has been coerced and warped, but our innocence and power can be retrieved.

We must renew our stillness and our silences, which are more electrifying and alive than the world that we perceive: that which has been passed down to us by our ancestors. It is vital that we cultivate our inner silence to such a degree that it sustains a perimeter of power around us that allows the inner self to witness the engagement of activity and not be fully engulfed by it, yet be enhanced by that which cannot be avoided.

The challenges that occur externally will also be manifested internally. They will most always have to be wrestled with and put aside, for this conflicted part of us has been dominant for way too long. Our inner beauty can sustain us, and that delicate and subtle resource, if focused on correctly, will break the confines of our waking dream.

Truth can be known and exists within the complexities that surround you at each moment. Pay into those fractal anomalies, for they will yield you the enlightenment that is your heritage. Even if the road you travel on delivers you extensive blows and hardship, stand up for your rights. Those onslaughts will only challenge you to sustain yourself within your integrity.

www.parallelperception.com

May you find friends who will nourish and support you till the very end, for they will enrich your life and enhance its meaning.

The onus is upon you. Move swiftly, without being noticed, so that you may not be tainted by those colors that wish to saturate your inner being. Fight for your life, fight for your existence, fight for your truth; yet be invisible, even to yourself. Your journey is at hand and you are responsible.

Lujan Matus

For information regarding workshops and private
shamanic tuition with the Nagual Lujan Matus please visit:
www.parallelperception.com

Printed in Great Britain
by Amazon